TAIWAN
National Identity
and
Democratization

At a moment when clashing forces of nationalism and heightened demands for political reform dominate the political life of many states, the democratization of Taiwan is a drama worthy of study. Since 1987, Taiwan has experienced a sequence of political changes that few thought possible and which standing theories of democratization assert could not happen. At issue is the persistent uncertainty about the national identity of Taiwan. This reflects the stark clash of nationalist visions: the Chinese nationalism manifested by the Mainlander elite in the ruling Nationalist Party (KMT), and the Taiwanese nationalism manifested by those who advocate that Taiwan be an independent state. By any measure, Taiwan has become a democracy despite the inability of the political elite to reach consensus about what is the national identity of the state.

This study examines the history of the democratization in Taiwan from the perspective of the national identity problem. Based on interviews with leading figures in the KMT and opposition parties, it elucidates the nature of the conflict among political elites about identity since the Nationalists came to Taiwan in 1947, describes how the conflict about identity has affected the course of democratization since the onset of reform in 1987, and explains why the political science theories about nationalism and democratization do not account for what has happened in Taiwan. The author has written to reach a broad readership and has not burdened the text with excessive jargon that would limit its accessibility. The historical discussion is interwoven with quotations from contemporary notables as well as commentary about conceptual matters pertaining to the process of democratization. This results in a work that will appeal to both the Taiwan specialist as well as those interested in national identity and the process of democratization per se.

TAIWAN IN THE MODERN WORLD

TAIWAN IN THE MODERN WORLD

TAIWAN

National Identity and Democratization

ALAN M. WACHMAN

An East Gate Book

M.E. Sharpe
Armonk, New York
London, England

An East Gate Book

Copyright © 1994 by M. E. Sharpe, Inc.

Library of Congress Cataloging-in-Publication Data

Wachman, Alan.
Taiwan : national identity and democratization / Alan M. Wachman.
p. cm.—
(Taiwan in the modern world) "An East gate book." Includes index.
ISBN 1–56324–398–9. — ISBN 1–56324–399–7 (pbk.)
1. Taiwan—Politics and government—1988– 2. Democracy—Taiwan.
I. Title. II. Series.
DS799.847b.W33 1994
305.8′00951—dc20 94–12659
CIP

Printed in the United States of America

The paper used in this publication meets the minimum requirements of American National Standard for Information Sciences— Permanence of Paper for Printed Library Materials, ANSI Z 39.48-1984.

MV (c) 10   9   8   7   6   5   4   3   2   1
MV (p) 10   9   8   7   6   5   4   3   2   1

For my father and mother

Contents

Preface

Just before the start of the Chinese New Year celebration, I sat in one of Taipei's ubiquitous Pizza Hut outlets trying to read as I ate my lunch. My concentration was disrupted by the frenzy of animated chatter and the festivity of excited laughter. Now and then as I looked up from the page, I noticed that the restaurant was bustling with young families and clusters of youths stylishly coifed and garbed in fashionable dress that any American raised on bargain basement wear would find lavish. The scene prompted me to reflect on all the ways Taiwan has changed since my first stay began in 1980.

At that time, there were no Pizza Huts on Taiwan, nor other Western food franchises for that matter. The prevailing wisdom then was that Chinese did not like cheese. Beyond that, people were not accustomed to spending what one must spend now for a side order of neon glitter with one's meal. At that time, there was nothing chic about the way people dressed. Adults often wore traditional blouses or jackets with high, stiff collars and knotted cloth buttons. Professional men tended to wear Chung Shan–style leisure suits and women wore frilly frocks with a hefty dose of lace. Students were perpetually seen in monotonous khaki, olive, black, or blue school uniforms. Unfortunate hatchet-job haircuts limited girls' tresses to the depth of the earlobe and kept all the boys in military stubble.

Indeed, in the eyes of a newly arrived American teacher, a severe and Spartan militarism pervaded daily life on Taiwan. Smartly marching military police with gleaming white helmets and automatic weapons strutted mechanically down city streets. Mail from abroad was intercepted and screened. Foreign magazines arrived with missing pages or offending paragraphs clumsily blacked out with the censor's magic marker. Local newspapers printed self-congratulatory pabulum.

Slogans promoting vigilance against communism and defending the moralistic crusades of the Republic of China (ROC) were posted in public spots. In movie theaters, the national anthem was played before the start of every movie while heroic images of navy frogmen storming beaches and fighter aircraft soaring majestically above Taiwan's mountain peaks were projected on the screen. From the walls of nearly every public office, a pair of framed portraits of Sun Yat-sen and Chiang Kai-shek glowered down with what I then took to be menacing vigilance.

Taiwan was dominated by the Nationalist Party (Kuomintang, or KMT), which gave the impression of being rigid, repressive, insecure, and intolerant. Superficially, Taiwan's political regime appeared to have far more in common with that of the People's Republic of China (PRC) than with any democracy with which the Nationalist Party claimed an affinity. When I arrived, the aftershocks of the Kaohsiung Incident were still rumbling across Taiwan's political landscape. During my first two years there, Professor Chen Wen-chen of Carnegie-Mellon University—a Taiwanese critical of the KMT—was found dead on the campus of Taiwan University under what are generally considered mysterious circumstances. Indeed, several of the individuals I ultimately interviewed for this study in 1991 and 1993 were in prison or in exile when I first came to Taiwan in 1980.

As one of the many innocent foreigners who passed through Taiwan after college, my rudimentary education about China left me with elevated expectations of encounters with antique Chinese aesthetics, philosophical sophistication, and relics of past cultural splendor. I was justifiably disturbed by what else I found to be true about Free China. I was confused by the gulf between rhetoric and reality. How silly it seemed that the whole country apparently abided by the fantasy propagated by the ruling party that it was the government of China and would eventually recover the mainland. The logic with which the Nationalists justified their sovereignty over the mainland made as little sense to me as the ravings of Lewis Carroll's Mad Hatter. I did not understand how the well-schooled and otherwise erudite individuals with whom I became acquainted could sound so daft. With time, I came to understand the emotional attachments that gave rise to such political ambitions. I also realized that other views existed but were held in check. Two years on Taiwan offered a glimpse of what it means to live in fear under systematic political repression.

As an inexperienced instructor in the Foreign Languages Department at Tunghai University in Taichung, I once had the temerity to suggest to a class of twenty-eight freshmen that they discuss in English their views of the U.S. recognition of the PRC and how that affected Taiwan. As is characteristic of Chinese college students, there was no immediate show of hands indicating a willingness to respond. Accepting the general reticence to speak voluntarily, I called on one student after another seeking an answer. None was able to say anything more profound than "I don't know, sir." Exasperated, I finally moved on to other matters.

After class, one student approached me hesitantly to say, "I'm sorry, sir. Please don't be angry with us. We have been taught by our parents never to discuss politics in public." This was more than a tidbit of social advice of the sort that one might get from a handbook on etiquette recommending that one not discourse about politics, religion, or sex at the dinner table. Rather, it was a parental admonition that reflected fear for a child's welfare in a state where dissent was not endured.

Stories circulated among the long-term foreign residents of the university that each class we taught had in it a student "spy," assigned by the campus party representative, whose job it was to monitor our political comments and attitudes. Indeed, there was apparently a teacher at Tunghai University some years earlier who had been asked to leave the country after repeatedly expressing unorthodox political views in class. The "spy" network was not only in place to catch wayward foreign English teachers. Students, too, could be reported to the campus authorities, who, like political commissars in the military, had extensive power within the university hierarchy that could be brought to bear on a miscreant.[1]

In the end, I learned far more from my students than they learned from me. They seemed exceptionally eager to take me to visit their villages, show off Taiwan's reputedly famous attractions, and invite me home for meals. It was during this gradual exploration of Taiwan in the care of irrepressibly hospitable students that I was initially exposed to the differences between Taiwanese and Mainlanders. At the time, I did not appreciate the political dimension of this regional distinction and saw it as simply another manifestation of China's rich cultural variety. I had not yet learned about the February 28 Incident, nor did I fully appreciate the significance of the affair in Kaohsiung the year before I arrived.

Learning about the lives of my earnest hosts, I was impressed that many of them spent their childhood in the sort of routine, rural poverty that one does not recognize until one is lifted to a state of plenitude. Then, the deprivations of the past are romanticized as the source of wholesome values that tempered the spirit. I was told that in the southern part of Taiwan, from which some of my students came, meat had been scarce and was eaten only once or twice a week. Few children had had much to wear beyond their school uniforms and often leather shoes were a luxury. Life on Taiwan then was simple and choices were few.

Since then, Taiwan's economy has flourished. Standards of living and popular expectations have soared. The range and quality of accessible goods, services, entertainment, and indulgences have expanded dramatically, and the ROC has joined Hong Kong, Singapore, and South Korea as one of Asia's four small dragons or tigers. Now, Taiwan is rich.

What sparked my recollection of Taiwan's not-too-distant past was the material I had come to the Pizza Hut prepared to read: the *Human Rights Report for 1993* issued by the U.S. Department of State. The section about the ROC began with the statement "In 1993 Taiwan continued its rapid progress toward a pluralistic system truly representing the island's population. Open political debate and a freewheeling print media contributed to a vigorous democratic environment."[2] As I read, I was struck by the impressive changes that have transformed Taiwan since I first visited.

The startling success Taiwan experienced in the economic sphere has now been matched by comparably stellar developments in the political sphere. What had been a cynical and repressive regime has been overhauled. Taiwan should now be regarded as one of the few places where the transformation from authoritarianism to democracy is proceeding successfully and with relatively little violence.

Perhaps the most remarkable dimension of Taiwan's political reform is the way the repressive Mainlander minority has delicately and gradually enabled the repressed Taiwanese majority to assume control of the central government apparatus. The State Department report notes,

> The disproportionate role of Chinese Mainlanders who had dominated both politics and government in Taiwan since 1945 through the Nationalist Party (KMT), already sharply reduced by the National Assembly

(1991) and Legislative Yuan elections (1992), was further curtailed at the KMT's 14th Congress in August [1993]. Factions led by Taiwan-born Chairman (and regime President) Lee Teng-hui won 80 percent of the seats on the Central and Central Standing Committees. Senior military officers were discouraged from seeking high KMT positions, thereby enhancing the political neutrality of the military.[3]

This outcome would have been unimaginable even a few years ago.

In the time I have spent conducting interviews on the island, many people have offered encouragement. I sense that people are pleased that their struggle is worthy of note outside Taiwan. For those who have been responsible for the maintenance of order and development, my questions offered an opportunity to boast about what has been a remarkably smooth transformation. For those who have suffered, the attention they falsely assume my research may attract is late but welcome vindication for their pain. For those who feel that the political situation on Taiwan has changed but has not fundamentally improved, my work bears witness to the unfairness they fear cannot be objectively represented except by someone who is not Chinese.

This work cannot possibly accomplish all of those lofty tasks, nor was that my intention in writing about Taiwan's democratization and the role of national identity. Foremost in my mind was the need to describe the conflict between Mainlanders and Taiwanese so that those who are not familiar with the complexities of this relationship will understand more about it. To do that with integrity, I strove to represent accurately the conflicting views of the individuals I interviewed and to analyze the nature of their conflict. I suspect that in an effort to do this I have characterized the views of some people in ways that they themselves will find objectionable. My efforts to render with precision a situation that is perversely complex and deeply divisive may offend some people who feel that I have failed to present Taiwan's situation as they themselves would.

To some degree, such flaws are unavoidable. The issues about which I have written are issues about which the people of Taiwan themselves bitterly disagree. That is the source of my interest in the relationship between national identity and democratization. If there was a uniformity of views on Taiwan, I would need only to report, not to analyze, what I heard. In this respect, the account that follows is colored by my own biases—some of which I recognize and some of which I do not.

After listening to a wide range of opinions about the matter of national identity and democratization, I recognize that it does not matter to me whether Taiwan remains an autonomous state or is reunified with the Chinese territory across the strait. The responsibility to negotiate the extent and nature of the Chinese polity or polities is, I hope, a privilege that will be reserved for those who will live there as citizens. I am, I confess, sympathetic to the calls for democratization, and I do care about the manner in which the dispute about national identity is resolved. From that perspective, this account is biased by my antipathy for authoritarianism.

This volume reflects interests nurtured and supported by several institutions. My first introduction to the issues dealt with in this work came from those at Tunghai University who inadvertently helped to educate me about Taiwan while leaving me with an abiding fondness for and attachment to the island. Subsequent research on Taiwan was funded by the Center for International Affairs at Harvard University in the form of a K.T. Li Dissertation Research Fellowship and supplemented with a grant from the Pacific Cultural Foundation. I benefited immensely from a different sort of fellowship, as well as sustenance and a commodious haven, at Quincy House, where I lived and worked during all the years I studied at Harvard.

The bulk of my impressions about the complex state of politics and matters of identity on Taiwan was formed in the course of interviews I conducted during 1990–1991 and 1993. I am exceptionally appreciative of the time, trust, patience, and warmth of those very busy individuals (listed in appendix 1 on page 265) who welcomed me into their offices or studies and shared their thoughts. Dr. K.T. Li, in honor of whom my fellowship was named, was uncommonly gracious and forthcoming with assistance. Certainly, I would not have progressed on Taiwan without the unflagging encouragement and wise counsel of Edith Coliver and Hope Phillips and the seemingly inexhaustible hospitality of Malcolm Riddell and Piper Tseng. For help translating documents and transcribing tapes, I turned in Taipei to Piper Tseng and Bella Chao, and in Cambridge to Huang Ming-chung, Leon Yen, and Loretta Zhang.

In subtle but essential ways, this work has been affected by a host of teachers and friends who have been especially influential during the period that I have been struggling to learn about Taiwan and Chinese civilization. Ch'en Li-li, Chiang Hue-na, Fan Mei-yuan, Kau Ying-mao, Lin An-chi, and Shih Chih-yü are among those who took seriously my interest in knowing more and devoted themselves to helping me see things with greater clarity than I might have without them. I am especially indebted to Wang Ching-yi, who was of incalculable assistance in shaping the way I view the interaction of identity and democracy in Taiwan. I have also drawn from the wisdom and insight of Nancy Abelmann, Jacques de Lisle, Huang Yasheng, David Kornbluth, Kevin Lane, Lin Wen-cheng, and the members of the "Pateh Road Research Institute" (David Boraks, Helena Ho, and Shelley Rigger), who provided a stimulating and comfortable forum in which to work out ideas while living in Taipei.

At Harvard University, I was fortunate to have the encouragement and guidance of Jorge Dominguez, Roderick MacFarquhar, Tu Wei-ming, and Ezra Vogel who read and offered perceptive advice about draft chapters of my doctoral dissertation that is the basis for this book. Each in his own fashion contributed immeasurably to the way I framed and explored the issues addressed in this volume and provided the emotional and institutional support I needed to complete this project. Finally, it is hard to imagine how this book would have reached completion without the assistance, friendship, and unfailing good sense of Nancy Hearst, the Librarian at the Fairbank Center for East Asian Research. I am pleased to be among the many students of China who are now beholden to her.

Anyone who has written a book such as this must recall that at the final stage one is overcome by an exhilarating sense of relief that it is done and a keen sense that it never would have been possible without the devotion of worthy teachers and the affection of valued friends. Foremost among all those to whom I feel thankful are my parents. They have been and remain my worthiest teachers and my most valued friends.

Notes

1. Douglas Mendel taught at Tunghai University as a Fulbright Scholar in 1961–1962. Several years later, he reported, one of his students met him in the United States and explained: " 'You didn't realize it when you were lecturing to

us . . . but Mr. X in the class was the KMT spy. . . . Naturally we were afraid to tell you these things because we knew you were being watched. . . . I am sure that other students were also afraid of talking politics with you, because to have too close relationships with foreign professors is to be suspected.' " Douglas Mendel, *The Politics of Formosan Nationalism* (Berkeley: University of California Press, 1970), p. 51.

   2. U.S. Congress, *Country Reports on Human Rights Practices for 1993* (Washington, DC: U.S. Government Printing Office, February 1994), pp. 620ff.

   3. Ibid.

TAIWAN

National Identity
and
Democratization

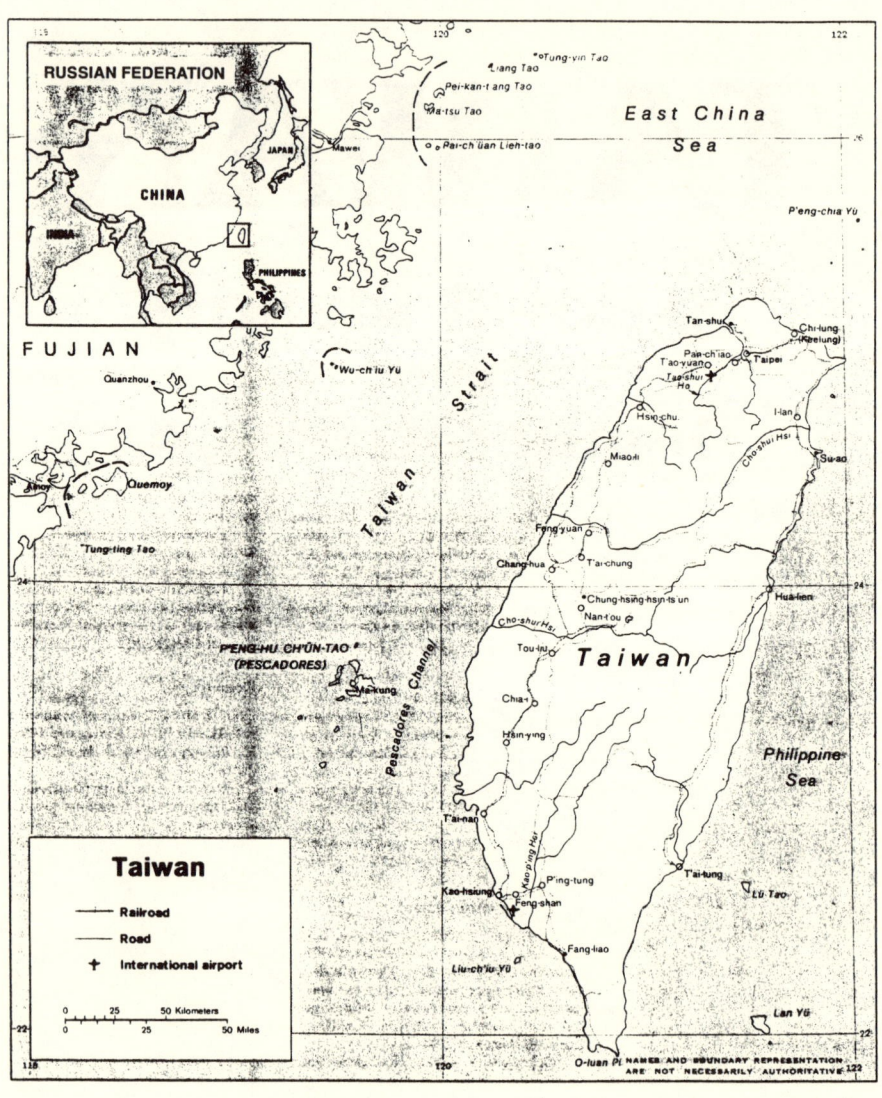

RUSSIAN FEDERATION

CHINA

JAPAN

INDIA

PHILIPPINES

FUJIAN

Quanzhou

Amoy

Quemoy

Tung-ting Tao

Mawei

Wu-ch'iu Yü

Liang Tao

Tung-yin Tao

Pei-kan-t'ang Tao

Ma-tsu Tao

Pai-ch'üan Lien-tao

East China Sea

P'eng-chia Yü

Tan-shui

Pai-ch'iao

Tao-yuan

Tan-shui Ho

Chi-lung (Keelung)

Taipei

Hsin-chu

I-lan

Miao-li

Cho-shui Hsi

Su-ao

Feng-yuan

Chang-hua

T'ai-chung

Chung-hsing-hsin-ts'un

Nan-t'ou

Hua-lien

Cho-shui Hsi

Tou-liu

Taiwan

Chia-i

Hsin-ying

Philippine Sea

T'ai-nan

Kao-ping Hsi

P'ing-tung

T'ai-tung

Lü Tao

Kao-hsiung

Feng-shan

Fang-liao

Liu-ch'iu Yü

Lan Yü

O-luan Pi

Taiwan Strait

P'ENG-HU CH'ÜN-TAO (PESCADORES)

Ma-kung

Pescadores Channel

Taiwan

— Railroad
— Road
✚ International airport

0   25   50 Kilometers
0   25   50 Miles

NAMES AND BOUNDARY REPRESENTATION ARE NOT NECESSARILY AUTHORITATIVE

Introduction

In February 1993, Hau Pei-tsun resigned as premier of the Republic of China (ROC) after a turbulent thirty-three months in office. Lien Chan, formerly the governor of Taiwan, was appointed to succeed him. With the resignation of Hau and the appointment of Lien, Taiwan took a symbolic stride into a new political era. This was not a revolutionary change, nor was it even the most significant of the many changes since 1987 that have carried Taiwan ever farther from its authoritarian past. It was, however, an indication that the system by which a ruling minority systematically suppressed the majority for four decades had been dismantled and that Taiwan is now cultivating its own style of democratic governance.

Considering that both Hau and Lien are of the same party and that both were selected to serve by the same president, Lee Teng-hui, it would be simple to overlook the import of this transition. The appointment of Lien to the role of premier was not the manifestation of a cataclysmic political shift, nor did it signal a discernible redirection of administrative policy. The appointment was the outcome of a process that had crept onward incrementally until 1987 and then, in a sudden eruption of activity, propelled Taiwan rapidly from its autocratic past and embedded it deeply in a democratic present.

The symbolic import of the change is that for the first time since the Nationalist party fled to Taiwan in the aftermath of the Communist victory on the mainland in 1949, the ROC is governed by a president and a premier who are both Taiwanese. This morsel of trivia may excite the political connoisseur, but to other observers it might seem just another iota of unprocessed news. The purpose of this volume is to explain how the developments leading to this event came to pass and why they are significant. This account draws on an understanding of

Taiwan's political history, on theories pertaining to the process of democratization, and on an elucidation of national identity as a motivating force in the struggle for power on Taiwan.

With the surety of hindsight, one might view the addition of a Taiwanese premier to the pantheon of political actors on Taiwan as simply an inevitable next step in the process of political reform. By 1993, many of Taiwan's political elite were Taiwanese. Indeed, once Lee Teng-hui became president in 1988 after the death of Chiang Ching-kuo, it might seem that the naming of a Taiwanese premier five years later was an inconsequential adjustment in a process of reform that was already well under way. As late as a few months before Lien's appointment, however, there was no reason to assume that such a change was possible, and only the most ardent and overconfident opposition partisans dared to proclaim that it would be inevitable.

The appointment of a Taiwanese premier was really the final flourish in a drama that had been unfolding since 1987. A principal characteristic of that period was the interplay between the determination to create a stable democracy and the contest between two competing views of national identity. This work is intended to acquaint readers with the symbolic world of Taiwan's politics and to offer a view of the events of 1987–1992 from the perspectives of the various actors in that realm. From that vantage, one can see that the four-decade-long struggle between two groups of Chinese on the island has unfolded in such a way that a striking reapportionment of power has been effected. As in other former authoritarian regimes, those who formerly enjoyed limitless power have been displaced by those who formerly had none. On Taiwan, however, this transformation was comparatively peaceful.

This political realignment did not occur by force of arms but by a steady, calculated struggle to redefine the rules by which Taiwan's political game was played. Whereas the struggle between the two groups concerns the distribution of political power, the polarization of the island's political elite into two groups stems from competing notions of national identity. These factors have been so entwined that it has not been possible to disentangle the quest for democracy from the quest for consensus regarding national identity. That Taiwan has become democratic despite the inability of its political elite to agree about national identity is a challenge to the theoretical literature about democratization. Theories of democratization have generally specified a sequence of development in which consensus about national identity is a condition that must exist prior to the consolidation of democratic institutions. The way democratization has developed on Taiwan suggests the need to reconsider and refine what is meant by consensus and to identify what in particular is at stake if there is no consensus before the emergence of democracy. As far as Taiwan is concerned, however, the absence of consensus has not prevented democracy from being established, although it has certainly affected how democratization came about, as this work is intended to demonstrate.

Taiwan's remarkable political development in the period after 1987 should be seen as a noteworthy accomplishment on a scale with the economic development of the island in the preceding decade. What has happened on Taiwan offers insight about how a state may move from authoritarianism to democracy, but this insight should not be misconstrued as providing a model for political reform elsewhere. The expectation that a reform process that worked in one state can be replicated in another is alluring but ultimately elusive. The peculiarities of each state's history, culture, and relationship to the international environment severely undermine the possibility that one state can expect to copy the process another state used to become a democracy.

Even trying to apply an understanding of what took place on Taiwan to the needs of the PRC will be unlikely to offer the sort of "lessons" that are frequently sought by policymakers and students of China. Taiwan's democratization is not solely the product of a scheme that was well planned and executed according to clearly identifiable goals. There were certainly principles articulated by leading figures on Taiwan who hoped to direct the process of political reform. The pace and sequence of these changes, however, emerged more from the interplay of intentions and *fortuna* than by the application of a model that might be emulated elsewhere.

Since the reforms on Taiwan got under way, there have been several commendable studies that clarify aspects of the process.[1] This study concentrates on one issue that previously has not attracted much scholarly attention: the influence of the national identity problem on the process of democratization. It is based on the premise that the dominant issues in Taiwan's national-level politics were (1) the demands by the formerly disenfranchised for greater participation, fairness, and equity in the political system and (2) the absence of consensus regarding national identity. This led to a concerted effort by the political opposition to drag Taiwan away from authoritarianism to democracy and in so doing to make the official view of Taiwan's political status conform to the attitude most Taiwanese have about their national identity.

Historical Context

Taiwan's Travails

Taiwan's most intractable problems are political and stem from differing views of the island's national identity. The roots of these matters lie deep in Taiwan's past. For one thing, Taiwan's political status has never been unassailable. China (understood as the mainland) has been governed in several ways: by Chinese exercising dominion over the entire empire, by Chinese exercising power in regions that competed for control of the whole empire, and by foreigners who wrested control of China from Chinese but who were ultimately routed and replaced by Chinese rulers. This has not been the case on Taiwan. Taiwan has not always been considered part of China, has often been governed by non-Chinese, and until the early 1990s had never been ruled exclusively by people who consider Taiwan their home.

Taiwan was first inhabited by Chinese immigrants in the seventeenth century but was then under the control of the Dutch until 1662, when the island was taken by a colorful figure known as Koxinga (Cheng Ch'eng-kung), the son of a Chinese pirate and a Japanese woman. The island was ruled as a separate kingdom until 1683, when it was conquered by forces of the Ch'ing, the Manchu dynasty that had taken control of China in 1644. Taiwan was then formally under the control of the Manchus, who were themselves alien rulers of China. Although the Manchus adopted Chinese manners, values, and administrative systems, they were foreigners. Even if one accepts that Ch'ing emperors had inherited the right to rule China, official representatives of the court in Peking who were stationed on Taiwan apparently exercised very little influence outside the cities where they lived.[2]

When China was defeated in war by Japan in 1895, Taiwan was severed from the rest of China and taken by the Japanese as part of the settlement exacted under the Treaty of Shimonoseki. From 1895 until Japan was defeated at the end of the Second World War fifty years later, Taiwan was a Japanese colony. The legacy of Japanese rule runs deeply among those residents of Taiwan old enough to remember and has shaped mannerisms and customs on the island. Many of Taiwan's elderly were educated in Japanese during the period of colonization. Japan's presence is visible even to those who have no personal memory of Taiwan's days as a colony, because Japan directed the construction of an industrial base and infrastructure that is often cited as a contributing factor in Taiwan's subsequent "miraculous" economic development.[3]

At the Cairo Conference of December 1943 and again at the Potsdam Conference of July 1945, it was determined that, following the defeat of Japan, Taiwan would be turned over to China. As Chiang Kai-shek and the KMT were generally accepted as governing the Republic of China, it was to KMT forces that the Japanese formally surrendered control of Taiwan on October 25, 1945. The KMT military administration that took control of the island initially plundered the island for booty, which was used to support the KMT's battle with the Communists on the mainland.

The relationship between the residents of Taiwan—newly freed from Japan's colonial rule—and the representatives of the KMT was sour from the start. Those who first arrived from the mainland to take control of the island were viewed as carpetbaggers, bunglers, or thieves. By 1947, the animosity had built to such a degree that a violent islandwide uprising erupted after government agents arrested a street vendor in Taipei. Residents of Taiwan lashed out against the KMT and other immigrants from the mainland. This outbreak of hostilities was brought under control and Taiwan was thereafter subjected to a brutal period of repression, retribution, and mass executions.[4]

In 1949, when the KMT lost control of the mainland to the Communists, between 1 million and 2 million civilian and military refugees retreated to Taiwan—which then had a population of about 6 million—where the Nationalist government set up shop. The KMT's intention was to use the island as a temporary haven from which to launch an assault to recover the mainland. In more than forty years, the KMT has been unable to realize its goal of national recovery. During that time, it thoroughly subjugated the island to its own purposes. A repressive authoritarian system dominated by the political elite who had escaped from the mainland was established without regard for the wishes, sentiments, or consent of the island's preexisting population. The Constitution of the ROC was suspended and the island was ruled under emergency provisions that institutionalized a prolonged period of martial law. Dissent of any form was suppressed and opposition severely punished.

Chiang Kai-shek ruled with impunity. After Chiang's death in 1975, his son Chiang Ching-kuo—first as premier and eventually as president—succeeded him as paramount leader. Chiang Ching-kuo was a more moderate, less doctrinaire soul than his father. Under his leadership, a range of programs was undertaken with the aim of invigorating the economy and the viability of the island itself. No longer was Taiwan viewed simply as a temporary base that might be disregarded once the mainland was recovered. As the island's economy developed, demands for political change increased in vigor and frequency, and the cost to the regime of suppressing dissent also increased. Toward the end of his life, Chiang Ching-kuo oversaw the initiation of dramatic political reforms that gave rise to a process of democratization.

The Turmoil of Change

Prominent among changes that were brought on by political liberalization on Taiwan was the liberty to address divisive questions concerning national identity that might have been considered taboo only a few years earlier. Free to express their genuine sentiments, people asserted political identities that threatened the cohesion of the polity in which they lived and complicated efforts to reform the political system by which it was ruled. Uncertainty about the political status of the island is tied to deep anxieties people on Taiwan feel about their own national identity. These anxieties have often been manifested intensely by people on Taiwan with very different notions of who they are and what their country is. This results from a clash of nationalist visions: the Chinese nationalism manifested by the old guard in the KMT and their supporters, and the Taiwanese nationalism manifested by advocates of an independent Taiwanese state.

Although the array of social and ethnic categories with which individuals on Taiwan identify extends far beyond the simple notions of Chinese (Mainlander) or Taiwanese, these are the two fundamental political camps that have been in evidence during the period of political liberalization and democratization. The conflict between these camps about national identity overrode other political disputes at the level of the central government and revealed ingrained hostility and mistrust between segments of the population that have threatened to destabilize Taiwan. The absence of consensus about national identity on Taiwan may be seen as both a contribution to rapid change and an outgrowth of change.

Despite the steady progress of democratization throughout the late 1980s, it was not possible to anticipate that the volatile uncertainties concerning national identity might be dampened by some means other than the exercise of self-determination. As repression gave way to liberty, problems that reflected conflicting notions of identity became more nettlesome, and the demands to rectify long-standing inequities across social divides intensified. While Taiwan faced many problems that may have appeared from the outside to be more pressing, underlying tensions related to national identity affected nearly every sphere of political and social interaction at the central level and guided the attitudes, decisions, and behavior of the political elite.

Residents of Taiwan have been impelled by changes in the political and social realms to reexamine their attitude toward China, toward Taiwan, and toward themselves. The simple truths to which they clung in the past no longer seem so simple and may not even be true. The nub of debate has been whether Taiwan itself is a country or whether it is, as the KMT on Taiwan and the Chinese Communist party (CCP) in the PRC have claimed, only part of a larger country: China.

Identity and Power

This controversy encompasses subsidiary questions that affect Chinese living beyond Taiwan as well as those on the island. The effort by Taiwanese to redefine their national identity challenges some of the most fundamental assumptions that Chinese elite have held. Once one admits the possibility that Taiwan and China are separate states, one must ask: What constitutes China? Is the PRC China? Is Taiwan China? Is it possible to differentiate "Taiwanese" from "Chinese"? Is it possible to be culturally Chinese and politically Taiwanese? Which Chinese—those on Taiwan alone, or all Chinese—should decide these matters, and by what means should they decide?

Viewed narrowly, this debate concerns a competition for power among the 21 million residents of Taiwan. Taken broadly, the debate pertains to the nature of China as a polity and the existence of the Chinese nation. These matters affect Chinese everywhere and reflect long-standing anxieties triggered by the dissolution of the empire at the end of the last century. In essence, what does it mean, now, to be Chinese?

Taiwan's most fundamental problem has been who should govern the island. This is a question of power. In earlier phases of the island's past, various forces have contended for control of Taiwan, notably, the Dutch, the Spanish, pirates, the court in Peking, Japan, the KMT, and the CCP. Those who lived on Taiwan had no say in the matter of who should rule the island. That was a decision made among powers based elsewhere. There was no thought that the island's residents had sufficient political standing to question such decisions; they were expected, simply, to acquiesce. For many Taiwanese, the contemporary competition for control of the island is indicative of a history of subjugation by forces that came from elsewhere. Repeated efforts to assert control over Taiwan by people from afar have made the people who lived on Taiwan prior to 1945 feel increasingly victimized and frustrated.

The hundred miles or so that separate Taiwan from the mainland also separate its people from the people on the mainland. People on Taiwan have developed a sense of belonging to a group defined by residency on the island. History has reinforced this distinction. Taiwan has been regarded by foreign powers and by governments on the mainland as different from China.

From the instant the KMT arrived on Taiwan, the conflict between it and the Communists concerning the control of Taiwan expressed itself in terms of the issue of reunification. Leaders in Taipei and Peking have been committed to the idea that, ultimately, Taiwan and the mainland should be reunified under a single authority. They disagree about which authority that should be and under what conditions the reunification should be effected, but they have shared a belief that Taiwan is a part of China.

From the perspective of the preexisting population of Taiwan, the effort by the KMT to reunify with the mainland was just another example of an exogenous force imposing its will on the people of the island. Some Taiwanese declared that Taiwan should be a separate state. They decried the absence of democracy on the island because they felt that if Taiwan were governed by the consent of the majority, the population would be at liberty to determine its own national identity and would reject the idea of reunification. Some Mainlanders supported the notion that Taiwan be governed democratically simply because they preferred democracy to repression.

Until the early 1990s, the island's residents were not able to participate in decisions that affected the determination of Taiwan's political status. That privilege was reserved for a tiny group of politically powerful rulers in the KMT. Most of them were men who emigrated to Taiwan in the late 1940s from the mainland or the offspring of such men. With a National Assembly newly elected in December 1991 and the Legislative Yuan elected a year later, popularly elected representatives were introduced en masse, and this laid the foundation for self-determination.

Considering that Taiwanese constituted more than four-fifths of the population of the island, self-determination was equated with democracy. A twofold assumption held sway: people would vote according to regional identification (Taiwanese would vote for Taiwanese and Mainlanders for Mainlanders) and if the political system were completely open, the Taiwanese would be able to exercise self-determination through the ballot box because, as a group, they outnumber Mainlanders. Repression by the ruling minority of the ruled majority and their demands for self-determination intensified the sense of identity Taiwanese felt as they differentiated themselves from the rulers who came from outside Taiwan.

This book examines the process of democratization as a contest for power between the Taiwanese and the Mainlanders. While this dichotomy is admittedly a simplification of a vastly more complicated reality, it is intended as a point of departure that may help readers to understand why democratization has come about on Taiwan as it has. Other works may do a far more thorough job of cataloging the fractious subethnic groups and political factions that exist on Taiwan or of explaining the intricate inner workings of the electoral or decision-making processes that resulted in Taiwan's form of democracy. This work is intended to contribute to that body of research by offering a perspective on the political world of Taiwan that approaches the way that the political actors themselves describe their interactions. For that reason, much of this volume is devoted to recounting and analyzing the way prominent figures in Taiwan's political realm describe the conflict between Taiwanese and Mainlanders and the effect of this conflict on the period of political reform from 1987 to 1992.

Gathering Impressions

To a considerable extent, the question of identity is a matter of perception. For that reason, I was eager to speak with people about their perceptions of national identity so that I could understand and explain the intensity of feelings that are expressed on Taiwan about this matter. In 1991 and 1993, I interviewed a number of Taiwan's prominent political figures as well as other thoughtful members of the political elite.

The interviewees fall into several categories. With regard to the ethnic composition of the people I consulted, I met with elderly immigrants from the mainland, the Taiwan-born offspring of such immigrants, elderly Taiwanese with memories of the arrival of mainland immigrants, younger Taiwanese, Taiwanese Hakka, and individuals who were born to one Taiwanese parent and one immigrant parent.

In terms of the political roles played by those I interviewed, I met with conservative KMT officials resistant to reform and supportive of reunification, moderate KMT officials committed to reform, moderate opposition officials who promote democratization but do not publicly identify themselves with the independence movement, radical opposition officials who promote independence, representatives of small and large opposition parties, former political prisoners, and dissidents.

In addition, I consulted with scholars of all stripes, political correspondents for television and print media, members of the business and professional elite (both Taiwanese and Mainlanders), and a host of professional non-Chinese observers in government service, business, and the press.

All told, I conducted more than fifty formal interviews and met informally with many others whose views and interpretations helped to shape my sense of Taiwan's political situation. The formal interviews were designed to promote conversation rather than to elicit responses to a predetermined list of questions. During each interview, five central topics were raised, but the approach and emphasis taken in each discussion varied depending on the informant's position, experience, and responsiveness. In most interviews, I raised the following major and subsidiary topics:

1. Is it possible to distinguish between Chinese culture and Taiwanese culture? What are the sources of cultural identity for Taiwanese and Mainlanders? What characteristics typify Taiwanese and Mainlanders?

2. How should we regard China in the present era? Is it a culture, a people (in the sense of a nation), or a place? What is the locus of political identity? Is it the locality in which people reside or the state?

3. To what degree is democracy compatible with Chinese culture? Will people be satisfied with a system that is fair, or is there a genuine understanding of and interest in establishing democracy?

4. How should the matter of Taiwan's political status be resolved? Should self-determination for the residents of Taiwan be a goal, or is the question of Taiwan's status to be decided by all Chinese? Is democracy a means or an end?

5. To what degree does the inability to resolve the matter of national identity impede the development of democracy on Taiwan?

The impressions derived from my discussions and interviews are woven into the text of this study.

The deepest impression left by these encounters is that the quest for democracy and the quest for consensus about national identity cannot be disentangled. As Taiwan's intellectual and political elite struggle to transform the old, authoritarian, repressive, and ideologically rigid state into a new, pluralistic system that responds to and is legitimized by broad public participation, they will be hounded at each step by the controversial matter of identity. Whether Taiwan is part of China or a separate state will be reflected in the kind of system they construct.

Notes

1. See, for example, Simon Long, *Taiwan: China's Last Frontier* (New York: St. Martin's Press, 1991); Peter W. Moody, *Political Change on Taiwan: A Study of Ruling Party Adaptability* (New York: Praeger, 1992); Tien Hung-mao, *The Great Transition: Political and Social Change in the Republic of China* (Stanford: Hoover Institution Press, 1988); and Tun-jen Cheng and Stephan Haggard, eds., *Political Change in Taiwan* (Boulder, CO: Lynne Rienner, 1992).

2. Douglas Mendel, *The Politics of Formosan Nationalism* (Berkeley: University of California Press, 1970), pp. 13–14.

3. Thomas B. Gold, *State and Society in the Taiwan Miracle* (Armonk, NY: M.E. Sharpe, 1986), especially chapters 2 and 3.

4. This incident in Taiwan's history is known as the February 28 (2–28) Incident and is the subject of Lai Tse-han, Ramon H. Myers, and Wei Wou, *A Tragic Beginning: The Taiwan Uprising of February 28, 1947* (Stanford: Stanford University Press, 1991).

1

Nationalism and Identity

Who Is Involved

Strong emotional ties bind people to localities in China, and it is with a particular place, as much as with China as a whole, that people tend to identify themselves. The place to which one is emotionally bound is not necessarily that place where one lives. Although there certainly are many who do identify most closely with the place where they live, the sense of identification has been governed more by an attachment to where one's forebears lived than by an attachment to where one currently resides. For those Chinese who live in the same village, province, or region where their ancestors lived, residence and ancestral home are the same.

Ties to an ancestral place (where ancestral links have been defined in terms of patrilineal relations) are reinforced by distinct local dialects, regional cuisine, and other discrete local practices that either cause or underscore one's sense of belonging to a social unit smaller than the state as a whole. In some cases, links to an ancestral home can be validated by written records and other evidence of continued inhabitation of a particular place. Where natural or political calamities have caused ruination and migration, people retained notions of their provenance through family lore and communal memory. In the course of China's history, there have been many episodes of upheaval and, consequently, waves of dislocation. That the political life of Taiwan has been shaped by the twin forces of upheaval and dislocation makes the tension on the island about national identity emblematic of a recurring theme in China's political history.

As it is among Chinese elsewhere, people on Taiwan categorize each other according to their place of origin: Taiwan or the mainland. The term *Mainlander* refers to Chinese on Taiwan who either came from the mainland in the late 1940s or early 1950s or are the Taiwan-born offspring of those people. It does not refer to Chinese currently living in the PRC.[1] One also hears the term *second-generation Mainlander* used to refer to those people born on Taiwan to Mainlander parents. Naturally, with the passage of time, the second generation spawned a third, and so forth.

Taiwanese does not refer simply to everybody living on Taiwan. It is a term used to denote only those Han Chinese who already lived on Taiwan prior to the wave of migration that occurred at the end of the 1940s and the offspring of those people. This dichotomous notion of labeling people is imprecise and, in any case, is more meaningful when applied to the generations alive in the 1940s and 1950s than to those born since. Not everyone living on Taiwan fits into one of these two neat categories, even though it is in terms of these categories that the political debate has been framed. For example, despite an earlier taboo against mixed marriages, a lot of people were born to one Mainlander parent (in the first few decades of intermingling it was generally the father) and one Taiwanese. This group defies simple classification and complicates any effort to calculate the number of Taiwanese and Mainlanders on Taiwan.[2] The more one examines these categories—Mainlander and Taiwanese—the more one realizes they are sloppy labels, at best, and do not offer an accurate manner of classifying people on the island. That the labels are only rough does not mean they have no value, but their applicability is limited. For example, there are people who have other identities. The Hakka migrated from Honan Province in central China about fifteen hundred years ago and, over several centuries, passed through Anhwei Province, Kiangsi Province, and Fukien Province. Eventually, many settled in Kwangtung Province.[3] During the successive waves of migration southward and after they settled in Kwangtung, they continued to speak their own dialect and to maintain a sense of communal identity that distinguishes them from their neighbors. Among those Chinese who came to Taiwan from the mainland in the sixteenth to mid-twentieth centuries, some were Hakka. Once they settled on Taiwan, they continued to see themselves—and were seen by others—as a distinct group. Among those Chinese who came to Taiwan from the mainland in the late 1940s there were also Hakka. Altogether, somewhat more than 12 percent of the population is thought to be Hakka. In some ways, their identity cuts across the Taiwanese/

Mainlander divide although one may still classify those who were on Taiwan before the late 1940s as Taiwanese and those who came afterward as Mainlanders.

Another group that does not easily fit the categories described are those who are not Han Chinese. Mainlanders and Taiwanese are all considered Han Chinese, but approximately 1 percent of the island's population of about 21 million are non-Han residents of several distinct ethnic groups who are referred to collectively as aborigines, *yuan-chu min*, literally "original dwellers." The status of these people is comparable to that of the Native American "Indians" in the United States. Their ancestors inhabited the island before the Chinese arrived. They were smitten by unfamiliar diseases and their communities violated by aggressive settlers. They have a marginal status in contemporary society and virtually no influence as a group on national politics.

The terminology used to refer to the various segments of the population can be confusing. Taiwanese are referred to as native or local people, *pen-ti jen*, literally "people from this land," or *pen-sheng jen*, literally "people from this province." This term refers to residents of any given province and is not to be confused with the term that denotes original dwellers, or aborigines. Mainlanders on Taiwan are known as outsiders, *wai-sheng jen*, literally "people from outside the province," a term also used elsewhere in China to denote those who come from another province.

Taiwan's population is generally described as slightly less than 85 percent Taiwanese, about 14 percent Mainlanders, and a bit more than 1 percent aborigines. In fact, the 1990 census states that the total population is 20,366,325, of which 87.11 percent are Taiwanese and 12.74 percent are Mainlanders.[4] Although the proportions are about right, the labels are not as meaningful as they might at first seem. A survey conducted by the government-sponsored research institution Academia Sinica found that when asked "Where are you from?" 76.1 percent of respondents identified themselves as Taiwanese, 12.4 percent said they were Hakka from Taiwan, 10.1 percent said they were from the mainland, and 1 percent identified themselves as aborigines. Asked "Where is your native place?" (a question that pertains more to the place from which one's father comes; the place one considers the province of family origin rather than the actual spot where one was born or raised), 78.4 percent listed a county or city on Taiwan, another 11 percent said only that they were from Taiwan, just 7.5 percent identified themselves as from the mainland, and about 2.5 percent identified themselves in other ways.[5]

National Identity and Party Affiliation

Before the initiation of liberalization, there were three political parties on Taiwan: the KMT, the Young China party (YCP), and the Democratic Socialist party (DSP). All three were formed on the mainland before 1949, but the YCP and the DSP have remained small parties of Mainlanders with little political clout. Since 1987, there has been a proliferation of political parties. During 1991, there were sixty-eight different parties, but, other than the KMT, the only party with any real political influence was the Democratic Progressive party (DPP); by early 1993, it claimed more than thirty-five thousand members.[6]

For many years, the KMT was seen as the party of Mainlanders and was predominantly concerned with the reunification of China. Until the onset of reforms in the mid-1980s, the KMT ruled with so few checks on its power that Taiwan was essentially a one-party state and the government of the Republic of China was virtually indistinguishable from the KMT. For that reason, Taiwanese felt that they were ruled, not represented, by the KMT.

This has changed. For one thing, by the late 1980s approximately 70 percent of the KMT membership of 2.4 million was Taiwanese.[7] Although it is true that a majority of the ruling party is Taiwanese, for many years the most powerful positions in the party apparatus had been held by Mainlanders. This remained true even after reforms had brought Taiwanese in at other levels.[8] By 1993, the very highest posts in the government were filled by Taiwanese, including the president, Lee Teng-hui, the premier, Lien Chan, and the president of the Judicial Yuan, Lin Yang-kang.

In addition, the party has been seriously divided about the pace and direction of reform. During the period under consideration, rigid traditionalists with a strong attachment to the mainland contended with the more moderate members of the KMT for control of the government and the reform process. These hard-liners in the KMT manifested a passion for order and control, a willingness to manipulate the organs of government to execute their will, and a visceral mistrust of anyone who seemed to disagree with them. They clung to old ideas and old ways, continued to enjoy spheres of power—although more circumscribed than in the past—and impeded the pace, if not the direction, of political liberalization. By the end of the 1980s, most of the hard-liners were elderly. They continued to take exceptional pride in what they saw as the KMT-led development of Taiwan. They genuinely feared that the loss of central control and the greater pluralism of contemporary Taiwan politics would lead to calamity.

Moderate members of the KMT, some of them younger Mainlanders and others of them Taiwanese, supported the need for the political reform of Taiwan and recognized that reform of Taiwan's political system could occur only with reform of the KMT itself. Their efforts to ease senior legislators and party officials into retirement were aimed at creating for themselves greater opportunities to influence the internal political structure of the party. To the degree that they succeeded in shaping the internal political system of the party—making it more democratic—they may have planted the seeds that ultimately diminished the power of the party itself.

By the early 1990s, the KMT was also fractured by a controversial relationship between the "mainstream" and "nonmainstream" factions. The mainstream faction was also known as the "Taiwan KMT" and the nonmainstream faction as the "China KMT." Roughly speaking, the former was composed primarily of Taiwanese and the latter of Mainlanders. In 1993, immediately preceding the KMT Fourteenth Party Congress, a small group of the party's most popular vote getters, most of them Mainlanders of the nonmainstream faction, splintered off from the KMT and formed the Chinese New party. Their avowed interest was in clean politics unsullied by the vote buying and other corrupt practices that had come to be expected of the KMT; however, it was also noteworthy that the key members of the Chinese New party were Mainlanders who could no longer depend on the KMT, which was by then more heavily influenced by Taiwanese, to protect their interests.

The DPP, the strongest opposition party during the period of reform after the mid-1980s, was the only party that offered any credible counterbalance to the KMT. It was formed in 1986 out of a loose coalition of opposition activists who sought to assert the interests of the Taiwanese, who had for so many years been restricted from effective participation in Taiwan's politics. The absence of experience by its leadership and the turmoil that results from the establishment of any new political party initially limited the DPP's effectiveness. The party was divided between those in the *Hsin Ch'ao-liu* (New Tide) faction, who were eager to promote Taiwan independence, and those in the *Mei-li Tao* (Formosa) faction, for whom democratization was a more urgent objective. There were also independent satrapies that operated under the umbrella of the DPP because they comprised Taiwanese opposed to the KMT, but their nominal association with the DPP did not imply ideological conformity.

From 1987 onward, the DPP earned the reputation for sponsoring visible public demonstrations, initiating melees in the parliament to embarrass the KMT, and standing up to unfair practices of the KMT at every turn. While these forceful and theatrical ploys attracted attention and support from disaffected Taiwanese in the early years of the party's life, the DPP came to be seen by many as lacking the capacity to take over the reins of government.

During this period of political reorientation, Taiwan's residents were most in agreement when talking about the need for improved social order and continued economic development. KMT officials gleefully suggested that the DPP undermined its own credibility by failing to address the concerns of the growing, commercial, middle class, which associated disorder with the opposition. After the elections of December 1991, the DPP recognized the need to alter its style and thereafter endeavored to appear more responsible.

What Is at Stake?

That Taiwan is populated by groups of people who identify with different ancestral locales and that it has a political system in which there are parties that have acrimonious relations are unremarkable. Nor is it these factors alone that affected the outcome of political reform and democratization on Taiwan. The reason why these factors are relevant to the democratization of Taiwan has to do with the efforts of each of the two groups, Mainlanders and Taiwanese, to impose on the other its own vision of Taiwan's political status.

The catechism of Chinese Nationalists, as embodied in Article 2 of the KMT charter, is that "the Kuomintang shall be a revolutionary and democratic political party charged with the mission of completing the National Revolution, carrying out the Three Principles of the People, *recovering the Chinese mainland, promoting Chinese culture*, aligning with other democratic nations, and building the Republic of China into a unified, free, peace-loving, and harmonious democracy based on the Three Principles of the People" (emphasis added).[9]

The recovery of China and the promotion of Chinese culture have been the focus of KMT policy on Taiwan since 1949 and the bane of many Taiwanese. For many Taiwanese, China is a foreign country. They see no need or advantage in unifying with it or subjecting themselves to governance from Peking. These goals of the KMT have manifested themselves in grand campaigns, symbolic gestures, as well as countless restrictions and requirements meant to embed these aims in the minds of Taiwan's population. Those who identify with China and the nationalism of the KMT view their efforts as a sacred trust. They express their interest in providing greater stability and opportunity to the next generation by ameliorating the tension between the PRC and the ROC, in playing a key role in the modernization of the mainland after the passing of communism, and in realizing a historic imperative to reunite China.

Chen Charng-ven (C.V. Chen), an influential attorney who has played a prominent role on behalf of the ROC as an intermediary between it and the PRC, expressed passionately the determination to reunify China:

> I'm for reunification of China. I know unification is extremely difficult if not impossible. Yet, on the other hand, I do know I am Chinese—by history, by blood, and also by [my] ideal[s]. . . . I know that if China could be united under a system comparable to what we have now [on Taiwan] . . . with freedom for the people . . . be it economic, political, or social . . . all Chinese, be it on Taiwan or on [the] mainland [would] have a great future. . . . But, I am not blind to the fact that if China is . . . ruled by the same leaders [who hold office now], we have a problem. But, I'm hopeful that if we all work hard, we may achieve something, not only for us [in] this generation, but also for the generations to come. That is the belief I have, that is the hope I have. Whether or not I will succeed, God knows, but I think that at least it is worth trying. What do we stand to lose? . . . We stand to lose very little, but [have] something to gain. Yet, on the other hand, if we now say we should go independent . . . that is really too provincial . . . if not irresponsible.[10]

Taiwanese who favor the continued autonomy of Taiwan, by contrast, view the possibility of giving up that autonomy to become unified with the mainland as irresponsible. For some Taiwanese, the quest for independence follows from a prior conclusion that Taiwanese culture and Chinese culture are different, even if related.

Chinese nationalists do not seem to accept as genuine the protestations of Taiwanese about the desirability of independence. They are incredulous that their promotion of Chinese culture and the recovery of the mainland are not universally accepted by all Chinese. For them, the concepts of a distinct Taiwanese culture, nation, and independent state are nonsensical and heretical. They fear that crafty local politicians have manipulated the notion of Taiwanese identity to veil a menacing quest for personal power which might accrue from an independent Taiwan.

Typical of the sort of skepticism one hears about the idea of a Taiwanese culture distinct from a Chinese mainland culture is a comment by Chu Chi-ying, director of the Cultural Affairs Department of the KMT and the party's spokesman. Chu suggested that for some of the Taiwanese who distinguish between the culture of China and that of Taiwan "there is a political motivation behind it. In their mind and heart they believe there is no such great difference between Taiwan culture and mainland culture. I believe they know Taiwan culture is rooted in mainland culture."[11]

Those who believe that Taiwan itself is a country challenge the long-standing belief in the unity of a Chinese culture, nation, and state. They identify themselves as Chinese—which they see as a cultural or ethnic designation—while identifying themselves as citizens of Taiwan. Taiwanese speak of their Chinese lineage or heritage (*hsueh-t'ung*), acknowledging their acceptance of a "blood relationship" to Chinese from the mainland while rejecting the idea that all Chinese must live under the same government within the same polity. They reject the idea of a Chinese nation-state. Some even reject the idea of a Chinese nation. Chinese, for them, is a cultural or ethnic category, not a political category.

Of course, "overseas Chinese" have for centuries lived in countries other than China while clinging to their essential Chineseness. The sense that they are "overseas" implies that their real home is China. They may identify politically with Malaysia, Thailand, or Indonesia, but they still view themselves as part of the Chinese nation. Their nationality as Chinese inheres even though they are citizens of non-Chinese states. This is not true, however, for those overseas Chinese who view themselves as overseas Taiwanese. Many of them have been involved in promoting the independence of Taiwan from the United States or Japan. They have formed political alliances and interest groups that lobby the U.S. Congress and provide financial and other forms of succor to their brethren on Taiwan.

Drawing a distinction between the Chinese nation—the people—and a single Chinese state is the foundation for the view that Taiwan is inhabited by Chinese but is an autonomous state. Some advocates of Taiwan's independence go even further. A commentator in a pro-opposition newspaper wrote "The Taiwanese nation is not the same as the Chinese nation; Taiwanese are not Chinese, just as Americans are not Englishmen."[12]

Hu Fo, a professor of political science at National Taiwan University, suggested two political concepts common to Mainlanders. *I-t'ung* is an ideal that the state, China, encompasses all regions and all ethnic groups under a single, unified moral system. It is a cultural perspective of oneness in which individuality and distinctiveness are surrendered to unity so that virtue may spread to the four seas. *T'ung-i* is the action needed to bring this about after China has been divided.

Hu observed that one legacy of the Japanese influence on Taiwan is that Taiwanese no longer abide by the notion of *i-t'ung* and already see themselves as having separate cultural and political identities. Many Taiwanese feel that Taiwan is already independent and that the Mainlanders and government should simply acknowledge that reality. Hu said that this practical assessment is unacceptable to Mainlanders whose sense of *i-t'ung* is an emotional attachment not subject to reason.[13]

Over the past four decades, politically active Taiwanese pressed for greater and more sweeping liberties on Taiwan and have pressured the KMT to loosen its control of the political and ideological restraints that had limited discussion and political participation. Taiwanese who hope to establish an independent Taiwanese state, as well as those who simply want to preserve the ambiguous status quo vis-à-vis the mainland, were united in their demand that they be given more opportunities to compete for political power. This is commonly expressed in terms of a desire for democracy.

Since 1987, those who hope to preserve a unified Chinese culture and promote the reunification of Taiwan and the mainland have struggled to moderate their inclinations to dominate Taiwan's political sphere so as to offer a controlled release for the hostility and frustration of their opponents. Still, some conservatives were disinclined to liberalize for ideological and temperamental reasons. Many in the KMT feared that democracy would enable Taiwanese activists to push for Taiwan independence, and that would invite a military response from the mainland.

Whether the KMT sincerely expected an attack by the PRC or whether this was the residue of an earlier ideological creed is difficult to gauge. KMT officials have asserted that greater democracy would lead to a rise in manifestations of Taiwanese identity, and that, in turn, would intensify demands for independence, which would incite the PRC to attack Taiwan. Opposition leaders have dismissed these alleged fears of a PRC attack as a ploy to restrain the pace of political liberalization; simply, a way for the KMT to retain power.[14] Questions of identity, therefore, were not idle matters. They spilled over into nearly every political debate at the central level and, in the years after liberalization began, were especially prominent in discussions of democratization and the political status of Taiwan.

Nations, Nation-States, and Nationalism

The Nation

Although the specific historical context in which Taiwan's democratization emerged is distinctive, the volatility of nationalism in Taiwan's society reflects a universal political phenomenon. As the modern conception of the state developed, so did the concept of the nation and nationalism.[15] At first, efforts to define a nation "emphasized the importance of a shared language, ethnicity or heritage."[16] With greater sophistication, theorists came to view a nation as evincing "shared identity and feelings of affinity, transcending though rarely eliminating allegiances based on locality, ethnic group, religion, or class."[17] In the case of Taiwan, the issue of transcending and eliminating has been critical. For most of the time since 1949, the KMT denigrated the identification Taiwanese felt toward Taiwan and imposed the expectation that all residents of Taiwan accept a transcending allegiance to China.

Ernest Gellner offers a view which rests on the premise that shared cultural traits are necessary, but insufficient, conditions of nationality. He claimed that, in addition, a nation must be composed of people who "recognize each other as belonging to the same nation. In other words, *nations maketh man*; nations are the artefacts of men's conviction and loyalties and solidarities. . . . It is their recognition of each other as fellows . . . which turns them into a nation, and not the other shared attributes . . . which separate that category from non-members."[18] John

Stuart Mill's commonly cited definition of nationality incorporates a sense of mutual interest that distinguishes a nation from other associations, the willingness of people who comprise a nation to cooperate, and their ambition of exclusive self-rule. "A portion of mankind may be said to constitute a Nationality, if they are united among themselves by common sympathies, which do not exist between them and any others—which make them cooperate with each other more willingly than with other people, desire to be under the same government, and desire that it should be government by themselves or a portion of themselves, exclusively." [19]

Nationhood is, at its root, a profoundly political concept. To ignore the power embodied in the concept of nationhood, with its implication of political unity, is to mistake national identity with religious, linguistic, or cultural affinity. It is true that "some confusion arises from the widespread legal or euphemistic use of the word 'nation' as a synonym for 'independent state.' "[20] When one speaks of a nation, one invokes a sense of political solidarity that goes beyond community and suggests a tie between social order and political power; perhaps even power tied to territory. Beyond any cultural, regional, or linguistic traits the people subsumed by the term *nation* may share, there is also an implication of political sovereignty.

In the end, it is extraordinarily hard to find an unambiguous way to capture the essence of nationhood. It is difficult to specify a list of objective characteristics that comprise nationhood. Regarding the subjective characteristics, one must take account of "voluntary adherence" and consent, even if it comes in response to "fear, coercion, [or] compulsion," as critical factors that contribute to the sense of solidarity that emerges within groups that share cultural traits. "Most persisting groups are based on a mixture of loyalty and identification and of extraneous incentives, positive or negative, on hopes and fears."[21]

Nationalism

Nationhood has to do with one's sense of shared identity. It is primarily a matter of association—a sentiment felt collectively by individuals. Nationalism, however, is "primarily a political principle, which holds that the political and the national unit should be congruent."[22]

Nationalism is not synonymous with tribalism, ethnicity, or shared cultural, religious, and linguistic identities. It deals only with the sentiments one has for the nation-state.[23] As a concept, nationalism must encompass "the distinctive set of ideals, myths, symbols, and values that can serve as the inspiration for a nation-state."[24] Unlike other primordial forms of association that may attract the intense loyalty of the individual, a nation must, in the end, be linked to a specific territory. It is a link either to the motherland of antiquity or to the current domain over which those people who consider themselves a nation, rather than "those other guys," feel they should reign.

As a political movement, nationalism often emerges first in the minds of an intellectual or political elite and is spread by them to the populace. It is the drive of the elite to create a nation, rather than the existence of such an association, that gives rise to a broader, popular sense of nationhood. This accounts for the common inclination of the nationalistic elite to "project future hopes into the present and the past, to persuade oneself that one is discovering what in fact one is trying to create. Nationalism . . . thus has often preceded the emergence of a nation."[25]

Indeed, the bases of nationalism are frequently invented. Traditions and histories are created or tailored to suit the political ambitions of an elite who use the potency nationalism can arouse among a people to advance a political program. "Dead languages can be revived, traditions invented, quite fictitious pristine purities restored. . . . The cultural shreds and patches used by nationalism are often arbitrary historical inventions. Any old shred and patch would have served as well. . . . The culture [nationalism] claims to defend and revive are often its own inventions, or are modified out of all recognition." [26]

Indeed, there is a propensity for the nationalist to view history "as a grab-bag from which he instinctively selects past themes that suit his present purpose."[27] This search for nationhood in the mythologies and folk ways of the past is a romantic effort to impart meaning to memories or fantasies that have the power to spark a sense of communality among a given group. "The whole point of nationalism . . . is its insistence on the importance of a special cultural group identity as the bedrock of political claims and actions. What is more it frames this insistence in terms of the recovery of some identity which has always been 'there' but which has been forgotten or abandoned or threatened."[28] On Taiwan, both the nationalism of the Chinese and that of the Taiwanese can be explained, in part, as a reflection of certain communal, psychological needs. Taiwanese nationalism is directed at the creation of a nation that never existed, while the nationalism of the KMT

—the *Nationalist* party—and indeed the Han chauvinism of Chinese elite is directed at the "restoration of a past state in which the nation was most fully itself."[29]

Each of the two forms of identity arose as the response of a community that felt that the place it viewed as its own polity was governed by an illegitimate regime that did not represent the community's own basic cultural values.[30] For Chinese nationalists, most of whom are Mainlanders, the alien regime they reacted against was the Communist one. The government they wished to have would encompass all China and be a Chinese nation-state that would restore a situation long undermined by the Communists, the Japanese, and the Manchus before them. Chinese nationalism reflects Mainlanders' efforts to cope with the competition they feel toward the Communists on the mainland and their reaction to a reality that they have not otherwise been able to control.

The nationalism of the Taiwanese was *their* effort to cope with the competition *they* felt toward the Mainlander elite on Taiwan and *their* reaction to the same kind of reality, which until recently *they* have had no other means to influence. Namely, the place they consider home was controlled by Mainlanders in the KMT who were unsympathetic toward and did little to preserve the Taiwanese nation. The government many Taiwanese hope to establish would be chosen by the majority of Taiwan's residents and would, quite likely, declare itself to be an independent state. It would constitute a Taiwanese nation-state, a political association that has never been permitted to exist before.

Matters of identity rest largely on sentiment, and one cannot quantify such sentiments. They are dynamic, not static. Sentiments change. These sentiments are worth examining even though they cannot be validated because so many other actions, decisions, and attitudes are dependent on these basic identities. Indeed, it is fair to state that during 1987–1992, questions of identity manifested themselves in most of the national political controversies on Taiwan.

Ultimately, the distinction between Mainlanders and Taiwanese is a matter of an individual's consciousness. There are Mainlanders who were born on Taiwan and even Taiwanese who were born on the mainland (as in the case of Premier Lien Chan). The link between provincial origin and party affiliation is also not absolute. There are some Mainlanders who have supported the DPP and many more Taiwanese who have supported the KMT. Beyond the KMT and the DPP, there are other parties. Beyond Mainlander and Taiwanese, there are other forms of identity.

Party affiliation with the KMT is not necessarily an indication of ideological commitment. As in any Leninist system, many benefits accrue from membership, and recruitment begins well before people are politically mature enough to have established an autonomous political identity. Some members of the party are members because they want what the party has to offer in the form of employment, influence, and prestige—KMT membership offered a way to get ahead. Undoubtedly there are members of the opposition parties who are more concerned with opposition to the KMT than with the specific ideology of the party they joined.

This work does not pretend to offer an exhaustive description of society on Taiwan. The aim is to understand the interaction between the forces of democratization and the "problem of national origin" (*sheng-chi wen-t'i*). To discuss the controversy, one must employ terms such as *identity, consciousness,* and *nation* because it is in these terms that the actors in this drama discuss the matter themselves.

When it comes to understanding the political developments during the period of democratization, however, these four categories (Mainlander, Taiwanese, KMT, and DPP) are the most salient. Even though there are other forms of identity, the contest between the Mainlanders and the Taiwanese dominated the period. Even though there are other political parties in Taiwan's political sphere, the interplay between the KMT and the DPP was the defining political contest of the period. Even though it is simplistic, from the perspective of the anthropologist or sociologist, to classify Taiwan's society in terms of just Taiwanese and Mainlanders, political symbolism is necessarily simplistic.

Notes

1. Tien Hung-mao, *The Great Transition: Political and Social Change in the Republic of China* (Stanford: Hoover Institution Press, 1989), pp. 35ff.

2. For a discussion of intermarriage between Taiwanese and Mainlanders, see Hill Gates, "Ethnicity and Social Class," in *The Anthropology of Taiwanese Society,* ed. Emily Martin Ahern and Hill Gates (Stanford: Stanford University Press, 1981), pp. 265–66.

3. See John F. Copper, *Taiwan: Nation-State or Province?* (Boulder, CO: Westview Press, 1990), p. 8; and Leo J. Moser, *The Chinese Mosaic: The Peoples and Provinces of China* (Boulder, CO: Westview, 1985), p. 237.

4. *China Post,* April 3, 1991, p. 1. According to census figures released in 1993, the population of the ROC as of December 1992 stood at 20,752,000. See *The Republic of China Yearbook: 1994* (Taipei: Government Information Office, January 1994).

5. Hsiao Hsin-Huang (Michael Hsiao), "Sheng-chi jen-ting yu sheng-chi wen-t'i" (Provincial Identification and the Problem of Provincial Origin), in *T'ai-wan ti-chu she-hui i-hsiang tiao-ch'a* (Survey of Social Attitudes in the Taiwan Area), ed. Chung-yang yen-chiu yuan (Nankang: Academia Sinica, January 1991), pp. 42–43.

6. *China Post*, February 16, 1993, p. 15. See also Tien, *The Great Transition*, pp. 64ff.

7. Tien, *The Great Transition*, p. 85.

8. Chen Jou-chin, "Premier's Version of Taiwanization Challenged," *Hsin Hsin-wen* (The Journalist), no. 224, June 30, 1991, in Joint Publications Research Service: China Area Report (JPRS-CAR)–91–057, October 18, 1991, pp. 40–42.

9. "The Charter of the *Kuo Min Tang* of China," Article II, in *Getting to Know the KMT: The Nationalist Party of China*, vol. 2, ed. Department of Cultural Affairs of the Central Committee of the *Kuo Min Tang* (Taipei: China Cultural Services, 1989), p. B4.

10. Interview with Chen Charng-ven, Taipei, June 24, 1991.

11. Interview with Chu Chi-ying, Taipei, July 4, 1991.

12. *Tzu-li Wan-pao* (Independence Evening Post), May 17, 1991, p. 4. See JPRS-CAR–91–039, July 5, 1991, p. 94.

13. Interview with Hu Fo, Taipei, June 13, 1991.

14. Republic of China Government Information Office, *A Study of a Possible Communist Attack on Taiwan* (Sanchung: Government Information Office, 1991).

15. John Breuilly, *Nationalism and the State* (Manchester: Manchester University Press, 1982), p. 45.

16. Rod Hague and Martin Harrop, *Comparative Government and Politics: An Introduction*, 2d ed. (Atlantic Highlands, NJ: Humanities Press International, 1987), p. 31.

17. Ibid., p. 32.

18. Ernest Gellner, *Nations and Nationalism* (Ithaca: Cornell University Press, 1983), p. 7.

19. John Stuart Mill, *Considerations on Representative Government* (Buffalo, NY: Prometheus Books, 1991), chapter 16. Originally published in 1861.

20. Dankwart Rustow, *A World of Nations: Problems of Political Modernization* (Washington, DC: The Brookings Institution, 1967), p. 21.

21. Gellner, *Nations and Nationalism*, p. 53.

22. Ibid., p. 1.

23. Lucian W. Pye, "Chinese Nationalism and Modernization," lectures by Wei Lun Visiting Professor to the Chinese University of Hong Kong, January 1991. First lecture: "The Challenge of Modernization to the Chinese National Identity," p. 3. I am indebted to Professor Pye for providing me with a copy of his lecture notes.

24. Ibid., p. 4.

25. Rustow, *A World of Nations*, pp. 25–26.

26. Gellner, *Nations and Nationalism*, p. 56.

27. Rustow, *A World of Nations*, p. 41.

28. Ibid., p. 28.

29. Breuilly, *Nationalism and the State*, p. 348.

30. Ibid., p. 349.

2

Democracy and Democratization

Ever since the seventeenth century, political philosophers have been hunting for the secret of an alchemical transformation from the brutish chaos of conflict to the serene life of cooperation.

—Adam Przeworski, *Democracy and the Market: Political and Economic Reforms in Eastern Europe and Latin America*

Democracy

For years the credo of the KMT was that the ROC was a constitutional democracy. In this way, the KMT distinguished itself and the ROC from the CCP and the PRC. However, the threat of attack by the Communist regime on the mainland impelled the KMT to invoke an elastic constitutional provision to create a legal framework that effectively imposed martial law on Taiwan. The ROC was an authoritarian regime from the moment it retreated to Taiwan in 1949 until July 15, 1987. On that day, President Chiang Ching-kuo lifted the decree that had enabled the regime to rule on an emergency basis, and he initiated a program of liberalization.

By the early 1990s, liberalization had resulted in the expansion of civil and political rights, the reform of state institutions, the erosion of the power of the KMT, and a shift from token contestation to genuine competition in elections for posts of political consequence. In 1987, Taiwan began evolving into a democratic state. By the early 1990s, it had achieved a noteworthy level of "electionism" and was well on its way to establishing the sort of legal and social structures necessary for democracy. Depending on one's definition of democracy, one might even say that with the elections of the Legislative Yuan in December 1992, Taiwan had become democratic.

Yet political theories suggest that it is especially difficult to sustain a democracy in a society where "political parties, interest groups, media of communication, schools, and voluntary associations" are determined along "religious, ideological, linguistic, regional, cultural, racial, or ethnic" lines.[1] In the past, the divide between the Mainlander and the Taiwanese was sufficiently stark that one could legitimately question whether democracy might be sustained on Taiwan. Despite the uncertainty about Taiwan's political status, the gap between Mainlanders and Taiwanese has narrowed in most spheres of life, and even in politics—where the distinction is most apparent—it has not impeded the development of democratic institutions.

However, as political reform accelerated in 1987, questions concerning Taiwanese and Chinese identities gained increasing prominence. The more open society became, the more openly these issues were debated and the more threatening this dispute became to the ground rules that enabled democratic reform to materialize. Taiwan's political and intellectual elite generally endorsed the furtherance of democracy, but they differed about what that really entails and how rapidly Taiwan should progress toward that goal. Hard-liners in the KMT were reluctant to give up too much or to give in too far for fear that the Taiwanese would overwhelm and unseat them at the ballot box. Taiwanese opposition figures pressed for more and faster democratic reforms because they, too, calculated their advantage in terms of numbers.

Once it became clear that authoritarianism was finished and democratic reform inevitable, the opposing camps turned their attention to the form of democracy that Taiwan should pursue. Throughout this period, the populace at large seemed motivated far less by ideological commitment than by the chance to ride the wave of consumerism and prosperity that had brought political reform to Taiwan's shores. Although there was a perceptible popular interest in change, the discordant and unpredictable manner with which democratization proceeded profoundly disturbed a population accustomed to well-established and constrained political norms. People were annoyed that their hard-earned wealth might be jeopardized by yet another political dispute.

One often heard complaints about the futility of change and the sense that inevitably the political elite would continue to reserve privilege and power for itself. Cynics felt that the new system, whatever it was, would be just as unfair to the common people as the authoritarian one it replaced. In the late 1980s and early 1990s, this cynicism about the nature of democratic reform was undergirded by a spreading sense of disorder that was seen as evidence that the efforts to change the political system might well result in a system that was even less satisfactory than the authoritarianism of the past.

In some manner, Taiwan's experience with this process was conditioned by factors that are peculiar to Taiwan. Other dimensions of the social and political turbulence that affected Taiwan are common to states engaged in the transformation from authoritarianism to democracy. By comparison to the massive instability and disruption to social order that was experienced by the Russians and Eastern Europeans in the aftermath of the demise of the Soviet Union, what Taiwan experienced was minor. By comparison to the political tinderbox of South Korea, Taiwan's transformation appears to have been relatively easy. In the PRC, too, the rapid economic growth of the early 1990s contributed to a rampant disintegration of order, corruption, and inflation that helped to nurture a nostalgia for the towering control of Chairman Mao. The sense of social instability that comes with a relaxation of state control is undoubtedly an uncomfortable phase of the transition from certainty and protection by the state to uncertainty and self-reliance. The choices and leniency that come with the dismantling of an authoritarian system are indeed threatening, even to those who promote a democratic alternative.

On Taiwan, though, the greatest uncertainty had to do with the status of Taiwan as a political entity, and the greatest choices had to do with the national identity of the populace. How it was possible for Taiwan to develop a democratic system despite the persistence of the unresolved questions about national identity is of considerable theoretical interest. Students of democracy have held that if there is not a commonly accepted view of the identity of the state in which a given population lives, it is not possible to transform that state into a democratic one. Taiwan's development from 1987 to 1992 challenges that assumption.

Definitions of Democracy

It is hard to define democracy unambiguously. Like other elusive political concepts—authority, liberty, justice, peace, and power, for example

—democracy may be brought into sharper focus by its absence than by its existence. It may even be easier to identify what is not democracy than what is. Some definitions frame the concept of democracy in opposition to whatever political system already exists as a way to explain what ought not to be or what could be in a perfectly functioning society. In this way, democracy is viewed as a normative ideal.[2] In common parlance, democracy is a fuzzy term and is often used without precision. It has become "a debased currency in the political marketplace. Politicians with a wide range of convictions and practices strove to appropriate the label and attach it to their actions. Scholars, conversely, hesitated to use it—without the addition of qualifying adjectives —because of the ambiguity that surrounds it."[3] Despite the difficulties of defining democracy, there have been many efforts to do so. Some definitions rest on the sources of democratic power and others focus on the purposes of democracy. Joseph Schumpeter departed from these approaches and focused on the procedural dimension of democracy. He described democracy as "that institutional arrangement for arriving at political decisions in which individuals acquire the power to decide by means of a competitive struggle for the people's vote."[4] Samuel Huntington added "By the 1970s the debate was over and Schumpeter had won. Theorists increasingly drew distinctions between rationalistic, utopian, idealistic definitions of democracy, on the one hand, and empirical, descriptive, institutional, and procedural definitions, on the other, and concluded that only the latter type of definition provided the analytical precision and empirical referents that make the concept a useful one."[5] Robert Dahl offered a more complex explanation, augmenting the procedural criteria with some attention to the efficacy of the system. He wrote that democracy is founded on a government's "continuing responsiveness" to the "preferences of its citizens, considered as political equals." This system would offer citizens the "unimpaired opportunities"

- to formulate their preferences,
- to signify their preferences to their fellow citizens and the government by individual and collective action, and
- to have their preferences weigh equally in the conduct of the government, that is, weighted with no discrimination because of the content or source of that preference.[6]

In Dahl's view, democracy is a condition that exists only as an ideal and is never fully realized. States may be classified according to the degree to which political decisions are determined by citizen participation and public contestation. A system that is both inclusive and competitive he labeled a polyarchy. By drawing a distinction between democracy as an ideal and polyarchy as a range of actual behavior, he hoped to avoid blurring the difference between the ideal and "the institutional arrangements that have come to be regarded as a kind of imperfect approximation of an ideal."[7]

For example, to hold free and fair elections for posts that have no power is not democratic. For that reason, Taiwan might not be considered a democracy during all the years prior to political liberalization even though city- and county-level officials were chosen by election. Even when elections were used to augment the National Assembly and Legislative Yuan, because such elections did not significantly alter the nature of the authoritarian system, Taiwan was not a democracy.

Dahl wrote "[I]n the absence of the right to oppose, the right to 'participate' is stripped of a very large part of the significance it has in a country where public contestation exists."[8] Juan Linz emphasized that democracy rests on the existence of "basic freedoms of association, information, and communication for the purpose of free competition between leaders to validate at regular intervals by non-violent means their claim to rule." He specified that democracy is not just a matter of holding elections for some offices and granting freedoms to some segments of society and outlined a broad array of necessary criteria.[9] Huntington offers a low threshold for the classification of systems as democratic, a classification based on contestation and participation that synthesizes the views of Schumpeter and Dahl.[10] He proposed that "a twentieth-century political system [is] democratic to the extent that its most powerful collective decision makers are selected through fair, honest, and periodic elections in which candidates freely compete for votes and in which virtually all the adult population is eligible to vote."[11] This definition comports with Dahl's notion that contestation and participation are essential. It is a narrow definition based on the procedures by which political decisions are made. The "civil and political freedoms to speak, publish, assemble, and organize" commonly associated with democracy—or mistaken for it— Huntington denoted as ancillary principles that make the system work.[12] In his view, this approach conforms to people's commonsense notions of what democracy is. He wrote that people understand "that military coups, censorship, rigged elections, coercion and harassment of the opposition, jailing of political opponents, and prohibition of political meetings are incompatible with democracy."[13]

Throughout this study, Huntington's definition is the standard by which Taiwan's political reforms are gauged. According to this narrower definition, a procedural one, Taiwan in the early 1990s can be considered democratic. However, democracy can be expanded and cultivated. Even states that are roundly identified as democratic, such as the United States, continue to nurture and refine their democratic system. No state is *fully* democratic. There is always an opportunity for a community to realize more completely the democratic ends toward which it aims. In this regard, Taiwan may be democratic, but it can continue to expand the scope of its democracy so that the level of democratic practice suits the majority of Taiwan's population. It is that aim toward which many political activists still aspire.

Preconditions of Democracy

Beyond seeking a way to define democracy, scholars have been deeply concerned about how democracy comes about. The determination to specify what factors affect the evolution of political life in a community so that a system that is not democratic becomes so has led to volumes of theories regarding the origins and progress of democracy as a process. Some analysts identify what it is that made democracy thrive in those states where it seemed firmly established. Theories of democratization seem to rest on a foundation of hope that if one could just put one's finger on those factors that make democracy grow at home, one could transplant it abroad like a "hothouse plant."[14] By reasoning from the specific to the general, early studies were concerned with a wide range of economic, social, and cultural forces presumed to be necessary as the bases of democracy. These included the importance of voluntary associations; the correlation between democracy and the existence of a strong bourgeoisie; mass communications as a determinant of cohesion; the attainment of a certain level of per capita income, literacy, and urbanization; the need for preestablished attitudes among the citizenry, especially consensus about fundamental principles or about procedural matters; people's willingness to participate in the system; the need for a civic culture;

and preexisting social and political structure.[15]

These efforts to specify minimal requirements for democracy that might be woven into a theory of democracy provide useful insights about the nature of democratic states, but not absolute "preconditions" of democracy. Most of the factors cited by various theorists turned out, under scrutiny, to be correlative factors, not causative ones. This realization led some contemporary theorists to reject as futile the entire problematik that saw as its goal the identification of preconditions for democracy. Such prescriptive efforts fail because the qualities that are commonly seen as preconditions of democracy are qualities that more probably emerge from the establishment of democracy.[16]

The central problem with the effort to define universally applicable preconditions is that democracy takes on different forms in different places and at different times. It is also hard to draw a causal link between the presence of certain factors and the existence of democracy. For example, it has become routine to suggest that certain levels of economic development, the existence of a middle class, cultural and religious inclinations favoring the autonomy of the individual apart from a higher order, and the articulation of social interests by civic associations are features of democratic states, but these are not causes of democracy. These are not even all the conditions necessary to promote or nurture a democracy. There are states where these factors are present in some measure where democracy is absent and other states where these factors are wanting, but where democracy exists.

If a high level of economic development is a precondition of democracy, it is puzzling that wealthy oil-producing states in the Middle East have not become democratic but India has. From a cultural perspective, it might be expected that states influenced by Confucian values would resist democracy because of the ingrained attitudes of deference to authority and group conformity. Yet, Japan has apparently been functioning in a democratic fashion and now Taiwan is, too.

It may be more productive to consider whether democracy results from a single set of preconditions or whether there are various combinations of social, economic, and cultural conditions that may spur democracy. If this is so, it may not be at all clear which, if any, of these factors is both necessary and sufficient for the emergence or sustenance of democracy. Regarding those democracies that have emerged since the "third wave" began in 1974, Huntington dismissed the attempt to specify a common package of preconditions. He advised:

1. No single factor is sufficient to explain the development of democracy in all countries or in a single country.

2. No single factor is necessary to the development of democracy in all countries.

3. Democratization in each country is the result of a combination of causes.

4. The combination of causes producing democracy varies from country to country.

5. The combination of causes generally responsible for one wave of democratization differs from that responsible for other waves.

6. The causes responsible for the initial regime changes in a democratization wave are likely to differ from those responsible for later regime changes in that wave.[17]

Contemporary analysts have begun to understand that the effort to identify preconditions of democracy ultimately fails to explain how the presence of such factors can cause democracy to emerge. This has led scholars to focus on democratization as a process rather than a condition that inheres once certain conditions are present.[18]

The processes by which democracy emerges are likely to vary according to the socioeconomic characteristics of the state as well as its political culture and institutional structures.[19] If one views democracy as a decision-making procedure that is accepted by a polity as a means to resolve political disputes and distribute political goods, for a state that has not been democratic to become democratic, not only must the populace be capable of learning a new mode of political decisionmaking, but it must also be capable of unlearning and disregarding its earlier means of doing political business. Quite apart from the presence of certain preconditions, the capacity of a state to adapt to the imperatives democratic processes impose on a community may affect the development of democracy.

Claims of some states that they are democratic simply because elections are held are fallacious. Such "electionism" is no substitute for genuine democracy that "offers a variety of competitive processes and channels for the expression of interests and values."[20] After all, democracy is a form of decision making in which

• conflicts and conflict resolution are acknowledged as a permanent feature so that many groups may organize to promote their interests, access to political institutions is itself institutionalized, and "losers who play by the rules do not forsake their right to keep playing";[21]

- conflicts are resolved according to explicit rules that specify criteria for participation, admissibility of political strategies, and criteria for "terminating the conflict"; rules that may be changed, but only according to the rules themselves;
- participants in the system have choices of political strategies (although not all strategies are admissible); and
- no political entity, either an individual or a group, can be assured of always prevailing in a conflict, because no outcome may be predetermined by the status of the participants—that is, incumbency is no guarantee of success—and all outcomes of conflicts are institutionally uncertain.[22]

For a regime that is rooted in a culture of authority such as the Chinese, dislodging long-held notions about order, and weaning power holders and citizenry from their habitual diet of certainty, is an exceedingly ambitious project. By comparison, it is relatively simple to rewrite the constitution and basic laws, redesign the structure of government, and impose new procedures for decision making. It will be more difficult to have people accept a system in which uncertainty about outcomes is regularized. The confusion of having to make decisions, having choices, having to accept responsibility for choosing the wrong options, and understanding that these uncertainties are outweighed by the benefits of an elusive notion of liberty may prove hard to accept by many of those who have been infantilized and repressed by a system designed to restrict political competition.[23]

Proponents of the democratic system have to justify their proposals and offer resistant power holders and confused citizenry tangible rewards for giving up the systemic certainty to which they have become accustomed. This does not mean that a state must be accustomed to coping with uncertainty to become democratic. It may be difficult for people to change the habitual inclinations they rely upon as the basis of political interaction but it is not impossible. To change, a polity must be patient. The first wavering steps toward democracy may appear tentative and unstable. It is not realistic to expect a community's first efforts to be otherwise. At first, people have no reason to trust that the system will work or that the decisions made will be universally respected by those who oppose them. Still, it is possible that "contingent consent and bounded uncertainty can emerge from the interaction between antagonistic and mutually suspicious actors and that the far more benevolent and ingrained norms of a civic culture are better thought of as a product not a producer of democracy."[24] This view complements Rustow's sense that to bring about democracy it is not necessary to "foster democrats" by "preachment, propaganda, education, or as an automatic by-product of growing prosperity." He believes that it is possible to "force, trick, lure or cajole non-democrats into democratic behavior" and that their attitudes and beliefs will be brought around in due course.[25] This is an argument for the establishment of democratic procedures; a sense that one becomes democratic by acting democratic. This is precisely how democracy came about on Taiwan.

Prior to the election for the National Assembly in December 1991, Ma Ying-cheou contemplated the possibility that the KMT might lose. He said that the party is ready to become an opposition party if their opponents take more than 51 percent of the vote because, in the end, "the system itself will either seduce us or force us to accept the reality."[26]

Democratization

> It is evident to all alike that a great democratic revolution is going on among us, but all do not look at it in the same light. To some it appears to be novel but accidental, and, as such, they hope it may still be checked; to others it seems irresistible, because it is the most uniform, the most ancient, and the most permanent tendency that is to be found in history.

> —Alexis de Tocqueville, *Democracy in America*

Difference between Democracy and Democratization

Whereas democracy is a social or political condition, democratization is a process. Processes occur over time, and, as such democratization may be seen to have several distinct phases. In distinguishing between democratization as a process and the condition to which it may lead, it is useful to bear in mind Dahl's distinction between democracy as an ideal and polyarchy as a functioning political system. It is not the case that democracy is established wherever democratization is undertaken.[27] There are situations in which democratization is undertaken and progress is made, but the polity resists democracy or reverts to its predemocratic condition.

Even where a community appears to have succeeded in establishing a functioning democracy, people intuitively understand that some systems are "more democratic" than others. The ease with which one may determine that a given state is or is not democratic is deceptive considering that democracy is defined in terms of ideals that are impossible to realize fully. In reality, democracy is attributed to a range of political behavior and to systems that may be governed in part by democratic procedures and in part by procedures that aim at other ideals. States that have long been democratic may still only be at a point along the course of democratization. The effort to maintain democracy requires constant vigilance, adjustment, and refinement.

Democratization is a long, unpredictable, difficult process. There are many pitfalls along the way. Like the child's game of chutes and ladders, a state may progress several steps up the path toward democracy, only to find the way obstructed or some fatal flaw in the preexisting structure of the polity impeding its progress, causing it to tumble back and sacrifice gains it had made. A fundamental disagreement among the political elite about what constitutes the national entity might be such a flaw.[28] Sometimes the dissolution of authoritarianism leads to "the restoration of a new, and possibly more severe form of authoritarian rule. The outcome can also be simply confusion, that is, the rotation in power of successive governments which fail to provide any enduring or predictable solution to the problem of institutionalizing political power."[29] When the effort to move toward democracy is thwarted and the polity reverts to a less democratic equilibrium, the setback may prove to be temporary. It may be that democratization operates in what one analyst called a "genetic" fashion, planting the seeds of change in one generation for the birth of that change in a succeeding generation.[30]

During the process of democratization, political institutions, actors, patterns of interaction, and values are all in flux simultaneously. This makes it difficult to articulate a theory of how democratization takes place. It does not happen in a regular, ordered fashion. Instead, it is a process characterized by a "high degree of indeterminacy embedded in situations where unexpected events (*fortuna*), insufficient information, hurried and audacious choices, confusion about motives and interests, plasticity, and even indefinition of political identities, as well as the talents of specific individuals (*virtu*), are frequently decisive in determining the outcomes."[31] For many states, the struggle with democratization has been the focus of political change, during the modern era. The vagaries of economic development are inextricably linked to political change and in places, Taiwan included, where there had been a concerted effort to build wealth and make the economy flourish, democratization seems to have slipped in through the back door to envelope the political actors in a process they are unable or unwilling to control. For Taiwan, as for most other states that focused first on economic development, democratization came about after an extensive period of liberalization.

Distinguishing Liberalization and Democratization

To clarify the difference between liberalization and democratization, one should note that both occur as part of a transition from what is certainly an undemocratic regime to an "uncertain something else."[32] That transition is a period when the "rules of the political game are not defined." Moreover, the rules themselves may become the subject of intense controversy as various actors sense that the rules and procedures that are agreed on in the course of the transition to democracy will determine their status and power after the transition has been completed.

In the case of authoritarian regimes, the rulers begin with most of the cards in their own hands. Liberalization is the process whereby the restraints on society with which the regime represses behavior, suppresses expression, and perverts the lives of its citizens are pried open to extract greater personal and political liberties for the populace. The first step from authoritarian rule to democracy comes when the authorities, "for whatever reason, begin to modify their own rules in the direction of providing more secure guarantees for the rights of individuals and groups."[33]

Democratization moves beyond simply opening up the regime and creating greater liberty. It aims to reformulate the political system as a democracy. Democratization entails a redefinition of the rules of the political game to enhance the two dimensions that Dahl identified as the pillars of democracy: participation and contestation.[34] With democratization, "rules and procedures of citizenship are either applied to political institutions previously governed by other principles (e.g. coercive control, social tradition, expert judgment, or administrative practice), or expanded to include persons not previously enjoying such rights and obligations ... or extended to cover issues and institutions not previously subject to citizen participation."[35] Liberalization, in fact, "is only one step in the process of democratization and should not be confused with it. The former can continue for some time without the latter taking effect."[36] Regardless of what liberalizing actions an authoritarian regime takes to demonstrate that it is not as repressive as it once was, liberalization does not become democratization until the most powerful political posts are filled by open and fairly contested elections.[37] This was particularly evident on Taiwan during the late 1980s before the National Assembly and Legislative Yuan were subjected to electoral competition on Taiwan. Until then, there had been much progress in opening up contestation for positions that did not, ultimately, have much control over the political system itself. Even after the Legislative Yuan elections of 1992, the DPP remained committed to forcing the KMT to open the presidency to direct, popular election. The president on Taiwan appoints the premier, who enlists a cabinet; therefore, the direct, popular election of the president would ensure that the government would remain accountable to the voters on nearly all issues of national significance.

Getting from a condition in which the political leaders of a state need only to negotiate among themselves to determine how their polity will be governed to the point at which decisionmakers are elected in periodic, fair, and open elections by the citizenry is an arduous and uncertain undertaking. It is an undertaking that commonly begins with liberalization and, when successful, slips into democratization.

According to Samuel Huntington, Brazil is one of the prototypical cases in which the transition to democracy ran smoothly. He wrote that "there was no clear break" between authoritarianism and democracy. "The genius of the Brazilian transformation is that it is virtually impossible to say at what point Brazil stopped being a dictatorship and became a democracy." By the early 1990s, it might be said that Taiwan had joined Brazil in this astounding seamless transformation.[38]

Phases of Democratization

Many of the hallmarks of the democratization process that theorists describe may be detected in the development of democracy on Taiwan. However, this does not mean that democratization has proceeded on Taiwan precisely as it has in other states. Nor does it imply that the democratization of Taiwan was easily predicted by theorists. Indeed, just as democracy is practiced differently in each state where it appears, democratization is a process that occurs differently in each state undergoing the transition.[39] A vast literature now exists by those who study the process of democratization. They have generated a wide array of proposals, but little consensus, about the precise way in which democratization occurs. In general, their works endeavor to explain the collapse of the preexisting regime, a search for alternatives, an effort to effect some reforms, and the institutionalization of those reforms.

Transformations, Replacements, and Transplacements

Among the many models of democratization, one that is especially helpful in assessing the progress Taiwan has made in the effort to move away from an authoritarian legacy to a democratic actuality is written by Samuel Huntington. He described democratization during the "third wave" as a pattern of interaction among several political actors: "standpatters, liberal reformers, and democratic reformers" in the ruling elite and "democratic moderates and revolutionary extremists in the opposition."[40]

In a generalization that accurately encompasses the situation on Taiwan, Huntington wrote that in "noncommunist authoritarian systems, the standpatters . . . [are] normally perceived as right-wing, fascist, and nationalist." In the case of Taiwan, the epithets "right-wing" and "nationalist" could easily have been applied to the "hard-liners" in the KMT. The reformers on Taiwan are those viewed as "soft-liners," people who favor democratization over continued authoritarian rule, but who wish to monitor the pace and direction of reform so that the transformation occurs gradually, peacefully, and in such a way that they are able to retain power for as long as possible.

Those in the opposition who favor democracy are the "democratic moderates," a label one might apply to the Formosa faction of the DPP. As to those in the opposition who oppose democratization, Huntington characterized them as "left-wing, revolutionary and Marxist-Leninist." Although there may be some members of the DPP or more radical opposition groups who are Marxist, class interests are not prominent among their reasons for opposing the KMT. The New Tide faction is probably more concerned with independence than democracy, and that may be revolutionary, but it is not Marxist. Overall, "[s]upporters of democracy in both government and opposition could be conceived as occupying middle positions on the left–right continuum."[41]

Huntington explained the phases of democratization as the shifting interplay among these actors. He noted that their goals and attitudes change in the course of the process as a reflection of their perceptions of how well their interests are served by each phase. Obviously, democratization proceeded more smoothly if the prodemocratic forces maintained the upper hand in both the ruling elite and the opposition. This facilitated a form of cooperation.

Huntington classified the transitions to democracy that occurred around the world since 1974 as fitting into one of three categories: relacement, transplacement, or transformation.[42] In a replacement, the regime is overthrown and the opposition takes power. The standpatters in government are stronger than the reformers, but the regime as a whole is weaker than the opposition. As there is little hope that the liberal wing within the regime—if one exists—will persuade the standpatters to budge on the matter of reform, there is no reform from above. Democratization occurs after the opposition gains sufficient strength to overthrow the government, as it did in the Philippines when the Marcos regime was ousted by "people power" led by Corazon Aquino.[43]

Huntington's second class of transition is transplacement, where "democratization is produced by the combined actions of government and opposition."[44] In this form of transition, the government must be dragged into changing; as there are no factions within the regime sufficiently powerful to initiate reform, but no element in the opposition strong enough to overthrow the regime. Transitions in Poland, Czechoslovakia, Korea, and Uruguay were characteristic of transplacements.[45]

Huntington's notion of a transformation best describes what happened on Taiwan during the period of political reform. In a transformation, the liberalization process is initiated by the regime itself, which decides it must "take the lead and play the decisive role in ending that regime and changing it into a democratic system."[46] This is a transition in which, initially, the prodemocratic faction within the ruling elite is able to exert greater control over the regime than the more conservative "standpatters" and in which the regime's capacity to regulate political behavior overall is stronger than the opposition's capacity to force a change. When a transformation of this sort occurs, as it has in Spain, Brazil, Mexico, Hungary, as well as Taiwan, it naturally leads one to wonder "why any regime with a monopoly on political power ultimately decides to share it."[47]

According to Huntington, this sort of transition occurs in five phases. During the first, a faction that favors liberalization and/or democratization emerges within the authoritarian regime and initiates reform because of the perceived desirability of ensuring a "graceful exit from power." This occurs when the ruling elite within the regime

- sees that the opposition has become more forceful, or
- recognizes that to hold on to power indefinitely brings with it increased risks to their lives, or
- deludes itself into thinking that it is possible to liberalize and thereby extend its hold on power, or
- hopes that liberalization will win the state greater international legitimacy and benefits that will earn the regime itself more legitimacy, or even
- comes to see democratization as the "right" thing to do.

In the second phase, the faction within the regime that favors democratization acquires greater power vis-à-vis the hard-liners, a process that can occur—as it did on Taiwan—when the founding figure in the polity dies and is succeeded by one who views the needs of the polity differently. Then, in the third phase, there is a brief interlude of liberalized authoritarianism that leads either to democratization or to a backlash against reform. This is followed by a fourth phase in which the hard-liners are subdued by those in the ruling elite who favor democratization. This involves "weakening, reassuring, and converting" them to neutralize their objection to further reform, which may occur when

- there is a "concentration of power in the reform chief executive" —as with Lee Teng-hui,
- there is a purge of the government, military, and party with replacements coming from the reform wing, and
- "standpatters" are persuaded that democratization is a "return to legitimacy" because the authoritarian period was never envisaged by the regime's founder as a permanent state.

This effort to legitimize the "return" to democracy because of the founder's intentions is one of the ploys used by the moderate KMT with reference to Sun Yat-sen's Three Principles of the People, which specified that genuine democratic governance would have to be preceded by a form of tutelary democracy. Where this sort of strategy was applied, "it legitimated the new order because it was a product of the old, and it retrospectively legitimated the old order because it had produced the new." This strategy may appeal to the extreme hard-liners, but not to the extreme in the opposition who, like the New Tide faction of the DPP and other Taiwanese pro-independence groups, have "no use for either the old authoritarian regime or the new democratic one."[48]

Finally, in the fifth phase of transformation, the opposition is coopted by the reform-minded ruling faction. This entails the negotiation of a pact—implicit or explicit—that emphasizes moderation and cooperation on both sides during the course of reform. It will "draw out 'responsible' elements of the opposition" with whom to work while "reminding radicals that they would play into the hands of hard-liners if they pushed too hard."

Huntington cited Taiwan as an example where such a pact was negotiated. He wrote that "in 1986 the government and the opposition arrived at an understanding on the parameters within which political change would take place and, in a week-long conference in July 1990 agreed on a full schedule of democratization." It may be that Huntington attributed to the "pact" greater efficacy than has proven real, but the negotiation process itself and the National Affairs Conference of 1990 that he mentioned suggest that efforts to draw the moderate wing of the reform party into dialogue—even if not wholly successful— may benefit the process of gradual democratization.[49]

Huntington observed that in practice, the only way to build a democracy is by using democratic methods. During the "third wave," transitions that ultimately established a democracy came about through "negotiations, compromises, and agreements, . . . demonstrations, campaigns, elections and through the nonviolent resolution of differences."[50] This suggests that a state that is determined to become democratic cannot practice by being something else. Huntington showed that democratization seems to work best when people practice the art of democracy—even if imperfectly—until it becomes widely accepted and habitual.

Still, this process is not one that states can undertake easily. The choices leaders must make are difficult and the outcomes unpredictable. To some degree, it may be possible "to craft democracies,"[51] but to an even greater degree, this process is affected by "elements of accident and unpredictability, of crucial decisions taken in a hurry with very inadequate information, of actors facing irresolvable ethical dilemmas and ideological confusions, of dramatic turning points reached and passed without an understanding of their future significance."[52]

Consolidation

Advocates of democracy hope to see the system consolidated (in Przeworski's words) or habituated (in Rustow's). This is a condition in which democracy has been sufficiently ingrained into the social and political life of the polity that most political decisions are made in a democratic fashion as a matter of course and that there is a popular expectation that this be the case.[53]

A range of impediments may keep a state from realizing the goals of democratization, among which are the political culture of the state and the degree to which national political leaders are committed to the process. The best test of this commitment is how they behave while in office. This raises the question of whether or not to believe a leader who claims to have an interest in democracy when no sign of that interest is evident from his past and current conduct as the national leader.

Huntington wrote that one prime obstacle to democracy is the political culture of the state that has had no previous experience with democracy. For Taiwan, and many other states in Asia, democracy is not a condition to which the state is returning but one toward which it is heading for the first time. Nothing in the cultural background of the polity offers much experience with democratic procedures or values.[54]

Finally, in considering reasons why democracy might not be consolidated on Taiwan, one must acknowledge the long-standing argument that Confucian cultures are incompatible with democracy. Huntington made this argument in his work, and it is even common to hear Chinese themselves offering in apology for their resistance to democracy the argument that Confucian values have conditioned them to be wary of the pluralism and egalitarianism inherent in democratic culture.

To pursue this Confucian excuse, one would need first to define what is meant by Confucian culture and then to establish that Taiwan is, in fact, a Confucian culture. Each of these exercises might be confounding. Even if one could satisfy the skeptics with an adequate definition of Confucian culture and establish that Taiwan had one, the premise of the argument is insupportable. The idea that to become democratic a state must have a cultural heritage that predisposes its people to think in democratic terms is ludicrous. In fact, just the opposite might be easier to support. It is in those states where repression and authoritarian rule have thrived that democracy has often emerged. Indeed, no state that is today democratic was so before it made the transition from something else to democracy. Every state that is democratic had to learn by trial and error how to become a democracy. Many of those states that are today democracies were, in the past, as rigidly authoritarian and as thoroughly conformist as are the states associated with Confucian culture.

Consensus and Consent

A final factor concerning the establishment and consolidation of democracy deserving consideration is consensus regarding national identity. To rule, every regime must be founded on some form of legitimacy—regardless of whether it is established by coercion or consent. Democracy differs from other forms of government, however, because "democratic stability requires a widespread belief among both elites and masses that democracy is the best form of government for their society and hence, that the democratic regime is morally entitled to rule."[55] For democracy to be consolidated, then, there must be general agreement about the propriety of the form of government. General agreement itself is consensus. Consensus about the propriety of the form of government is consent that confers legitimacy. The conundrum currently confronting Taiwan is whether it is possible for there to be a consensus about the form of government without agreement about the identity of the polity to be governed.

In a statement highly suggestive of the current problems on Taiwan, Dankwart Rustow wrote "[t]he vast majority of citizens in a democracy-to-be must have no doubt or mental reservations as to which political community they belong to."[56] His rationale for this conclusion reflects his understanding of democracy as a system governed by "temporary majorities." Whether or not there is in fact an alternation of power between rival political forces, that alternation must, in principle, be possible. The possibility that a popular regime will be voted out of office is the essence of the uncertainty of which Przeworski wrote.[57] A party or leader may be reelected, but the system can be considered democratic only if the electorate had the choice of replacing one regime or leader with another.

Rustow maintained that for this system to function "the boundaries [of the polity] must endure, the composition of the citizenry be continuous."[58] He claimed that "national unity" is a precondition of democracy. It does not matter how or how long before the onset of democratization this unity was agreed to, but democracy will not take root without a commonly accepted sense of national identity. On Taiwan the fundamental controversy dividing the regime and the opposition revolves around the identity of the state. Many countries have disgruntled minorities that hope to secede from the state, but on Taiwan it is still unclear whether the place is a polity itself or the seceded portion of another state.

Rustow avoided using the term *consensus* about the sentiment of identification that he described as essential "because that implies a consciously held opinion and deliberate agreement." He viewed the common, popular sense of how the polity is constituted as a "background condition" that is most effectively satisfied when it is "accepted unthinkingly, is silently taken for granted."[59] Moreover, Rustow doubted that residual questions of national unity could be resolved by democratic means. He implied that if there is no unity, it is unlikely that democracy will emerge and become "habitual." In his words, "the hardest struggles in democracy are those against the birth defects of the political community."[60]

Sidney Verba, in an essay about political culture, commented that political identity may be "the most critical political belief" that people hold. Political identity enables one to determine "of what political unit or units does the individual consider himself a member, and how deep and unambiguous is the sense of identification?" Verba emphasized the significance of this component of a person's self-conception. "It is not merely a question of the physical location an individual assigns to himself, as he might identify himself by saying, 'I live on such and such a street.' Rather the identification with the nation may be and often is one of the basic beliefs that serve to define an individual for himself."[61] Verba stated this more forcefully, asserting that "the first and most crucial problem that must be solved in the formation of a political culture, if it is to be capable of supporting a stable yet adaptable political system, is that of national identity." This must take the form of a "commitment that the political elites can arouse" among the populace to the political system "over and above its actual performance."[62] For the political elite, "the problem of national identity may be the first one that must be faced. Unless they are sure of their identity the many other problems of change will have to wait. . . . For whatever reasons, it seems clear that the problem of identity for the members of a nation is one that cannot be postponed."[63] Here the views of Rustow and Verba converge. Verba suggested that national identity corresponds to territorial boundaries and that it is just as important for a people to have a clear and unambiguous notion of their identity as of their territory. For him, the tendency for people to live within a state but identify primarily with some group other than the state "such as a family or tribe or region" is less characteristic of a modern society in which people are "concerned with the central units of political integration."[64] Moreover, "[p]olitical change and development add a new dimension to the issue of identity. Whether or not the members of a political system have a strong and positive identification with their nation becomes important."[65]

Although Verba was not thinking primarily of a situation like the one facing Taiwan, he was aware that uncertainties about identity can be manifested in many ways. Verba described not only those states in which people have a primary loyalty to a subnational political unit, which is "the major source of cultural conflict within nations," but also situations in which the problem with national identity arises because "there is some ambiguity in the definition of that unit." He cited the case of Germany, where "the lack of coordination between cultural, linguistic, and political boundaries has caused serious identity problems."[66]

Both Rustow and Verba made clear that it is difficult for the latter to take place until the former is accomplished. According to Verba, "Other problems are likely to be pushed aside until the central problem is met; 'What is my nation?' must be answered before 'What kind of a nation?' The histories of divided nations such as Italy and Germany . . .

suggest the power of the identity problem, for almost invariably the problems of unity and independence—problems basic to identity—push other problems such as democracy and social reform aside."[67] This point is echoed by Eric Nordlinger, who wrote, with respect to democratization, "to maximize the probabilities of a political system's developing in a non-violent, nonauthoritarian form and ultimately achieving democratic stability, a sense of national identity should precede the institutionalization of the central government." He added, "Not only might the procedural values be readily challenged if governmental institutions were formed before a sense of national identity had emerged, but the legitimacy of the central government's mere existence might be called into question when parochial groups tried to secede or refused to accept the authority of the governmental incumbents."[68]

Verba also perceived the primary issue as procedural. He explained that agreement about national identity is particularly important as a foundation for democracy because two hallmarks of a democratic system are uncertainty and impermanence. Political outcomes are, a priori, uncertain, and "whatever is legislated today can be overturned" by subsequent generations of legislators working within the framework of democracy tomorrow. Democracy depends on flexibility and does not function well when lawmakers of today attempt to bind future lawmakers to unpopular or fiercely contested positions. Conversely, democracy breaks down if current lawmakers continuously undo whatever was done by past legislators.

Although some policy domains may tolerate the reversals that come with successive generations of legislators, it is not clear that the national identity and the public policies that emerge from the international status of a polity are as flexible. Verba concluded that while it is probably not appropriate to view agreement about national identity as a precondition on which the consolidation of democracy absolutely depends, it is also too volatile an issue to be subjected to the repeated buffeting associated with the democratic process.[69]

By 1992, it seemed that Taiwan had established a set of democratic institutions and was engaged in the process of consolidation. Despite this progress, there was still no overt resolution of the question about Taiwan's national identity. Indeed, the question about national identity seems to have been deferred—though not forgotten—while the political elite struggled to hammer out a democratic alternative to the authoritarian system they had acknowledged was obsolete.

It is highly unlikely that Mainlanders and Taiwanese will arrive at an overt consensus about national identity. In the abstract, it is difficult to imagine that a system can be established to govern on the basis of the consent of the governed when the governed and their governors do not agree about the identity of the country in which they all live.

Regarding Taiwan specifically, once it was clear that liberalization would give way to democratization there was some tension about whether the KMT would permit a genuine democracy to be established or not. There were two reasons to question whether the KMT was serious about democracy. One was the simple issue of whether KMT officials were really willing to tolerate challenges to their power and privilege. The greater source of consternation is whether the KMT would enable democratization to proceed to such a point that even the question of Taiwan's political status could be put to a vote.

The precarious and ambiguous political status of Taiwan and the unresolved matter of what its political system should become cannot persist indefinitely. As one considers the development of democracy on the island, one must question whether the Taiwan case undermines the theories that specify the primacy of consensus about identity. Alternatively, it is possible that, despite rhetoric to the contrary, Taiwan's political elite have already achieved tacit consensus about the matter of national identity. If that is the case, then Taiwan is an independent state.

Notes

1. See Arend Lijphart, *Democracy in Plural Societies: A Comparative Exploration* (New Haven: Yale University Press, 1977), pp. 1, 3–4.

2. Giovanni Sartori, "Democracy," in *International Encyclopedia of the Social Sciences*, vol. 4, ed. David Sills (New York: Macmillan and The Free Press), pp. 112, 115.

3. Philippe C. Schmitter and Terry Lynn Karl, "What Democracy Is . . . and Is Not," *Journal of Democracy*, vol. 2, no. 3 (Summer 1991), p. 75.

4. Joseph A. Schumpeter, *Capitalism, Socialism and Democracy* (New York: Harper and Brothers, 1950), p. 269. Sartori distinguished modern democracy from its classical origins by writing that the former is "based not on participation but on representation; it presupposes not direct exercise of power but delegation of power; it is not, in short, a system of self-government, but a system of control and limitation of government." Sartori, "Democracy," p. 115.

5. Samuel P. Huntington, *The Third Wave: Democratization in the Late Twentieth Century* (Norman: University of Oklahoma Press, 1991), pp. 6–7.

6. Robert Dahl, *Polyarchy: Participation and Opposition* (New Haven: Yale University Press, 1971), pp. 1–2.

7. Ibid., p. 9, n. 4.

8. Ibid., p. 5.

9. Juan J. Linz, "Totalitarian and Authoritarian Regimes," in *Handbook of Political Science*, vol. 3: *Macropolitical Theory*, ed. Fred I. Greenstein and Nelson W. Polsby (Reading, MA: Addison-Wesley, 1975), pp. 182–83.

10. Samuel P. Huntington, "Will More Countries Become Democratic?" *Political Science Quarterly*, vol. 99, no. 2 (Summer 1984), p. 195.

11. Huntington, *The Third Wave*, p. 7.

12. Ibid., p. 9.

13. Ibid., p. 8.

14. Dankwart Rustow, "Transitions to Democracy: Toward a Dynamic Model," *Comparative Politics*, vol. 2 (April 1970), p. 339; Giuseppe Di Palma, *To Craft Democracies: An Essay on Democratic Transitions* (Berkeley: University of California Press, 1990), p. 14.

15. Zehra F. Arat, "Democracy and Economic Development: Modernization Theory Revisited," *Comparative Politics*, vol. 21 (October 1988), p. 21.

16. Myron Weiner, "Empirical Democratic Theory and the Transitions from Authoritarianism to Democracy," *PS*, vol. 20 (Fall 1987), p. 861; and Terry Lynn Karl, "Dilemmas of Democratization in Latin America," *Comparative Politics*, vol. 23 (October 1990), p. 3.

17. Huntington, *The Third Wave*, p. 38.

18. Tun-jen Cheng and Stephan Haggard, "Regime Transformation in Taiwan: Theoretical and Comparative Perspectives," in *Political Change in Taiwan*, ed. Tun-jen Cheng and Stephan Haggard (Boulder, CO: Lynne Rienner, 1992), p. 2.

19. Schmitter and Karl, "What Democracy Is . . . and Is Not," p. 76.

20. Ibid., p. 78.

21. Adam Przeworski, "Some Problems in the Study of the Transition to Democracy," in *Transitions from Authoritarian Rule: Comparative Perspectives*, ed. Guillermo O'Donnell, Philippe C. Schmitter, and Laurence Whitehead (Baltimore: Johns Hopkins University Press, 1986), p. 56.

22. Ibid., p. 57. See also Schmitter and Karl, "What Democracy Is . . . and Is Not," p. 82.

23. See, for example, Stephen Engleberg, "East Bloc Treading Water in a Sinkhole of Lethargy," *New York Times*, April 8, 1992, p. 1.

24. Schmitter and Karl, "What Democracy Is . . . and Is Not," p. 83.

25. Rustow, "Transitions to Democracy," p. 344.

26. Interview with Ma Ying-cheou, Taipei, July 3, 1991.

27. Adam Przeworski, *Democracy and the Market: Political and Economic Reforms in Eastern Europe and Latin America* (Cambridge: Cambridge University Press, 1991), p. 51.

28. Huntington, *The Third Wave*, pp. 15–21.

29. Guillermo O'Donnell, Philippe C. Schmitter, and Laurence Whitehead, eds. *Transitions from Authoritarian Rule: Tentative Conclusions about Uncertain Democracies* (Baltimore: Johns Hopkins University Press, 1986), p. 3.

30. Rustow, "Transitions to Democracy," p. 345.

31. O'Donnell, Schmitter, and Whitehead, *Transitions from Authoritarian Rule: Tentative Conclusions*, p. 5.

32. Ibid., p. 3.

33. Ibid., pp. 6–7.

34. Dahl, *Polyarchy*, chapter 1.

35. O'Donnell, Schmitter, and Whitehead, *Transitions from Authoritarian Rule: Tentative Conclusions*, p. 8.

36. Ibid., pp. 6–11.

37. Huntington, *The Third Wave*, p. 9.

38. Ibid., p. 126; O'Donnell, Schmitter, and Whitehead, *Transitions from Authoritarian Rule: Tentative Conclusions*, p. 11.

39. Rustow, "Transitions to Democracy," p. 345; Karl, "Dilemmas of Democratization," p. 5.

40. Huntington, *The Third Wave*, p. 121.

41. Ibid.

42. Ibid., chapter 3, especially p. 113, table 3.1.

43. Replacements also occurred in Argentina, East Germany, Portugal, Romania, and the Soviet Union. Huntington, *The Third Wave*, pp. 142–51.

44. Ibid., p. 151.

45. Ibid., pp. 151–63.

46. Ibid., p.124.

47. Cheng and Haggard, "Regime Transformation in Taiwan," p. 2. See also Huntington, *The Third Wave*, pp. 124–42.

48. Huntington, *The Third Wave*, pp. 137–39.

49. Ibid., pp. 139–41.

50. Ibid., pp. 164–65.

51. See Di Palma, *To Craft Democracies*.

52. O'Donnell, Schmitter, and Whitehead, *Transitions from Authoritarian Rule: Tentative Conclusions*, pp. 3–4.

53. Przeworski, *Democracy and the Market*, p. 51.

54. Huntington, *The Third Wave*, p. 295.

55. Larry Diamond, Seymour Martin Lipset, and Juan Linz, "Building and Sustaining Democratic Government in Developing Countries: Some Tentative Findings," *World Affairs*, vol. 150, no. 1 (Summer 1987), p. 7.

56. Rustow, "Transitions to Democracy," p. 350.

57. See Przeworski, "Some Problems in the Study of the Transition to Democracy," in *Transitions from Authoritarian Rule: Comparative Perspectives*, ed. O'Donnell, Schmitter, and Whitehead.

58. Rustow, "Transitions to Democracy," p. 351.

59. Ibid.

60. Ibid., p. 360.

61. Sidney Verba, "Comparative Political Culture," in *Political Culture and Political Development*, ed. Lucian W. Pye and Sidney Verba (Princeton: Princeton University Press, 1965), p. 529. Although Verba used the terms *national identity* and *political identity* to describe an individual's identification with a polity and Rustow wrote of national unity as a collective consciousness about the polity, it is fair to surmise that they were writing about different dimensions of

the same belief. See also Lucian Pye, *Politics, Personality and Nation Building: Burma's Search for Identity* (New Haven: Yale University Press, 1962), p. 15.

62. Verba, "Comparative Political Culture," p. 529.

63. Ibid., p. 530.

64. Ibid.

65. Ibid., p. 531.

66. Ibid., p. 532.

67. Ibid., p. 533.

68. Eric Nordlinger, "Political Development: Time Sequences and Rates of Change," in *Political Development and Social Change*, 2d ed., ed. Jason L. Finkle and Richard W. Gable (New York: John Wiley and Sons, 1966), pp. 459, 464.

69. Sidney Verba offered these reflections about his earlier theoretical work during a discussion in Cambridge, Massachusetts, on February 13, 1992.

3

Conflicting Identities On Taiwan

Identity and Views of the "Other"

To consider matters of identity, one must depart the world of facts and enter a realm of sentiment and beliefs. As one begins to probe, it soon becomes evident that the convictions people have about their own identity are not necessarily consistent with reason. For that reason, the following discussion necessarily simplifies the depiction of identity because it is in terms of the simplification—rather than the complex reality—that the political battles are waged.

Identities are driven by emotion, they are dynamic, and they are seldom exclusive. Individuals have multiple, overlapping, or sometimes competing identities, and the bases for a person's disparate sentiments of identification may differ.[1] Discussions with members of Taiwan's political and intellectual elite suggest that people also have different notions about what it means to identify with a particular social category. For instance, one person may believe that being Chinese encompasses cultural, national, and political factors. Another person may distinguish between being culturally Chinese and being politically associated with a country other than China. There is no list of criteria by which one may determine who is *really* Chinese when people from Vancouver to Penang, Tsingtao to Lukang all claim the same label.

The inability to define who is Chinese may make for interesting academic discourse, but on Taiwan it has caused considerable political discord. Such pluralism may be acceptable in other contexts, but conformity and unity have long been prized in Chinese society. Collective consciousness rather than idiosyncratic expression is still valued highly. On contemporary Taiwan, the expectation of uniformity—rather than pluralism or polarity—persists, albeit less than in the past. Political liberalization has weakened the KMT's capacity to enforce a single view of such matters as Taiwan's political status or the cultural and political identities of Taiwan's residents. By the early 1990s, no other group had yet to emerge with sufficient moral suasion to succeed the KMT in that role.

When one begins to probe how residents of Taiwan view themselves, one finds that some seem clear that they are part of the Chinese nation—where nationality is defined in terms of "shared identity and feelings of affinity."[2] This sense of belonging cuts across the divide between Taiwanese and Mainlanders and across class boundaries, too. Others acknowledge their Chinese origin but identify themselves as Taiwanese. This group, in turn, is divided into those who consider Taiwan as their nation and those for whom Taiwanese is an ethnic category within the Chinese nation. In short, there is an absence of consensus.

The disparity of views has made people on Taiwan highly sensitive to the origins of others with whom they interact. Hill Gates observed some years ago that in social settings "new acquaintances were usually 'placed' for me . . . as Taiwanese or Mainlanders. The common social chat among strangers attending dinner parties begins by establishing the origins of all persons present with jocular references to foods, speech peculiarities, or personality traits supposedly characteristic of each ethnic group."[3] The intensity of differences that Gates observed may have dissipated with time and Taiwan's youth may be less concerned about these matters than were their parents, who remember the dislocation that came from immigration or the transition from Japanese to KMT rule. For most of the first four decades of KMT governance, however, the state employed administrative procedures that encouraged people to identify themselves on the basis of their ethnic identity.

In keeping with Chinese patrilineal traditions, one's ethnic identity has been defined in terms of one's father's ancestral origin and, until the early 1990s, this information was recorded on the identity card carried by all people older than fifteen.[4] With the mounting pressure to reform, the government swept aside this regulation, but that has not eliminated the inclination to pigeonhole people as either a Mainlander or a Taiwanese, even though it was much easier to do so in the years soon after the KMT retreated to Taiwan. At that time, the distinctions were fairly obvious and the criteria for labeling a person rather simple.

With time, intermarriage, and the birth of subsequent generations, these distinctions have become more difficult to draw and the criteria rather tenuous.

From the late 1940s to the mid-1980s, the prejudices between Mainlanders and Taiwanese were fairly ingrained. This has changed. People demur at the suggestion that stereotypes of Taiwanese and Mainlanders persist. One influential journalist, a second-generation Mainlander, recalled, "When I was young, when I talked to people, I used to ask, 'where are you from?' But now that question never jumps into my mind. I just look at [the person to see] whether he is very well educated, is he boring, is he articulate, is he interesting? It is not the first question which jumps into my mind, 'is this stranger Taiwanese or Mainlander?' "[5] Indeed, by the early 1990s blatant prejudices had been supplanted by a rediscovery of Taiwanese ethnicity that became possible only with the development of a more liberal society.[6] In that regard, restaurants featuring Taiwanese cuisine, teahouses, and pubs now re-create the ambiance of Taiwan's past. Books about Taiwanese culture, politics, and literature line the shelves of local bookstores, and courses about these topics are offered in Taiwan's universities. Popular arts and culture now explore issues of Taiwan's past. All of this is new and none of this would have been tolerated only a few years ago.

Although distinctions on the basis of identification are not as overt as in the past, one cannot escape the impression that people on Taiwan are at least still aware of a "we" and "they" dichotomy, even if this distinction is not paramount in people's assessment of others. The propensity to classify people in "we" and "they" categories is a reflection of the division between Taiwanese and Mainlanders and manifests itself most prominently in politics. The distinction between these groups is sometimes cultural, sometimes national, but nearly always political.

The legacy of four decades during which these distinctions were sharply drawn abides. A television series on one of the three national television networks accentuates the stereotypes that many claim no longer matter. A television critic wrote that the series is imbued with Han chauvinism. "It emphasizes the superiority of Mainlanders and, as the plot unfolds, blurs a number of factual situations regarding the Taiwanese and even makes them feel inadequate. Throughout the plot, every law-abiding and just person, every reasonable person, and every cultivated person seems to be played by a Mainlander and the hoodlums, petty thieves, snobs, money-grubbers, and vacillators, seem to be Taiwanese."[7] For some people these distinctions may be more consequential than for others. In some contexts the distinctions may be more apparent than in others. In the political context—especially among the political elite—the distinction between "we" and "they" is both consequential and apparent.

Who Are "They"?

When prodded to describe how one distinguished between Mainlanders and Taiwanese, people called up characterizations of the "other." The assumption that underlies these prejudices is that one's place of birth determines one's identity and world view. Crude distinctions between Mainlanders and Taiwanese do not always make a great deal of sense, and one must remember that the identity a person feels—or attributes to others—is an emotional attachment, not a carefully reasoned position.

For example, when Taiwanese described Mainlanders, they described them as a monolithic group. Many Mainlanders, however, emigrated from the same provinces from which the Taiwanese trace their own origins. As an illustration, consider that many of the old, redbrick family compounds that were constructed by rural families on Taiwan centuries ago are still standing and inhabited. These multigenerational homes are built around a courtyard and oriented so that a pavilion in which the family's ancestral tablets are preserved is the centermost chamber of a generally symmetrical array of buildings. Over the main door to the central pavilion, a place of architectural focus and symbolic import, one commonly finds a plaque on which is inscribed the name of the village on the mainland from which the family originated. Family crypts may also bear an inscription of the location on the mainland from which Taiwanese families came.[8]

Not only is the effort to distinguish between Taiwanese and Mainlander on the basis of original locale questionable, but these categories are too broad to have much meaning. A Taiwanese whose family came from Fukien in the seventeenth century may have much more in common (dialect, diet, and deities) with a Mainlander who arrived from Fukien in 1949 than that Mainlander might have with someone from Szechwan or Shantung who arrived on Taiwan at the same time. There is also a tendency to blur the distinction between the Mainlander elite who came from the mainland as the cream of China's intellectual, commercial, and political crops, and the Mainlanders who came as soldiers in the ragtag army of the KMT. The former were privileged and powerful. The veterans and their families led much simpler lives, some in deprivation.

The real line of demarcation affecting people's identity is not province of origin, although that is relevant, but time of arrival on Taiwan and attitude about Taiwan's political status. Among those who were adults in 1945, the criterion is generally a matter of where they lived at that time. If they were already on Taiwan, their political identity was probably shaped by their experience under Japanese rule and as the object of KMT control in the years that followed. They are unlikely to have much interest in reunification, may or may not actively support the Taiwan independence movement, but almost assuredly hope to preserve and expand Taiwan's autonomy under any guise that will work.

If they were on the mainland in 1945 and then made their way to Taiwan, it is likely that they associate themselves with the policies of the KMT—particularly the promotion of reunification, as many left parents, siblings, spouses, children, and friends on the mainland. More importantly, Mainlanders have feared that their fate hinges on the KMT remaining as the ruling party. If the Taiwanese opposition gains control, Mainlanders worry that they will rapidly begin to feel the minority status the KMT has been able to shield them from for the past four decades.

P'eng Ming-min, who returned to Taiwan in November 1992 after being in exile for more than two decades, said that "Mainlanders have been manipulated for forty years to support the KMT" regardless of whether it was in their best interest or not. The KMT operated along the principle of divide and rule and thereby persuaded Mainlanders that as long as it was in power, they would be safeguarded. P'eng said that the KMT encouraged the belief that if Taiwanese were to govern the island, Mainlanders would all be thrown into the sea. P'eng explained that the "sense of crisis" and "siege mentality" among Mainlanders now is thoroughly unfounded. If Taiwanese were to run the state, the only ones who might lose out are the Mainlanders who have held the positions of power and privilege that Taiwanese now seek. The common Mainlanders certainly have no reason to be uneasy. P'eng pointed out that there are a number of counties with

Taiwanese chief executives and a number of cities on Taiwan with Taiwanese mayors. P'eng asked rhetorically, "Are Mainlanders persecuted" in those places?[9]

The sense of the other as different persists. Taiwan has been separated from China for so long that there evolved a set of social mores peculiar to Taiwanese. This sense of difference causes Taiwanese to see themselves as belonging to a group of which the Mainlanders are not a part, even if they cannot agree about the principal differences. Personal traits, body language, and demeanor were all described as clues about who is a Mainlander and who is Taiwanese. While many people dismiss the possibility of distinguishing between Mainlanders and Taiwanese on any basis other than language, there is still a belief in some quarters that "you can just tell." This is not a phenomenon limited to the people of Taiwan.

> Between groups and subgroups of the Sinitic peoples there are ... clearly established behavioral stereotypes. The alleged personality differences between the people of each province and/or dialect group are spoken about by Chinese as assuredly ... as are the differences in "national character" within Europe by Europeans.[10]

In discussion about these matters, people also indicated that the ability to distinguish between Taiwanese and Mainlanders was easier in the past than it is now. For some Mainlanders, the difference between themselves and the Taiwanese was a matter of economic class distinction. One second-generation Mainlander explained that as a schoolgirl she carefully chose her friends from among other second-generation Mainlanders because she could communicate with them and because she saw them as more polite than the Taiwanese children. She said that their family backgrounds were similar.

> We [have] very similar lifestyle[s], we can share the same life experience; ... usually the Mainlanders will teach their kids very politely. Filial piety is very important in a Mainland[er] family. You say, "good morning," [and] "good night." When guest[s] come, you have to come out to say, "hello," bring tea, [and] bring slippers. You have to do all kinds of those things. But, I don't know if the Taiwanese kids are trained that way. I never lived with them. Maybe they do in a big, rich family. But usually in the rural area[s], I don't think they really teach kids to do that.[11]

This woman pointed out that her attitude toward Taiwanese began to change when she reached junior high school and encountered better educated and more refined Taiwanese. Still, she recalled enjoying the occasional opportunity to accompany a Taiwanese friend to a religious ritual at which there was a lot of praying and eating. Her description suggested that she viewed Taiwanese folk customs as quaint or exotic.

This, of course, is the view of a Mainlander who is one of the political elite. The distinction between the KMT soldiers who followed Chiang Kai-shek to Taiwan and their "earthy" Taiwanese compatriots is not so clearly a reflection of class differences or social polish. The veterans and their families who live in military villages and retirement homes and the vast cohort of aging single men who either left wives on the mainland or never married on Taiwan came from the lowest rungs of China's society before 1949. If one is to measure by reference to social polish, there is probably less of a difference between them and the Taiwanese farmers than between them and the Mainlander elite. All of this is to say that the distinctions between Mainlanders and Taiwanese are simplifications that mask a wide range of actualities.

For those born on Taiwan after 1945 (those who constitute the "second-generation" Mainlanders and their offspring, the Taiwanese, and all those who were born to mixed parentage), identity revolves largely around the issue of Chinese unity. Many Taiwan-born Mainlanders feel that they are just as Taiwanese as the Taiwanese. They complain that they are excluded from Taiwanese society because one or both of their parents was born on the mainland. Some even fear that because they are considered by Taiwanese as second-generation Mainlanders, not Taiwanese, they may be persecuted and deprived of their present social standing if Taiwanese extremists come to power.

One influential professional born on Taiwan to Mainlander parents said he "belongs" on the island of Taiwan and regards it as his home. He maintained that he shares a sense of Taiwan consciousness with Taiwanese and resents being excluded from the Taiwanese category because of his reliance on Mandarin and his parents' province of origin. He found it difficult to accept that in the eyes of Taiwanese he represents a class of repressors and expressed frustration that Taiwanese did not consider him to be a compatriot. He said that after a recent trip from Taiwan to the mainland, he felt more intensely than ever his association with Taiwan and said he would happily fight alongside Taiwanese to defend the island against any assault from the Communists. He fully identified with Taiwan as his home. Still, he hopes that ultimately Taiwan may be reunified with the mainland. He also revealed that he was very concerned about what would happen to him professionally when Taiwanese control the government.[12]

C.V. Chen said that he was born in 1944 in the city of Kunming in Yunnan Province on the mainland, but moved to Taiwan when he was five years old. Technically, he is not a member of the second generation but asked, after more than forty years on Taiwan, "Am I not a local Taiwanese?" He believes he is. He sees no contradiction between his identification with Taiwan as his home and his identity as a Chinese that impels him to push for reunification. For many Taiwanese, however, C.V. Chen is the archetypal, privileged power holder from the mainland whose interest in Taiwan is overshadowed by his greater concern for unification.[13]

Taiwanese vehemently distrust Mainlanders like C.V. Chen who are committed to promoting reunification. Conversely, Mainlanders deeply resent and distrust Taiwanese devoted to working toward independence. Each group sees the other as foolishly irresponsible, tempting fate, and spoiling a good thing. The visceral repugnance people who identify with one group—whether Mainlanders or Taiwanese—hold for the activists and extremists of the other group contributes to a general characterization of "we" versus "they."

Chen Shui-pian, a Taiwanese lawmaker in the Legislative Yuan, rejected the notion of classifying the population into Taiwanese and Mainlanders. For him, as long as an individual identifies with Taiwan, even if the person lives abroad, then that person is Taiwanese. He said that regardless of whether a person is a so-called aborigine, Hakka, *Minnan jen* (a Taiwanese with roots in Fukien Province), or Mainlander who arrived after 1949, that person can be considered Taiwanese if he or she identifies with the island. He declared that other than the aboriginal population of Taiwan, "strictly speaking, all of us are Mainlanders." He explained that "[W]e all emigrated. It's only a matter of coming earlier or later. Regardless whether you came earlier or later, as long as you identify with this place, we don't consider that only those who came earlier are Taiwanese and those who came later are not."[14] Chen's disclaimer notwithstanding, the inclination to classify people as either Taiwanese or Mainlander—even though the categories do not make as much sense today as they may have in 1949—still expresses itself in the ordinary affairs of politics. The prominence of the "we" and "they" distinction in politics has to do with the role the KMT claimed for itself on Taiwan, the conflict between the KMT and the CCP for the right to rule the mainland, and the unresolved matter of Taiwan's political status. It is not surprising, then, that people claim that the distinction between Mainlanders and Taiwanese is no longer a conspicuous factor in their daily lives, but it remains an essential ingredient in the political sphere.

Where Do We Live?

Although people may have clear convictions about their identity as either Chinese or Taiwanese, there is considerable uncertainty about the identity of the polity in which they live. The term used in Chinese to connote the problem is *kuo-chia jen-t'ung*, which one might translate as "national identity" except that it does not really pertain to the nation as "the people" as much as to the nation as "the country." That is, the term is applied to the identity of Taiwan, not to the residents of the island.

Taiwan's ambiguous status makes it difficult to know whether the island is a country itself or only part of a larger country. It is equally difficult to determine what is meant by China. If China is synonymous with the mainland, it implies that Taiwan is not part of China. C.V. Chen once stated, "If Taiwan is a part of China, then the mainland is also a part of China." That is, "only when the Chinese in Taiwan and the mainland are added together will China be complete."[15]

This notion, too, is imprecise. What, afterall, is meant by "the mainland," and what territories must be unified for China to be complete? Are the territories of the PRC—with the addition of Taiwan —coterminous with what is considered to be China? Chen Shui-pian asked which China is now viewed as the standard by which to know whether China is unified or not? Rhetorically, he asked whether China should be measured by the boundaries of the Chin dynasty of the third century B.C. or the boundaries that existed when the Republic of China was established at the end of the Ch'ing dynasty? He pointed out sarcastically that China has had a lot of dynasties. "Should we use the T'ang Dynasty as the standard or the Han dynasty or the Yuan dynasty?" He said that if the Yuan dynasty is viewed as the measure, then China's territory is quite expansive and even includes contemporary Moscow and segments of the Middle East. He pointed out that there were times in China's past when the entire Korean peninsula and what is now Vietnam were also Chinese, yet nobody seriously expects that contemporary China should be "unified" to include all that territory.[16]

Chen's point is that the idea of *i-t'ung*, the great unity of China which gives rise to the sentiment espoused by the Mainlanders that reunification is an important end, is specious. China's boundaries have expanded and receded with the passage of time. There is no reason why Taiwan must be part of the Chinese state for China to be complete.

As they try to define their sense of identity, people blur the distinctions between different dimensions of identity. They mingle references to their identity as Chinese or Taiwanese (cultural, ethnic, or national identity), to the identity of the political entity to which they feel a sense of attachment, and to the identity of the polity in which they live. This confusion hints at the problem contemporary Chinese have reconciling their emotional attachments with political realities. For the elite, it is difficult to define either China or Taiwan as a political unit without tripping into ambiguity. To define their political identity, people conjure rationales comprised of two key ingredients: history and pragmatism.

Those who appeal to the past cite historical data or theories to justify their views. For example, some endeavor to show that Taiwan was always a part of China and therefore should not be considered an independent state today. Hau Pei-tsun, who served as premier during the most tumultuous period of political transformation, explained that the fate of Taiwan is inseparable from that of the Chinese mainland. He said, "More than three hundred years ago, because the Ming dynasty was in decline, Cheng Ch'eng-kung [Koxinga] came to Taiwan." The change in circumstances on the mainland led Koxinga to take control of the island. In a similar fashion, Hau continued, at the conclusion of the Sino-Japanese War of 1894–1895, "the Ch'ing dynasty lost so the Ch'ing gave Taiwan to Japan. We can say that the change in the fate of Taiwan was because the Ch'ing governors on the mainland lost the war with Japan." A major turnabout in Taiwan's fate was determined again at the end of the Second World War, when Japan was forced to return Taiwan to the ROC. "It is not that Taiwan was itself able to control its own fate. In these circumstances that was not possible. The changes in the circumstances of the Taiwan region were all the results of changes in the circumstances of the mainland."

Hau said that in 1949, because of the "luck" of the CCP on the mainland, the KMT lost and then came to Taiwan.

> But, because the KMT brought talent, 600,000 soldiers, gold, and whatever to Taiwan, the CCP could not control Taiwan. So, today's KMT, the ROC government, took root and stood its ground firmly and stayed in Taiwan because of changes in circumstances on the mainland. But, if in 1949 the former president, President Chiang, did not bring the 600,000 soldiers to Taiwan, didn't bring talent from the mainland to Taiwan, Taiwan would have been governed by the CCP since 1949 and would not have had the democratic development of today and would not have seen the development of the DPP.[17]

Alternatively, others argue that for the past three hundred years Taiwan was rarely under the effective control of the Chinese court and therefore should not relinquish its de facto independence now. P'eng Ming-min pointed to the past century. From 1895 to the present, he said, "Taiwan has been legally, economically, geographically, totally independent from China except for four years: 1945–1949." Taiwan and the mainland were only unified and under one government for that four-year stretch. In P'eng's view, "separation is the normal state."[18]

In this debate, both sides assume that if they accrete sufficient evidence that the way things were accords with their view of how things should be, then the weight of history itself will be persuasive. Those who appeal to pragmatism seem less concerned with how well the present and future mimic the past, and more concerned with what can really be accomplished given the international context and domestic conditions that inhere. For instance, it is common for advocates of reunification to criticize those who demand independence, saying that the latter are impractical and irresponsible because they neglect the adamant views of the Communist authorities in Peking who oppose an independent Taiwan. They claim to fear that the PRC will use military force against Taiwan if it even seems that the ROC government has relaxed its opposition to independence.

Those who advocate independence, on the other hand, claim that the notion of reunification is unworkable because of the tremendous gap in the standard of living, political liberties, and opportunity that exists when the mainland and Taiwan are juxtaposed. They view official attempts to improve relations with the mainland as opening the door to a settlement in which Taiwan may be absorbed by the Communists and denuded of its assets. They wonder what Taiwan has to gain by sacrificing its autonomy to be a junior partner in an enterprise it will not easily influence. P'eng Ming-min asked what reason there is for Taiwan to reunite with China, "except that our culture is Chinese." He said that nobody ever points out concrete advantages to reunification, even though the disadvantages are numerous.[19]

In the end, opponents of reunification are skeptical. They charge that the KMT claims to fear PRC military reprisals as a ruse to keep Taiwan from becoming democratic. Chang Chun-hung, secretary-general of the DPP during the period under consideration, said the KMT does not, fundamentally, want to reunify with the mainland, but hoists the banner of reunification to justify its claim to rule Taiwan as part of China.[20] In that the KMT came to Taiwan claiming to be the sole legitimate government of all China, its primary source of legitimacy on Taiwan was that claim, as it had no mandate from the people of Taiwan. To reinforce that worldview, the KMT emphasized that Taiwan was a part of China and therefore that it, the KMT, was justified in continuing to govern the island. Even today, Taiwan maintains a provincial government as well as a national government, even though the territory controlled by each is nearly the same.

The difficulty is that both those who appeal to history and those who claim to be more pragmatic are selective in their reading of the past or present. How one presents historical evidence or assesses contemporary political realities depends as much on the view one espouses as on the evidence. Evidence used to underscore one position can be countered easily by other evidence or an alternative interpretation that undermines that position.

Perhaps there is no correct view of the past or the present. There may be no truth to which one can appeal nor any way to determine who is right and who is wrong. Indeed, in some ways each claimant is partially right and partially wrong. Yet each side dismisses the arguments of the other as a distortion of the past, a misreading of the present, a cunning effort to deceive, or a foolishly idealistic crusade. There has been very little effort to empathize with the other, to understand why others make the claims they do, or to reconcile one's own perceptions with the views of one's opponents.

Legislator Chen Shui-pian, however, commented about this mutual insensitivity, observing that "[s]ome people cry out that we should call a truce about the reunification/independence issue. My own view is that it is impossible to call a truce. The reunification/independence problem will exist forever and you can never evade it." Chen said that these two views were not like two train tracks that would run parallel to each other but never intersect. They cannot but intersect.

> What I mean is, you have to face this problem and while there are indeed many voices advocating Taiwan independence, one cannot deny that there are also those who think that China should be unified. Each position has its own supporters. If you insist that you absolutely want Taiwan to be independent and you do not give a damn about the views of those who advocate reunification, you do not care, you simply want Taiwan to be independent, then I believe that there will be problems. If you do not pay attention to these voices who advocate that China should be unified or if you ignore them on purpose, it may lead to another disturbance in Taiwan.
>
> Whether you ignore their existence or not, they still exist. Therefore, their voices will continue to be heard. If you suppress them or oppose them absolutely, it will be just as it was in the past when those of us who advocated that Taiwan should be independent were suppressed by the previous leaders of the KMT, the China KMT, who advocated re-unification, who suppressed us, imprisoned us, executed us, sent us into exile, put us on a black list and prohibited us from returning to Taiwan. It would be the same.
>
> So, we believe that those who advocate Taiwan independence should consider the position of those who advocate reunification. And the same goes for those in the KMT who advocate reunification, it's fine to do so, that is your political view, but you also ought to think of the other side and consider why it is that there are people who advocate an independent Taiwan and not habitually suppress them.[21]

Different Views of China

Taiwan's historical association with the mainland is an exceptionally thorny issue. Those who favor reunification look to the past to empha-size how long Taiwan has been (de jure) under the control of the Chinese court. Those who favor independence for Taiwan emphasize how the island has, in the past, maintained (de facto) autonomy. Since 1949, one of the few things about which officials in both Peking and Taipei have concurred is that Taiwan was and is a part of China.

One's identity as either Chinese or Taiwanese is tied to how one views China and Taiwan. For some people, China exists as a place; for others it is a concept. Often, though, the line between China as a concept and China as a territory is blurred. Tsiang Yien-si, secretary-general of the Office of the President, wrote that "more and more people would now accept the view that China is a trinity of culture, nation, and state."[22] Shaw Yu-ming asserted that in addition to being the name of the country, the word *China* also "symbolizes a cultural system of which Confucianism has long been a fundamental ingredient. . . . Since ancient times, the notion of one unified China has been deeply embedded in the minds of all Chinese. Perhaps alone among the major world civilizations, China is marked by a single, unbroken line of cultural identity.[23] For many Mainlanders, particularly the older ones who were adults when they took refuge on Taiwan, China consists of the mainland and Taiwan together. This has been the official view of the KMT. Tsiang Yien-si wrote:

> For more than forty years, we consider ourselves—the Republic of China—the legitimate representative for the entire Chinese nation, including both the mainland and Taiwan. In other words, we have never given up our sovereignty over mainland China.
>
> You may not understand why we maintain our claim of sovereignty over the mainland. But why should we give up that claim? What good would it bring us? In fact the claim is a reflection of our sense of responsibility, as long as we maintain our sovereignty, we would never forsake our duty in bringing freedom, democracy and prosperity to our compatriots on the mainland.[24]

People who hold this view object to the idea that Taiwan should be a separate political entity. To them, Taiwan used to be part of the empire and, therefore, *is* part of China. Former premier Hau Pei-tsun spoke with great conviction about the importance of unity in Chinese history. He said that China "can represent our history, culture, territory, and also includes our society, and political system." He linked the idea of geographic unity to the unity of the Chinese people. Hau explained:

> We Chinese have been one unified state since the Chin dynasty. The Yuan dynasty is not considered because it was extended to Europe and India. You can say that it was in the two hundred years of the Ch'ing dynasty that the borders of the Chinese people were defined and the Chinese people were unified. This is the common history of the Chinese all over the world, including the overseas Chinese. . . .
>
> This rationale was established on the foundation of the concept of unity of the Chinese people. So, . . . beginning with the Shang dynasty,

> Chou dynasty, at that time there were many divisions and unions. From division to unity . . . this became part of the culture of the Han people and formed a major stream of the culture of the Chinese people. . . . So China is a cultural, historical, political, territorial [entity]. This is the common desire of the entire Chinese people.[25]

Many Taiwanese, by contrast, oppose this view and claim that for most of the time Han Chinese inhabited the island, they were not under the jurisdiction of the central authorities on the continent. Taiwanese also feel it is hypocritical for the KMT, a party that traces its roots to a revolutionary ideology aimed at overthrowing the alien Ch'ing emperor, to claim Taiwan as part of China because it was taken more than three hundred years ago by forces who were themselves foreign rulers of China.

Ma Ying-cheou said that for government officials China is synonymous with the ROC. However, the ROC government has acknowledged that "there is a[nother] political entity in actual control of the mainland area to which we cannot extend our jurisdiction. That we understand. And we have gone so far as to acknowledge that. But the other side [the CCP] has not done that. They still refuse to recognize, or at least acknowledge, the political entity here. And they said, 'if you *are* a political entity, then you are a subentity.' "[26] C.V. Chen objected to the common misconstruction of China taken to mean the PRC. He said that the Communists have long claimed that because the PRC is larger than Taiwan it is, indisputably, China. Chen discounted the idea that merely because the territory and population of the PRC is larger it necessarily represents China.[27]

A senior official in the Foreign Ministry explained that traditionally China was seen as a politically unitary state. Development has engendered several different forms of China: a Hong Kong–China, a Taiwan–China, an eastern seaboard China, a southern China, and a middle China. He believes that no Chinese really want to see their country divided into a "China A, China B, and China C," and, in spite of these different notions of China, the ideal of a unity persists. This forms the core of China's nationalism: the view of a single, grand, unified China dominated by a central government.

The official said that "in people's hearts, honestly [we] feel we are still one China." Then he admitted that it may no longer be practical to think in terms of one China. He discussed the idea of a Chinese federation and suggested that during much of China's history, there actually was some sort of federation of feudal states loosely allied under an emperor to whom they all paid tribute.[28]

As an extension of this line of reasoning, anthropologist Li I-yuan said that while the notion of China as a unified political and cultural entity has been destroyed by the current political division, "culturally, every Chinese is in search of a kind of equilibrium, a total system of equilibrium."[29] This view is expressed by many Taiwanese and second-generation Mainlanders who view China as a concept. It is the homeland of their ancestors and the source of their cultural heritage, but it does not currently exist in a political sense. Ming Chu-cheng said, "We don't know who we are. Taiwanese are losing our own identity, yet we have not erected a new one."[30]

For those who promote reunification, the concept of unity is the highest ideal and a prominent theme in Chinese political thought. A high-ranking KMT official summed up this line of thinking by paraphrasing the opening passage of the epic novel *Romance of the Three Kingdoms*: "A world long divided must unite and when long united must divide."[31] Knowledgeable Mainlanders, however, distinguish between unity as an ideal and unity as a historical reality. They reject the view of China as a predominantly unified realm and describe how frequently China was divided as regional power holders contended for control. Despite this reality, division was ultimately viewed as intolerable; unity remained the objective.[32]

People who hold this view are reluctant to identify China as the mainland alone, because that would exclude Taiwan and play into the hands of those who promote Taiwan independence. At the same time, they would never say that China is only Taiwan. Their view of China is of a unity—the mainland and Taiwan subsumed in a single political entity. They vehemently oppose becoming citizens of the PRC and are viscerally disinclined to communism. Yet, they cannot envision a China that does not encompass the mainland.

In their view, China is now divided as Korea is and as Germany was. This line of reasoning has spawned its own debates and has frequently been featured as the subject of commentaries and editorials in the press. Some, like opposition leader Hsu Hsin-liang, say that the reunification of Germany occurred only because both West and East Germany were internationally recognized political entities with equal status and, therefore, it is important for Taiwan to have de jure independence as a precondition to any negotiations with the authorities on the mainland. Others, like KMT central committee member and National Assembly deputy Kao Hui-yu, point out that even though Korea is now divided, the residents of both North and South Korea see themselves as Koreans and are eager for the reunification of their state.[33]

P'eng Ming-min pointed out that the bid for Taiwan's independence is not like Quebec's desire to secede from Canada. Quebec, he said, "is an integral part of the territorial structure of Canada, that is not the same with Taiwan which has been separate from China for years." He went on to say that the desire for independence is not an effort to force a separation, but rather to recognize the status quo. By contrast, he said the efforts to reunify China are really a KMT quest to annex mainland China. "The idea that Taiwan cannot be separate from China is the result of brainwashing by the KMT to see the situation as separation. The KMT purposely plants this confusion."[34]

Independence: Autonomy or Sovereignty?

> The people in general don't care about reunification or independence.
> ... They want to be a sovereign state ... [in the] international community. They want to have their passport accepted in every country. Just like [people from] other countries. That's all.
>
> —Chiang Chun-nan

Through the Eyes of the Unifiers

Opponents of the Taiwan independence movement, fearful of the PRC's threats to use force to combat extremist Taiwan separatism, reason that Taiwan—as a part of the ROC—already is independent. The declaration of independence sought by proponents of independence will not improve the political standing of the island in the international community. Taiwan does not need to declare independence to be politically, socially, or economically autonomous.

The KMT has not wavered in its view of independence over the years, but has adjusted its rationale for seeking reunification. Shaw Yu-ming, while he was still the official spokesman of the government, explained the reasoning of the party about both unification and independence. He said that extremism, by which he meant the promotion of independence, will never become the mainstream on Taiwan. Indeed, he believed that the Taiwan independence movement would eventually die out. The government position, on the other hand, is more responsible, in part because reunification is inevitable. He, too, pointed to the reunification of Germany and the negotiations regarding normalization of relations between both parts of Korea and asserted that China and Taiwan will ultimately follow the same path.[35]

However, although the government believes in reunification as an ultimate goal, Shaw was quick to say that as leaders of a postindustrial society with an annual per capita income of U.S. $10,000, he and his associates do not believe that anyone is still prepared to die for reunification. Needless to say, this is a far cry from the war whoops of Chiang Kai-shek's era when dying for reunification was very much on the national agenda.

The way the government views the situation now is if Taiwan becomes "truly democratic, economically free, and socially pluralistic," it will be so "full of vitality" that it will be able to bargain with the mainland for better terms when the "final day of reckoning" arrives. Shaw said that "we may be militarily weak, but we must be politically strong."[36]

One premise of the KMT argument in the early 1990s is that totalitarian regimes around the world are crumbling under their own weight and that the PRC is destined to collapse, too. Shaw said they are waiting now in Taipei for this eventuality with confidence that the Communist system on the mainland is not going to last forever and will eventually collapse. He said, "the heavier they are, the more violent the[ir] collapse. China can change too, perhaps even before the year 2000. But whatever happens, it won't be long before it collapses."

Shaw said it is impossible for the regime to last indefinitely because it is opposed by an overwhelming majority of its educated elite. This view was strengthened after the China spring movement in Tiananmen Square and the June 4 incident of 1989. Before that, he said, there was always some speculation about the popularity of the government in Peking. Now, he said, it is very clear that it is unpopular and will eventually fall. When the PRC does collapse, Taiwan wants to be poised to pick up the pieces. For that reason, Shaw said, the full development of Taiwan's economy, society, and democracy will enable it—more than any other province of China—to play a role in the reconstruction of the mainland.

Shaw compared Taiwan's situation to a bank with thirty-five

branches. "If there is a vacancy in the general manager's post, the one selected should be the best manager." He said that Taiwan wants to become that manager. For that reason, the people of Taiwan "must be perceived as Chinese nationalists—not as separatists." Shaw added, "Either we will be back in the driver's seat or will get a fair share of the pie."[37] After reunification, "if we're perceived as true sons and daughters of China, how can we but fare well? How could the mainland Chinese become our enemies?" "We're not aggressive," he said. Then, "if we're on top, okay. If not . . . we'll still show them we can play the game."[38]

One frequently hears Mainlanders, especially those in the KMT, deride the Taiwan independence activists as extremely foolish or naive. Shaw said that the independence activists are leading Taiwan down a dead-end path. "They must accept what is coming," he claimed. "They are currently swimming against the tide. Against all odds." According to Shaw, their movement is an exercise in futility. In the short term, it might provoke a fatal blow against Taiwan because the mainland regime would not sit by idly and watch the island become more and more independent.[39]

Shaw said this was a serious warning. If a real clash emerged between the government of Taiwan and the pro-independence activists, and if the PRC perceived the government of Taiwan as soft on independence or the activists gaining ground, he feared the PRC might "attack Taiwan." This would be disastrous. "If there is a blockade, there will be a repeat of the Hong Kong syndrome in which the rich and the educated will leave. They don't want to take chances. They can make better money in Southeast Asia. They can be more secure in the U.S., Canada, [or] Europe. Our wealthy people have all sorts of connections. So, don't disturb the sleeping dog."[40]

Although the KMT is committed to reunification, Shaw offered the KMT disclaimer that "it does not have to happen soon. There is no big hurry." Taiwan now must devote itself to "finish the unfinished plan of constitutional reform" to fulfill the dream of the May Fourth Movement. He did not understand why the DPP and the Taiwan separatists are so irresponsible. He admitted that the KMT had many shortcomings and made many mistakes that the DPP could attack if it wanted to play the role of a genuine opposition party. He did not understand why the opposition focuses on the matter of independence.[41]

Taiwan is the future of China. Shaw said that those on Taiwan were much better educated, more skillful, and more experienced than the mainland elite. He boasted, "[W]e are actually ... the real elites among the mainland population. So if a genuine reunification takes place, how can we be the victims of that?"[42] On the contrary, those who oppose the Taiwan independence movement are fearful that a declaration of independence will adversely affect the autonomy the island already enjoys by inviting a PRC response; they hope to avoid confounding the diplomatic fictions that enable Taiwan to function as a political entity apart from the PRC.

An Opposing View

Chiang Chun-nan, publisher of a weekly political journal entitled *Hsin Hsin-wen* (The Journalist), said that KMT efforts to promote reunification were dangerous for Taiwan and "if they don't keep their cool ... [t]hey will make Taiwan like Hong Kong; then we will have no bargaining power." Chiang compared the attitude of the Mainlanders in the KMT and the authorities in Peking toward reunification to a traditional Chinese marriage. It is as if two people are determined to get married and the woman says to the man, "We have to get married. You don't have to love me. You can keep everything, you can keep your girlfriend, you don't need to live with me. But let's go to register as a married couple and let's get everybody his own key to his own room. We don't [even] have to sleep together."[43] Chiang suggested that there is no advantage for Taiwan in this sort of arrangement. He said that those who promote a political marriage do so on the basis of tradition. They believe that "[i]t is a tradition to get married; ... you have a responsibility to history." Chiang said he believes in a modern marriage where a couple only marries if they have established that they have some affection for each other. He mocked the "Chinese" (as opposed to Taiwanese), saying "They don't care about love or feelings. They say 'you can keep your security [forces], you keep your army, you keep your economy, you keep your [political] system.... But officially register as a couple.' "[44] In his view, Taiwanese have everything to lose and nothing to gain from that sort of obligatory relationship.

He decried the attitude of some of the Mainlanders—like Shaw Yu-ming—who claim it is "inevitable" that Taiwan will be reunited with the mainland as one China. He said that the belief of that sort of

Mainlander is that Taiwan should "behave very respectfully and make the central government—make Peking—more comfortable with us and then they will grant us more power, more authority, more autonomy. That's the best [we can] hope of them."[45] Not surprisingly, Chiang stated that this is unacceptable to Taiwanese. He said with indignation, "We submit ourselves and *then* they will be more generous to us. We are a sovereign nation already, why should we submit to them and then ask them to give us more power?"[46]

The view of many Taiwanese is that "Taiwan is already independent, why not just recognize that reality?" In fact, Chiang Chun-nan said, "We are separate already. We do not need to do much to make another separation. We just recognize the status quo. Nothing will change. We just don't want to go back to China."[47] While that would be a practical perspective on the matter, the difficulty is that for many Mainlanders, the desire to see China unified is an emotional, not reasoned, attachment to the idea of *i-tung*. For that reason, there is a conflict between those who hope to take a practical approach to the problem of Taiwan's political status and simply declare Taiwan to be what everyone knows it is—independent—and those who still hold out hope that conditions will, one day, be propitious for the realization of their ideal of *i-t'ung*.[48]

This has caused some confusion for the people of Taiwan—even those who support reunification. At the same time that the KMT and the government have relentlessly drummed into the minds of the people their obligation to reunify with the rest of China, they have earnestly tried to reinforce the idea that the communist system and the leaders of the PRC are evil. For years, the official and semi-official press on Taiwan referred to the leaders of the PRC as *Kung-fei*, or Communist bandits. The KMT created little incentive for people to view reunification as a desirable aim.

Hsiao Hsin-huang, a sociologist at Academia Sinica, explained that the KMT has consistently denigrated the PRC, saying, "Oh, the PRC is terrible. Look at their way of life—it's terrible, it's hell, [people there live behind an] iron curtain." In the next breath, people are told that they share the same cultural identity and heritage as the Chinese on the mainland and are prompted to think that reunification must take place. Hsiao said it is very confusing for most people. One reaction is to wonder, "[I]f things are so terrible there, why should we want to have anything to do with them? What advantage is there for us in reunification?"[49]

This is a reflection of the KMT's own confusion. Hsiao said that for years it was not really possible to express identification with a real place. If one identified with the mainland, one might be branded or persecuted as a Communist. If, on the other hand, one identified with Taiwan, one would be labeled or suppressed as one of the pro-independence activists (who were assumed to have ties to the Communists anyway).[50] So, the KMT's virulent anticommunist propaganda ended up sabotaging its own efforts to promote a popular sense of identity with the mainland. Now, in an effort to assert the need for unity with the mainland as a political entity, the KMT is contradicting its long-standing view that Taiwan is only a part of China and is promoting the distinctiveness of Taiwan as a separate polity.

Sincerity or Sophistry

Chang Chun-hung alleged that the KMT attitude is deceitful. In his view, the KMT has used the issue of reunification and the emphasis on the common Chinese identity of those on both sides of the strait to dominate Taiwan. He said that most members of the DPP understand that the KMT is not interested in reunification but in maintaining itself as the ruling elite on Taiwan. In this way, the two parties really do not differ on the issue of Taiwan's status. Both want it to remain independent.[51]

Extrapolating from Chang's statement, one can see that if the KMT wants to maintain Taiwan's independence, it does not want to admit it because that would undermine its credibility. The DPP, on the other hand, wants to force the issue precisely so that it can destroy the legitimacy of the KMT and, presumably, replace it as the ruling force on the island.

Those who favor Taiwan independence are not really arguing that the island is now dependent. Their concern is not for the island's current political status (although they are troubled by its standing in the international arena), but rather for two other problems. Advocates of Taiwan independence want to ensure that the island and its people are not subjected to rule from beyond by the mainland. To them, the KMT represents a threat to this ambition. As long as the KMT rules, the official government policy will be that the island should be ruled as part of a larger political entity, that Taiwan should sacrifice the autonomy it currently enjoys to subject itself again to rule from outside. After everything that has happened to the Taiwanese this century, this would be intolerable. Nevertheless, at present, Taiwan is an autonomous political entity, and the source of conflict is not its current but its future status.

Some members of the opposition hope that independence will be a step on the road to renegotiate some form of confederation or commonwealth with the rest of China. Even the most ardent advocates of independence, however, do not deny that Taiwan has been governed autonomously for the past four decades. This suggests that the real issue for those who promote independence may not be autonomy—which they have enjoyed under KMT rule—but sovereignty, Taiwanese sovereignty over Taiwan. They hope to displace as rulers the Mainlanders who favor reunification and interpose Taiwanese or those who are sympathetic to the sovereignty of Taiwan.

This is not a question of determining the status of the island vis-à-vis the mainland, for, in real terms, that status has been determined by the international community. By caving in to pressure from Peking, the international community has denied Taiwan the status it seeks. The KMT has not been able to dictate how the ROC is treated by international bodies or by other states that hope to have commercial intercourse both on Taiwan and on the mainland. That has been largely determined by Peking. In fact, the status in international forums or the recognition by other states that supporters of Taiwan independence claim an interest in seeking has been sought over the years by KMT leaders, despite their ambition to reunify Taiwan and the mainland.

A more immediate and, in some ways, fundamental problem that Taiwanese opposition activists are aiming to rectify is a matter of nationalism. Leaving aside the future ambitions of the KMT and considering only how that party has been perceived by Taiwanese, the KMT seems to have protected most the interests of the Mainlander elite and their values. To some extent, this perception has eroded as the process of "Taiwanization" (increasing the number of Taiwanese in the KMT power structure) has proceeded. However, it is difficult to dislodge in several years an impression that was formed over several decades.

From the perspective of Taiwanese nationalism, the continued dominance of Taiwan politics by Mainlanders has become unacceptable. Taiwanese have a sufficiently intense view of themselves as a distinct national group—regardless of how valid their claims for distinction may be—that they can no longer abide by a government that is dominated by a group they perceive to be different. This is not a matter of policy preference; it is not a matter of demanding autonomy from a power on which the island is currently dependent. It is simply a matter of a community demanding the right of self-determination so that it may govern itself. As democratization proceeds, Taiwanese have come closer to realizing this ambition in part by changing the very nature of the political party that they opposed.

Identity and Polity

On Taiwan, the conflict between the two visions of China is not limited to abstract, scholarly ruminations. It is the stuff of daily political struggle. This debate may not be prominent in the minds of the majority of Taiwan's residents, who concern themselves primarily with earning a livelihood, but among politicians, officials, intellectuals, and any people who travel beyond Taiwan this matter is of pressing importance. It affects people's views of a wide range of choices that must be made about Taiwan's ongoing political and social development.

From the perspective of the observer, the stalemate between advocates of unification and advocates of independence seemed a burlesque of exceptional complexity. Those who claimed to favor reunification readily confessed that they did not expect to resolve the matter any time soon, not as long as the Communists continue to rule in Peking. For them, the status quo—a tacit acceptance of Taiwan as an autonomous, sovereign state—was a necessary evil that they would not admit is preferable to reunification (as long as the mainland is governed by Communists). The status quo enabled them to perpetuate themselves in political power by invoking their role to keep the extremists in the opposition at bay. They could not tolerate an outright declaration of independence, even though, for all practical purposes, Taiwan is already independent. They claimed to fear that the PRC would use force to drag Taiwan back into the Chinese fold. It may be that they simply wished to create a sense of impending calamity that would cause the populace to resist the entreaties of the opposition and enable the KMT to maintain some degree of legitimacy to rule the island.

Those who demanded independence insisted that there be a formal acknowledgment of Taiwan's independent status so that the Mainlander-dominated KMT could be dislodged from power and a government could be elected from among Taiwan's populace with

Taiwan alone as its purview. Simply accepting that Taiwan has been independent even without a formal declaration was insufficient, because as long as the island was governed by a Mainlander-dominated KMT the threat of reunification remained. The advocates of independence believed that a formal declaration that Taiwan is independent—while unlikely to alter Taiwan's actual autonomy—would discredit and displace the KMT and allow a Taiwan-elected government to prevail. It would also bring to Taiwan the international status that many feel the island nation has for a long time deserved.

Not all supporters of independence see it as the most pressing objective. P'eng Ming-min is one who advocates that the argument about independence be postponed. According to P'eng, there is no point arguing about it at this stage of Taiwan's development and instead, leaders should concentrate on democratizing the political structure and strengthening the nation's ability to defend itself from the PRC. He claimed that education and the expansion of military power are of greater urgency.[52]

Chen Shui-pian, however, derided those who urge that the problem be "put in the refrigerator for twenty years, for thirty years, and not talk about it." In Chen's view, not talking about the issue of national identity does not mean that the problem has been solved: "During a time when we are promoting democratic reform, relations across the Taiwan Strait and the policy toward the PRC, what should we do? We want to join the United Nations. What name should we use? Is it possible to lay the problem aside? Questions like these will inevitably be related to the sensitive 'national identity' problem so it is inevitable. So, it would be better to face the problem than to avoid it. You've got to face this independence/reunification problem and the national identity problem."[53]

Identity and the "Rectification of Names"

Beyond the self-conscious responses people offer about the nature of their own identity, one can learn something from the words people choose to describe themselves and their polity. In Chinese, there are several terms that refer to the nation, each of which carries political import. The term *Chung-kuo*, literally "central kingdom," is generally used to identify the entity that, in English, is China. The term *jen* means "man," or, in the generic sense, "person," and when appended to *Chung-kuo* creates the term *Chung-kuo jen*, which, in English, is translated as "Chinese"—referring to the people, not the language.

The Chinese language is replete with terms that describe like phenomena or objects that are similar, but not identical. In this vein, there is another term, *Hua*, which is used to describe "Cathay," a poetic, archaic reference to China. This term is more conceptual. While *Chung-kuo* implies a centralization of power in a single state and reflects the way the Chinese empire actually emerged out of a morass of smaller, sovereign states, the term *Hua* evokes an indistinct image of splendor that might be more appropriately applied to the Chinese nation and its culture than to the Chinese polity. For this reason, Chinese people who do not want to associate themselves with the Chinese state may identify themselves as *Hua jen*, not *Chung-kuo jen*.

One official noted that an overseas Chinese in the United States is likely to identify himself as an American, indicating his country of citizenship, and also as a *Hua jen*, indicating his identification with the Chinese nation. It is unlikely that he will call himself a *Chung-kuo jen*, as that would imply that he is a citizen of China, not the United States.[54] As an illustration, Yao Chia-wen said that because he is Taiwanese, he does not identify himself as a *Chung-kuo jen*. "I prefer to say, 'I am a *Hua jen*.' A Chinese, yes . . . but a *Chung-kuo jen*, no."[55] His concern for linguistic propriety and symbolism manifested itself in conversations with others about identity.

Ma Ying-cheou raised another issue of terminology. He said that the KMT and the DPP make subtle political statements in the words they choose to describe the other side of the Taiwan Strait. Ma said that the KMT refers to the other side as "the mainland" whereas the DPP makes a conscious effort to call it "the Chinese mainland." By adding the term *Chinese*, the DPP hopes to distinguish Chinese from Taiwanese. The KMT, on the other hand, regards both the mainland and Taiwan as Chinese.

Ma observed that Chinese from the PRC residing abroad use the term *kuo-nei*, (meaning "internal") to refer to the PRC. People from Taiwan—even those who oppose Taiwan independence—use the same term *internal* to refer to events in Taiwan. In this way, those from Taiwan who consciously oppose designating Taiwan as a separate state inadvertently imply that it is so by using the term *kuo-nei*. As Ma explained it, "Since mainland China is also part of the idea of *kuo*, . . .

we have to be very careful and we try to avoid terms like 'third country' because that would imply that the Chinese mainland is the second country. Actually, we don't consider that [the mainland is] a second country.[56] Sometimes, this attention to terminology causes amusing verbal gymnastics. For instance, the English-language *China Post* reported that the ROC minister of transportation at that time, Eugene Y.H. Chien, commented, "Flights between Taiwan and mainland China will not be called domestic routes or international routes, but will be 'mainland routes' once direct aviation links across the Taiwan Straits are established."[57]

Identity, Socialization, and Culture

An especially significant source of tension pertaining to people's identity as either Chinese or Taiwanese is the KMT effort to socialize the population of Taiwan. When the advance guard of the KMT arrived on the island after the surrender of the Japanese in 1945, it considered that many of the residents had been overly influenced by Japan. In response, and out of suspicion about the loyalties of the island's population, the KMT established policies that were intended to resinicize the Taiwanese. The KMT promoted a form of orthodox, Chinese gentry culture and represented it as national culture—the culture of all Chinese. China's monuments and geography, the high culture of its elite, the Mandarin dialect adopted as the national language, and the history of its heroes, achievements, and development dominated the school curriculum and were validated by public, official expressions in word and deed. Taiwan, and all that is distinctive about it, was largely ignored.[58]

Taiwanese have been alienated by the incessant, pervasive focus on China as a whole at the expense of Taiwan. Chiang Chun-nan's experience is illustrative:

> My daughter now is in high school. She has to memorize all the cities, all the agricultural products, and industrial products of every province [of China], the weather, the rivers, and the natural resources. Everything. We had to memorize all this before, thirty years ago. I forget everything. Now, my daughter . . . has to memorize what I had memorized and we know so little about Taiwan. . . . We are forbidden to learn. We have no access. No resources. Some get into trouble when

they began to know about Taiwan. When you begin to identify with Taiwan . . . people feel you are associated with independence or the opposition.[59]

There is considerably more information about Taiwan and its history publicly available now than ever before. Although this material now proliferates in journals and books, several generations of Taiwan's residents have been shielded by the KMT from learning about their past. This effort to direct people's attention away from Taiwan to the mainland has left scars and resentment.

Chiu I-jen, of the DPP New Tide faction, recalled that when he was in junior high school there were six semesters over the course of three years. During each semester students were issued a history text and a geography text, but in those twelve volumes, there were only two chapters that mentioned anything about Taiwan's history and only two that mentioned anything about Taiwan's geography.

Curricula are standard on Taiwan, and most schools assign texts used islandwide for each course in each grade. It was reported that in the twelve volumes used to educate elementary school students about social studies, about 30 of approximately 1,200 pages mention Taiwan. These passages emphasize the importance of Taiwan as a base from which to recover the mainland but depict the island as simply a temporary refuge. The standardized college entrance exam, required of any student hoping to get a college education, also deals sparingly with Taiwan. In 1987, of the forty-two items pertaining to geography, four were related to Taiwan, and of the thirty-two items dealing with history, only one dealt with Taiwan.[60]

In January 1991, the Ministry of Education announced that it would revise geography textbooks to bring them into line with "factuality." One report stated, "[C]urrently, Taiwan students . . . are taught the old names of mainland China places, railways, and administrative divisions. They learn names that were used before the ROC government relocated to Taiwan forty-two years ago." These names will be revised to reflect current PRC usage, but the changes will appear only in the appendices of the texts, where the differences will be explained.[61]

These illustrations are suggestive of the imbalance between the attention given to the mainland and that given to Taiwan in public school curricula of which Chiu spoke. This sort of indoctrination is effective when people are young, but after they graduate and take up roles in society, people are confronted with a reality that does not match the lessons they were taught in school. This leads to a feeling of betrayal that has resulted in a degree of animosity directed toward the KMT.

This sentiment was validated by National Taiwan University Professor Hu Fo, who said that according to popular opinion surveys he has conducted, he found that people begin to break away from the orthodoxies fed to them by the KMT during a critical period between the second and third years of high school and the second and third years of college. Before that time, children display no signs of challenging the attitudes they are expected to adopt about China. By the time many complete college, however, they attest to feeling as though they were deceived by the KMT about political and cultural realities. This, Hu said, is the cause of intense anxiety.[62]

People resent that they are caught between an abstract notion of a remote China, about which they know many facts, and a concrete reality on Taiwan, about which they know too little to make sense of their experiences. This emphasis on Chinese culture, Chiu suggested, results from the KMT's efforts to strengthen a Chinese identity and assimilate the Taiwanese. By purveying a false sense that there is a single Chinese culture and by denying the possibility that Chinese culture comprises many local variants, the KMT inadvertently fostered the development of Taiwanese identity.[63]

When questioned about the effort of the government to create a unified sense of Chinese culture on Taiwan, the influential Tsiang Yien-si responded,

> No effort as [far as] I know of was ever made to "unify" Chinese and "Taiwanese" culture. . . . However . . . we would not deny that we Chinese are always very proud of our culture and treasure our tradition and heritage. . . . The ROC Government on Taiwan . . . made urgent efforts to promote what is known as the "Chinese Cultural Renaissance Movement" to counter any possible devastation of the [Communists' Cultural] "Revolution.". . . The purpose of our renaissance movement has always been to affirm and restore those traditional value[s] in the Chinese culture which would help to enrich our spiritual life in a rapidly developing society that can become also increasingly materialistic.[64]

Dr. Tsiang's disclaimer notwithstanding, it seems evident that the KMT has fostered a particular view of China, history, and culture associated with a value system that validates the adoption of the appropriate—

Chinese—identity and denies the legitimacy of any rival, subordinate, or alternative construction of cultural identity. At first this resulted in an effort to reorient the Taiwanese "from Japanese to mainland influence by installing a Nationalist curriculum and culture." After decades of failing to eradicate the Taiwanese cultural element, "Nationalists gradually began to accommodate cultural localism, but still defined Taiwaneseness as just one local variant of a national Chinese culture."[65]

It is easy to understand that the KMT hoped to promote a set of attitudes, attachments, and beliefs that would perpetuate Chinese culture as the political elite knew it and advance the cause of reunification —an aim dependent on popular identification with the mainland. What the KMT did not anticipate is that by promoting Chinese identity as exclusive and trivializing or denying the validity of sentiments Taiwanese had for their own subcultural forms, the KMT ended up emphasizing, rather than muting, the differences between its view of culture and that of the Taiwanese. The very effort that the KMT made to foster a sense of identity—because it insisted on the exclusivity of that identity—impelled Taiwanese to cling to and cultivate their own sense of self.

P'eng Ming-min claimed that this "total confusion about political, ethnic, and cultural identity" was intentionally fostered by the KMT. He suggested that "many Taiwanese think that we are Chinese because the KMT has confused them and they feel that it is a betrayal of our ancestors to be split off from China." P'eng emphasized that Taiwan is an immigrant nation. However, it is very much unlike the United States and Canada, which are also immigrant nations. In those places, P'eng explained, there are all sorts of ethnic groups represented in the population: Irish, Germans, Italians, and so forth. He asserted that these ethnic groups are all proud of their ancestral origins even though they are now citizens of a different state. Most Americans and Canadians have never even been to the place from which their ancestors came and, if asked, he said, they will identify themselves as Americans or Canadians, not as citizens of the state from which their forebears came.

The attachment to the new state, the United States or Canada, is not superficial. P'eng observed that in most cases, people are willing to fight and die for the country in which they are a citizen. He said that General Eisenhower was of German heritage, yet he led the U.S. troops to defeat Germany in the Second World War. Indeed, the U.S. armed forces were composed of immigrants from Italy, Germany, and Japan—

all three of which were enemies of the U.S. during the war. In sum, P'eng declared that "it is important to distinguish between political identity and cultural identity."[66]

P'eng is correct that these forms of identity have been conflated and mixed up. That it was completely intentional, however, may be difficult to demonstrate. There are some fundamental differences between Mainlanders and Taiwanese that may have contributed to the insensitivity of the KMT to the Taiwanese notion of identity. It is understandable that the Mainlanders who came to Taiwan in the late 1940s would have a difficult time valuing the distinct identity of the Taiwanese. The Mainlanders themselves were not a single cohesive group. They emerged from different regional subgroups within China, and their own experience of China was of a single nation that comprised an amalgam of different regional identities. The peculiar claim of regional distinctiveness of the Taiwanese was no more compelling than that of the Hunanese or the Cantonese.

Conversely, it is easy to appreciate why the Taiwanese do not automatically consider themselves as Chinese when to be Chinese is equated with being like those from the mainland, who, while different enough from each other, are collectively distinguishable from the Taiwanese. The central distinguishing characteristic is that the Mainlanders did not share the communal experience of the Taiwanese. They did not understand what it meant to live on Taiwan.

In contemporary Taiwan, those Mainlanders or "second-generation" Mainlanders who do identify themselves as Taiwanese identify with Taiwan as a state, whereas for many of the Taiwanese, their identity is not just political. Being Taiwanese is as much a cultural consciousness as it is a political identity. Taiwanese share the communal legacy of living on Taiwan; no Mainlander, not even one born on Taiwan, can feel this in the same way. Naturally, those people born on Taiwan since 1949—regardless of their ancestral origin—have also experienced what it means to live on a post-1949 Taiwan. That commonality may bind them to the island in a way that even Taiwanese who were adult in 1949 do not necessarily appreciate, because the generations born since 1949 have experienced a very different sort of Taiwan than existed before.

Once the KMT came to Taiwan, it defined the state in terms of the experience and ideology it brought from the mainland. Dru Gladney, who provided insight about China's vast Muslim population, wrote that "the notion of *Han zu* or *Han min* (Han nationality) is an entirely modern phenomenon—it arises with the shift from empire to nation." It is a consciousness of "Chineseness," which gained acceptance with the spread of Sun Yat-sen's ideology, an ideology that focused on the ideal of China's ethnic unity as a means to distinguish the Chinese from the Manchus.[67]

Gladney suggested that, "by invoking the argument that the majority of the people in China were Han, Sun effectively found a symbolic metaphorical opposition to the Manchu to which the vast majority of peoples in China would easily rally." Oddly, this is precisely the motive that has prompted leaders of the Taiwan independence movement to promote the notion of Taiwanese identity.

While Sun understood that China was home to five great peoples, "his ultimate goal was still assimilationist, to unify and fuse all the peoples into one Chinese race. . . . While the idea of the unity of the Chinese state and/or country certainly existed before, it was the stress upon cultural and national unity, with the rising importance of the Han nation, that was a crucial component of Chinese nationalism in the early twentieth century."[68] Gladney explained that because Sun was Cantonese, he needed to find a way to overcome the loyalty Chinese have to their own locale so that he could forge the nationalist movement that would be needed to overthrow the regime of Manchurian outsiders and establish a Chinese nation. "Dr. Sun found an ingenious way to rise above deeply embedded north–south ethnocentricisms. The use and perhaps invention of the term *Han minzu* was a brilliant attempt to mobilize other non-Cantonese especially northern Mandarin speakers and the powerful Chekiang and Shanghainese merchants into one overarching national group against the Manchu and other foreigners threatening China during the unstable period following the unequal treaties."[69] In this respect, the KMT is not just Chinese; it is Sun-ist in that it is ideologically devoted to the ideals of Sun Yat-sen and his vision of China: a China that never existed before but was under construction when the Japanese invaded in the 1930s. Taiwanese of the early part of the century may not have accepted that notion because they were already under the control of Japan and had been identified by the Japanese as Chinese. Taiwanese notions of being Chinese and those of the KMT, which came from the mainland, may have been sharply different from each other.

The different attitude that Mainlanders and Taiwanese may have about their identity as Chinese certainly is the foundation for the conflict about national identity. However, the friction generated by these differences has been exacerbated by the emergence of a distinct Taiwanese identity that is the by-product of interaction between the two groups on the island.

Notes

1. This and other passages benefited from discussion with Professor Benjamin Schwartz of Harvard University.
2. Rod Hague and Martin Harrop, *Comparative Government and Politics: An Introduction*, 2d ed. (Atlantic Highlands, NJ: Humanities Press International, 1987), p. 32.
3. Hill Gates, "Ethnicity and Social Class," in *The Anthropology of Taiwanese Society*, ed. Emily Martin Ahern and Hill Gates (Stanford: Stanford University Press, 1981), p. 254.
4. Ibid., p. 255.
5. Interview with Kao Hui-yu, Taipei, May 24, 1991.
6. Edwin Winckler, "Taiwan: Changing Dynamics," in *China Briefing, 1991*, ed. William A. Joseph (Boulder, CO: Westview Press in cooperation with the Asia Society, 1992), p. 165.
7. Liu Fang, "As People of Integrity, Taiwanese Should Refuse to Watch the Excesses of the TV Series 'Love,' " *Tzu-li Wan-pao* (Independence Evening Post), March 11, 1991, in JPRS-CAR–91–028, May 22, 1991, p. 109.
8. I am indebted to Wang Ching-yi, a journalist and scholar from Kang Shan Township in Kaohsiung County, for pointing out to me the significance of these architectural features.
9. Interview with P'eng Ming-min, Taipei, August 23, 1993.
10. Leo J. Moser, *The Chinese Mosaic: The Peoples and Provinces of China (Boulder, CO: Westview, 1985), p. 6.*
11. Interview with Kao Hui-yu, Taipei, May 24, 1991.
12. Understandably, this subject asked that he not be cited by name.
13. Interview with Chen Charng-ven, Taipei, June 24, 1991.
14. Interview with Chen Shui-pian, Taipei, August 25, 1993.
15. "Taiwan Feelings, Chinese Heart," *Yuan Chien* (Global Views Monthly) 62 (July 15, 1991), p. 123.
16. Interview with Chen Shui-pian, Taipei, August 25, 1993.
17. Interview with Hau Pei-tsun, Taipei, August 27, 1993.
18. Interview with P'eng Ming-min, Taipei, August 23, 1993.
19. Ibid.
20. Interview with Chang Chun-hung, Taipei, May 28, 1991.
21. Interview with Chen Shui-pian, Taipei, August 25, 1993.
22. See appendix 2: Letter from Tsiang Yien-si, July 8, 1991.
23. Shaw Yu-ming, *Beyond the Economic Miracle: Reflections on the Republic of China on Taiwan, Mainland China, and Sino-American Relations* (Taipei: Kwang Hwa, 1989), pp. 6–7.

24. See appendix 2: Letter from Tsiang Yien-si, July 8, 1991.

25. Interview with Hau Pei-tsun, Taipei, August 27, 1993.

26. Interview with Ma Ying-cheou, Taipei, July 3, 1991.

27. Interview with Chen Charng-ven, Taipei, June 24, 1991.

28. The individual who made these observations asked that he not be cited by name.

29. Interview with Li I-yuan, Taipei, July 2, 1991.

30. Interview with Ming Chu-cheng, Taipei, March 11, 1991.

31. Lo Kuan-chung wrote *Romance of the Three Kingdoms* (*San-Kuo Yen-i*) in the fourteenth century about the period of chaos following the collapse of the Han dynasty in the third century.

32. Interview with Ma Han-pao, Taipei, March 9, 1991.

33. Interviews with Hsu Hsin-liang, Taipei, June 3, 1991; Kao Hui-yu, Taipei, May 24, 1991.

34. Interview with P'eng Ming-min, Taipei, August 23, 1993.

35. Interview with Shaw Yu-ming, Taipei, June 15, 1991.

36. Ibid.

37. Ibid.

38. Ibid.

39. Ibid.

40. Ibid.

41. Ibid.

42. Ibid.

43. Interview with Chiang Chun-nan, Taipei, May 20, 1991.

44. Ibid.

45. Ibid. Actually, Shaw Yu-ming stressed that "we cannot make too many waves" in relations with the PRC. Interview with Shaw Yu-ming, Taipei, June 15, 1991.

46. Interview with Chiang Chun-nan, Taipei, May 20, 1991.

47. Ibid.

48. Interview with Hu Fo, Taipei, June 13, 1991.

49. Interview with Hsiao Hsin-huang, Nankang, July 3, 1991.

50. Ibid.

51. Interview with Chang Chun-hung, Taipei, May 28, 1991.

52. Interview with P'eng Ming-min, Taipei, August 23,, 1993.

53. Interview with Chen Shui-pian, Taipei, August 25, 1993.

54. Interview with Soong Chu-yu, Taipei, June 28, 1991.

55. Interview with Yao Chia-wen, Taipei, June 7, 1991.

56. It was revealing that in his explanation about the use of the terms *kuo* and *third country*, Ma used the terms *mainland China* and *Chinese mainland*. He reflexively used terms that he had just explained were tainted with political implications he hoped to avoid. Interview with Ma Ying-cheou, Taipei, July 3, 1991.

57. See *China Post,* November 27, 1991, p. 1.

58. Richard W. Wilson, *Learning to Be Chinese: The Political Socialization of Children in Taiwan* (Cambridge: MIT Press, 1970); Lin Yu-t'i, *T'ai-wan chiao-yu mien-mu 40 nien* (Faces of Taiwan's Education Over Forty Years) (Taipei: Cultural Division of *Tzu-li Wan-pao* [Independence Evening Post], 1987).

59. Interview with Chiang Chun-nan, Taipei, May 20, 1991.

60. Lin, *T'ai-wan chiao-yu mien-mu 40 nien* (Faces of Taiwan Education Over Forty Years), pp. 117–19.

61. *Free China Journal*, January 7, 1991, p. 3.

62. Interview with Hu Fo, Taipei, June 13, 1991.

63. Interview with Chiu I-jen, Taipei, March 21, 1991.

64. See appendix 2: Letter from Tsiang Yien-si, July 8, 1991.

65. Winckler, "Taiwan: Changing Dynamics," p. 165.

66. Interview with P'eng Ming-min, Taipei, August 23, 1993.

67. Dru Gladney, *Muslim Chinese: Ethnic Nationalism in the People's Republic* (Cambridge: Council on East Asian Studies, Harvard University Press, 1990), p. 82.

68. Ibid., pp. 83–84.

69. Ibid., p. 85.

4

The Origins of
Taiwanese Identity

At many turning points in Chinese history, underlying subethnic factors, perceptions of group interests at the regional level, and local value systems have been crucial elements in events that shaped the future of the nation.

—Leo J. Moser, *The Chinese Mosaic:*
The Peoples and Provinces of China

Influential Factors

Competing claims of identity on Taiwan reflect the consternation that is nearly universal among Chinese intellectuals this century about what it means to *be* Chinese. A good deal has been written about Chinese nationalism and the titanic battle with communism. Taiwanese national identity, by contrast, has been much less studied, and comparatively little has been written about it, especially in English.[1]

If Ernest Gellner is correct, it is the collective consciousness that "we" are a group that is the basis of a national spirit. To locate the source of Taiwanese national identity, then, would be to identify reasons why Taiwanese think of themselves as a group distinct from other Chinese. There are many. Among those factors Taiwanese themselves commonly see as shaping their identity are:

1. The separation from the rest of China and the collective memory of succeeding periods during which forces came from elsewhere to impose control on the island's people;

2. The friction between the KMT and the Taiwanese stemming from persistent memories of initial misperceptions and early conflicts;

3. The sense that a distinct Taiwanese culture and consciousness differs from Han culture and Chinese consciousness, and

4. a legacy of frustration resulting from the authoritarian nature of KMT rule, which seemed to favor Mainlanders and their interests over the Taiwanese, and which, in an effort to resocialize Taiwanese as Chinese, inadvertently reinforced mutual perceptions of difference.

How one assesses the origin and development of Taiwanese identity, how one regards Taiwanese nationalism, the weight one accords to the various contributing factors, and how one sees their mutual influence depends largely on one's identity and consequent worldview.

Separation from Mainland China and Alien Rule

As an island, apart from the continent, Taiwan has been subjected to political, military, and commercial forces that did not affect Chinese living across the Taiwan Strait. It may be that people who are separated from others by natural boundaries—like those who live on an island—sense a kinship with those who share the same territory and an alienation from others who do not. The people of an island cannot help but view themselves as distinct from all others who might claim them as compatriots because they are divided from those others by more than a town line or provincial boundary. Even though there are visual and social similarities between Taiwan and, say, Fukien Province, there is no way to get from the mainland to Taiwan without feeling that one has left one place, traveled across an expanse of neutrality, and arrived in another. It is likely that the residents of Taiwan have been conditioned to view themselves vis-à-vis the mainland in a manner that reflects this spatial dimension.

Chang Chun-hung portrayed the initial migration from the mainland to Taiwan in the seventeenth century as a process of fleeing from adversity. He mused that the common sense of having taken refuge on the island contributes to an identity that distinguishes the people of Taiwan from those across the strait: "The reason why Taiwan consciousness succeeded is because they had fled to a place from which they could no longer flee, because they had to have an identity for the sake of survival, and because they were dominated by outsiders, which prompted a rather strong emotional reaction."[2]

However, the development of a distinct Taiwanese identity was not a product of simply being isolated on the island. From the earliest times, succeeding waves of invaders have tried to sever the island from the rest of China and break what were seen as tenuous bonds to the authorities who governed Chinese on the mainland. Taiwanese have inherited a legacy of subjugation by aliens: Spanish, Dutch, pirates, Manchurians, Japanese, and, in the minds of some, the KMT and refugees from the mainland.[3]

The most enduring foreign influence for Taiwanese with memories that reach back before 1945 is the Japanese, stemming from a period of occupation. In 1895, at the conclusion of the Sino-Japanese War, Taiwan and the Pescadores were ceded to Japan in perpetuity, a period that lasted only until Japan's defeat at the end of World War II.[4] The fifty years of Japanese occupation affected Taiwanese in a significant and complex manner. Detached from China, residents of Taiwan were effectively exiles in their own homeland. There were repeated efforts to oppose Japanese occupation and other indications that the residents of the island saw themselves as Chinese at heart. This sentiment emerged from the wistful poetry and songs composed during the occupation that expressed a longing for China.[5]

During the period of occupation, the Taiwanese were obliged to use Japanese language in the schools and were tightly restricted politically and economically on the basis of their identity as Chinese.[6] Taiwanese who recall the period of occupation claim that the Japanese forbade Chinese from studying law or politics. A promising student would be directed to medicine or commerce, and higher education for the best was often available only in Japan. This practice frustrated Taiwan's intelligentsia because, for the entire period of Japan's rule, few had any opportunity to play a role in the governance of the island.[7]

Japan brought order and development to Taiwan but may also have affected the growth of a nationalist sentiment among Taiwanese.[8] Japanese occupiers discriminated against the Taiwanese and monopolized high-ranking posts in the government, military, state-run industrial enterprises, and schools. Managers, teachers, and policymakers were predominantly Japanese even though the population was overwhelmingly Taiwanese. A Spanish priest, Bartoleme Martinez, who lived on Taiwan through much of the Japanese occupation observed, "[T]he more stupid Japanese always gets any available government position first, can rise higher, and is paid from fifty to eighty percent more for the same work than a Formosan [Taiwanese]."[9]

The period of Japanese occupation was the first period during which the entire island of Taiwan was governed effectively in a unified fashion. By severing Taiwan's ties with China and establishing a system of education, commerce, agriculture, and law, the Japanese succeeded in raising the standard of living on the island significantly. These factors all contributed to a growing sense of identification among the Chinese on Taiwan with the island itself. In addition, the growing trends of "urbanization, along with the rise of an articulate middle class, helped to weld the Formosan [Taiwanese] population together at the same time that the irritant of the Japanese presence further united it."[10] The mentality of isolation coupled with the experiences of being ruled by outsiders contributed to a sense of group consciousness among Taiwan's residents. This identity evolved more fully and was politicized after the KMT arrived on the island.

Friction with the KMT

The first encounters with the Mainlanders who arrived to replace the Japanese after the Second World War caused some Taiwanese to acknowledge, with chagrin, that in many ways the Japanese were superior to the Chinese. It also caused them to see themselves as different from the Mainlanders. Those old enough to recall the transition of power once the Japanese had left Taiwan recounted how an air of jubilation prevailed in anticipation of being rejoined with their homeland and governed again as Chinese by Chinese. These high spirits quickly sagged on seeing the Nationalist troops.

Having looked forward to a restoration to the Chinese realm, Taiwanese were disappointed to see the gap between Japanese values and those manifested by the Chinese. P'eng Ming-min recalled watching the first Nationalist troops disembark at a welcoming ceremony staged by the vanquished Japanese colonial forces.

> The ship docked, the gangways were lowered, and off came the troops of China, the victors. The first man to appear was a bedraggled fellow who looked and behaved more like a coolie than a soldier, walking off with a carrying pole across his shoulder, from which was suspended his umbrella, sleeping mat, cooking pot, and cup. Others like him followed, some with shoes, some without. Few had guns. With no attempt to maintain order or discipline, they pushed off the ship, glad to be on firm land, but hesitant to face the Japanese lined up and saluting smartly on

both sides. My father wondered what the Japanese could possibly think. He had never felt so ashamed in his life. Using a Japanese expression, he said, "If there had been a hole nearby, I would have crawled in!"[11]

Another eyewitness wrote that after the soldiers arrived on Taiwan they were expected to fend for themselves "No camps had been set up to receive them. Clusters of dank hovels—improvised with coconut palms, flattened rusted tins and flimsy bamboo strips—sprouted in back alleys all over town. Cowering soldiers, ashen and skeletal, some only 14 or 15, others decrepit with age, limped around unshod, in tattered uniforms stiff with filth and dried sweat. Local residents shunned them, and if they ventured to better areas of town the police shooed them away brutally as they did unsightly beggars."[12] Chang Chun-hung recalled this episode from his perspective as a young boy.

> We all took up flags and went to welcome them [the KMT] . . . President Chiang has come to take over Taiwan! That was really how we felt— entering the embrace of our fatherland. But although we genuinely accepted the mainland takeover, we immediately began to sense the conflict of culture. Moreover, that conflict of culture was extremely intense. It was discovered that the Japanese culture which we had originally loathed was, as compared to the culture of our fatherland, a strong culture, a superior culture. And the culture of the rulers [the KMT] is a worthless, inferior—an inferior kind of barbaric culture. . . . That kind of conflict was extremely intense and transformed us from the heights of identification to the heights of hostility.[13]

One Taiwanese, now a highly placed senior official in a government ministry, observed that the Japanese had promoted a set of social values that had been derived long ago from China but which had been corrupted on the mainland. When the KMT arrived and began to set up institutions to govern the island, Taiwanese elite who had assimilated the standards and values with which the Japanese had imbued them were disheartened to see that their Chinese brethren were corrupt, decadent, and backward as compared with the Japanese. One commentator wrote, "Although we bitterly detested the brutal colonial rule of the Japanese, we cannot deny that, under Japan's perfected system of civil service, obedience to the law and administrative efficiency made the Japanese incomparable to the KMT's corrupt feudal regime. Even though it was the rule of a different race, Taiwanese of the older generation believed in the fairness of the Japanese courts. How many today believe in the judicial system manipulated by the KMT?"[14] Initially, Taiwanese hoped that the Japanese surrender would signal the start of a happier phase of life on Taiwan. Mutual misperceptions, corrupt and inept leadership, misconduct on the part of the KMT soldiers, and a host of other irritants soon soured the views of the residents of Taiwan toward their mainland cousins and reinforced whatever notions of Taiwanese identity already existed.[15]

One hears different tales about the first encounters with the Mainlanders. Nationalist soldiers were perceived by Taiwanese as unsophisticated country bumpkins. Some Taiwanese claim that Taiwan had been more highly developed by the Japanese than almost anywhere on the mainland and that urban residents on Taiwan were far more "modern" than the Chinese who came from across the strait.

Chang Chun-hung, in an assertion that mirrors what Mendel wrote, said that in the 1920s and 1930s, per capita income on Taiwan exceeded that in Japan. He argued that the standard of living on Taiwan was much higher than that on the mainland and suggested that this was one factor affecting the first interactions between Taiwanese and Mainlanders. He expressed this with some resentment of the claim often made by the KMT that it should be credited with having engineered Taiwan's economic success. In his view, if Japan had continued to rule Taiwan, the current standard of living on the island would be even higher than it is.[16]

The sense that many Mainlanders who arrived with the KMT were not as sophisticated as the Taiwanese was evidently widespread. Several people explained with great mirth how a Mainlander soldier—having never seen running water before he arrived on Taiwan—purchased a spigot, took it home, forced it into the wall, turned the knob, and was angered that no water flowed from it. Furious, and feeling that he had been cheated by the Taiwanese merchant who sold him the fixture, he returned to the store where he bought it and threatened the proprietor with violence for having deceived him. This story is emblematic of the sentiments some of the urban Taiwanese had with regard to the Mainlanders.[17]

In a similar vein, Huang Hsin-chieh, once the chairman of the DPP, said, "The people that came over from the mainland appeared outwardly very noble minded and intelligent, but actually their general knowledge was far below ours. For instance, when they went to the toilet, they all used bamboo sticks to clean themselves while we here use toilet paper."[18] There are various approaches to explaining the tension that emerged between the Taiwanese and the Mainlanders. Objectively, it had less to do with inherent characteristics and initial impressions of one group vis-à-vis the other and much more to do with the quality of their early interactions. Certainly the mythology of cultural superiority and inferiority is affected by the perceived differences in economic status. That is, the Mainlanders who arrived in the late 1940s and early 1950s were composed of two distinct groups: the educated, polished, cosmopolitan elite and the simple, uneducated, unwashed soldiers. Taiwanese, too, may be divided into simple rural types and more sophisticated urban elites. Characterizations of Mainlanders and Taiwanese must be calibrated by reference to the status of the one doing the characterization and the one being characterized.

The relationship also suffered from the confrontation of expectations and reality. The residents of Taiwan recall welcoming the Nationalist troops as liberators, but the leaders of the KMT apparently suspected that the Taiwanese had collaborated with Japan while the KMT had been battling Japanese savagery on the mainland. The KMT also feared that Taiwan had been infiltrated by Communist provocateurs. Given the KMT's stunning loss to the Communists on the mainland, it is easy to appreciate how reasonable this insecurity seemed to them at the time. Although Taiwan seemed a bountiful base from which to operate, it also was viewed as a "peripheral frontier province dangerously exposed to Japanese influence and dangerously populated by what was perceived as a dissident intelligentsia."[19]

Owing in part to the preexisting skepticism about the trustworthiness of Taiwan's intelligentsia, once the Japanese were expelled from the island, the KMT appointed newly arrived Mainlanders who had had experience governing in other provinces—rather than natives of Taiwan—to assume positions of responsibility for the welfare of the island province. The preference for mainland immigrants over native Taiwanese in positions of legal or administrative responsibility was easily justified in terms of the dearth of trained Taiwanese lawyers or public officials.

One Mainlander explained that, during the Japanese occupation, no Chinese on Taiwan were permitted to hold management positions. Even those who oversaw the crews of laborers who gathered the nightsoil were Japanese. When the Japanese left, this Mainlander claimed, Taiwanese were not even capable of managing the collection of human excrement by themselves and were dependent on Mainlanders to regulate society.

Despite its humiliating defeat on the mainland, the KMT still saw itself as the government of all China, of which Taiwan, in its view, was a small, backward part. That individuals with significant experience in the administration of the whole of China should assume positions of leadership once they arrived on the island was natural, as they did not consider themselves to be governing the island only, but saw themselves as the rightful government of the Republic of China, which had been chased off the mainland by the Communists.

This perception contributed to the clash of expectations. The Chinese who had lived under Japan's rule on Taiwan saw the KMT as a liberating force and expected to gain from the KMT what they were prevented from having by the Japanese. The KMT, however, did not view itself primarily as a liberating force. It was preoccupied with a profound and pervasive sense of crisis and an abiding fear of an imminent attack from the Communist-controlled mainland. Those Mainlanders who came to Taiwan were there out of necessity, not desire, and viewed themselves as temporary residents of the island. Those who held positions of responsibility may have had a strong sense of entitlement about their role and probably gave little thought to the way in which their presence would be perceived by the Chinese who had been living on Taiwan prior to their arrival. It is unlikely that they viewed themselves either as liberating or as suppressing the local population.

The February 28 Calamity

Another episode in the early contact between the Taiwanese and the Mainlanders contributed to an intensification of the mutual hostility and a Taiwanese sense that the Mainlanders were determined to eliminate any possibility that the Taiwanese could govern themselves. On February 27, 1947, there was a confrontation between investigators of the Monopoly Bureau (a government agency that monopolized the sale of alcohol and tobacco) and a woman who was illegally selling matches and cigarettes on a Taipei street. Unexpectedly, the incident turned ugly and a government officer unintentionally shot a Taiwanese bystander. That night, and all the following day, mobs of Taiwanese in Taipei and other cities across the island went on a rampage assaulting Mainlanders and destroying their property.

The violence continued for two weeks as Taiwanese vented the anger, frustration, and hostility toward the Mainlanders that had mounted in the year and a half since the KMT came to Taiwan. This was followed by several months of terror imposed by the KMT, which had troop reinforcements sent from the mainland to Taiwan. What actually happened may never be fully known. The perception among Taiwanese is that the KMT authorities systematically wiped out the political and intellectual elite of Taiwan.[20] When it was over, thousands had been executed.[21] The precise number of executions, if it was ever known by the authorities, has not been released. Estimates run from a conservative one thousand dead to an extreme of more than a hundred thousand. An official account says sixty-three hundred and there is a popular conception that approximately ten thousand were executed. In any case, the KMT claims that it was quelling a rebellion and that the lives of many Nationalist troops and those of innocent mainland refugees were lost as well.

With this bloody preface, the story of Taiwanese and Mainlander animosity unfolded as the two groups were riveted to opposing camps. The whole episode is referred to on Taiwan as the 2–28 Incident (for February 28, the day the killing started in earnest) and impeded subsequent efforts at integration because of residual hostility and mistrust. Until the end of the 1980s, it was not even permissible to discuss this matter openly on Taiwan. Now, as many other things have changed, this taboo also has been shunted aside.

In 1990, a film, *City of Sadness*, won popular acclaim for its startlingly frank depiction of the period of "white terror." The government has gone a long way in recent years to deal with the animosity generated by the 2–28 Incident. President Lee Teng-hui and Hau Pei-tsun, while he was premier, each addressed the matter in public—a momentous step. An official commission was impaneled and a report about the matter has been issued publicly. In 1993, the government offered a formal apology, acknowledged the KMT's role in the affair, announced plans to construct shrines in memory of the victims, and committed itself to provide reparations to the families of the victims.[22]

Searching for a cause of the 2–28 Incident in the Taiwanese identity, Chang Chun-hung explained,

> Originally [Taiwanese] thought that the culture of their fatherland was noble. This sort of esteem is just like that of a son who has for a long time been cut off from his parents and . . . in his thoughts his father is exalted, noble, and abounding [in fine qualities]; so, when the son enters back into the embrace of his father he is full of excitement and illusions; to be let down from such a high point of illusion is really dreadful; to discover suddenly that the parent for whom you yearned, whom you held up with such illusions is actually quite low class and lacking in fine qualities—the impact of that was a factor in the eruption of the 2–28 Incident and a reason why the heights of acceptability were transformed into the heights of animosity; it produced an extremely serious fissure.[23]

One gathers from conversations with Taiwanese—even those too young to have any memory of the 2–28 Incident—a severe sense of victimization. The failure of the KMT to address adequately the anger Taiwanese felt about the random, pervasive terror associated with the crackdown by Nationalist troops caused this sense to fester. Memories of the 2–28 Incident also provided a rallying point for the opposition movement, an effective tool to mobilize support for Taiwanese nationalism. The indignation Taiwanese repressed since the KMT crackdown in 1947, a gnawing sense of hatred, was fed at each turn by any perceived impropriety or inequity in which Taiwanese were victimized by Mainlanders. Regrettably, the KMT fanned the flames of resentment and animosity in the forty years since it came to Taiwan both by actions that wronged Taiwanese and by inaction.

Some academics point out that the friction the Taiwanese had with the KMT was not so much a clash between the native population and Mainlanders as much as it was an example of the way the KMT behaved wherever it took power. There are those who say that before the KMT came to Taiwan, its relations with the local people of Nanking and Chungking were also soured by brutality and high-handedness. Speaking of those who now advocate independence on Taiwan, Chu Chi-ying said, in an astoundingly candid remark, "During World War II when the central government was seated in Szechwan . . . Szechwanese had such [an] element, such sentiment. . . . It was fortunate that [the] Japanese occupation . . . only last[ed] eight years. Had it lasted for forty years, probably [there] would be some kind of Szechwan Independence Movement.[24] The indignations the Taiwanese feel they have suffered at the hands of the KMT have probably been the most potent source of group consciousness. In this sense, even though the notion of Taiwan consciousness is couched in terms of cultural distinctiveness, it is essentially a political phenomenon.

Taiwanese Culture, Taiwanese Consciousness

Some Taiwanese have justified their demands for independence by claiming that Taiwanese culture and Chinese—or Han—culture are different. For example, according to Hsieh Chang-t'ing, "Taiwan's traditional culture originated from the Han culture of mainland China. But because it was separated from the mainland for long periods of time, and also due to its oceanic location, it was able to absorb foreign cultures easily and it gradually developed a lifestyle and values that were suited to its own survival. Thus, in many ways there was a significant difference between it and the original Chinese culture.[25] Chiu I-jen acknowledged that Taiwanese culture is similar to the culture of Fukien Province. However, the KMT worked hard to foster a sense of unity, to eradicate any source of Taiwanese opposition, and systematically repressed any expression of Taiwanese history, dialect, folk-operatic forms, songs, and so forth. In reaction, Taiwanese who felt that their sense of identity was being smothered arose to assert their differences. The implication is that, had the KMT been more inclusive, less suspicious of Taiwanese cultural forms, and tolerant rather than repressive, there would have been little impetus for Taiwanese political action and, therefore, a weaker sense of Taiwanese identity.[26]

Chang Chun-hung agreed that "[b]asically we cannot deny that Taiwanese culture is an extension of Chinese culture." He accounted for the emergence of Taiwanese identity, not in cultural differences, but in persecution and repression.[27] It would be wrong to attribute the animosity and distrust between Taiwanese and Mainlanders today to cultural differences, as some have tried to do. Essentially, Taiwanese culture is a regional variation of Chinese culture. It is not unique and shares a good deal with the culture of southeastern China, particularly of Fukien Province, across the Taiwan Strait.

Cultural anthropologist Li I-yuan suggested that at a basic level, Taiwanese are like Chinese from elsewhere in that they abide by the same notions of the temporal, supernatural, spatial, and cosmological dimensions as manifested in such common practices as fortune-telling (*suan-ming*) and geomancy (*feng-shui*). Their attitudes toward interpersonal relations—in the family, the community, and the state—are the same as Chinese elsewhere, as are their attitudes toward food and health. Li suggested that these similarities affirm that the culture of Taiwan is Chinese.[28]

The identity Taiwanese feel and the reason why some have tried to promote the idea that Taiwan has a separate culture has to do with Taiwanese reactions to political repression. The frustration Taiwanese have endured has caused them to challenge the legitimacy of the KMT and all it represents. That has created an atmosphere in which regional distinctions that might otherwise have been ignored have become potent symbols of a group consciousness, or identity, that empowers Taiwanese to see themselves as different.

It is evident that Taiwanese differ from most Mainlanders in that they speak a different dialect, worship different deities, have cultivated a self-referential literature, perform distinct forms of folk opera and puppetry, and practice different funeral and burial customs. What some Taiwanese refer to as Taiwanese culture is most easily characterized as the transported culture of Fukien Province (from which most Taiwanese families trace their roots), leavened with bits of other southern Chinese cultural ingredients and flavored with the peculiar historical experiences of Taiwanese interactions with Japan and the West.

Every civilization that extends over a wide territory and a vast population is bound to have regional variations and discernible differences in practice, customs, and beliefs. These differences do not necessarily constitute a different culture. That Taiwanese distinguish between their own expressions of culture and the ways of Mainlanders may have to do with the gap between the folk culture of Taiwan and the elite, gentry culture that the KMT has portrayed as Chinese national culture. This gap, naturally, has led Taiwanese to see themselves as different but may not necessarily be attributed to the existence of a distinct Taiwanese culture.

Ch'en Li-li wrote about the cultural elite's perception of China during the period that the KMT first came to Taiwan. She offered insight about the gap between the Han culture purveyed by the KMT as national culture and Taiwan's indigenous culture. The elite believed that Chinese civilization:

resembled a tree, and China at any given generation was a cross-section of the trunk with concentric rings. Occupying the core was the cultured elite—erudite gentry and well-born scholar officials. . . . Less cultured groups occupied successive outer rings with the outermost ring occupied by the untutored masses. Generation after generation of descendants kept their places in their appropriate rings.

Horizontally, in good times, the core sent its sap outward to nourish the other rings, but when the times were bad, outreaching altruism could be retrenched and the core need only protect its own survival. . . . Vertically, each generation's core must pass on its values and cultural heritage to the next generation's while constantly harkening back for sustenance to its predecessors. As long as the continuity was maintained, Chinese civilization would be safe.[29]

From the perspective of those about whom Ch'en wrote, imbuing Taiwanese with the essence of Chinese civilization was something they were obliged to do for their own survival. Of course, there are some Taiwanese who view the KMT effort to assimilate the Taiwanese into "Chinese" culture as an effort to smother any indigenous Taiwanese culture with the form of nourishment that Ch'en described.

As liberalization proceeded on Taiwan in the late 1980s, a flood of publications gave voice to the Taiwanese need to redefine their culture and to rectify the problems with contemporary Taiwanese society that stem from the abiding uncertainty people feel about their identity.[30] Many Taiwanese seem willing to acknowledge that Taiwan's culture evolved from the Han culture of the mainland but claim that the peculiar circumstances of Taiwan's history have resulted in the emergence of a new cultural form that must be accepted for what it is, rather than be molded to suit an idealistic notion of what Chinese culture must be. Many intellectuals object to the idea that Taiwanese must be remade in the KMT's image of what Chinese used to or should be. Taiwanese social critics view contemporary society on Taiwan as profoundly unhealthy because for forty years people have strained to maintain a false sense of attachment to China when they are mired in a society on Taiwan that they have been cued by socialization and propaganda to disregard or disdain.

Taiwanese intellectuals make the plea that all residents of Taiwan—Mainlanders and Taiwanese alike—must accept the culture they live with as a new form of Chinese culture. The culture of Taiwan, a departure from the Chinese culture of the past, is depicted as arising from the struggle of Taiwan's people to cope with the pressures of adapting traditions to suit modernity. This is an embracing ideology that looks from the present forward to what Taiwan must be, rather than from the present backward to cling to an ideal that was not realized. It is a declaration of cultural independence that is intended to offer the residents of Taiwan a more realistic image of themselves and their future. It is a new identity that has vital political import. "Taiwanese have been a prisoner of the yoke of Han culture for almost 400 years, especially after 1949. Large-scale traditional culture was forced onto the Taiwanese by a fascist regime and today . . . finally there is a turning point for a complete reform in Taiwanese society. Taiwanese have had all kinds of new consciousness and they are alive and bravely pursuing freedom, emancipation, egalitarianism, and self-respect."[31]

The author of this passage, Lin Yang-min, dismissed the focus on national recovery that has served as the essence of KMT ideology and the plinth on which its legitimacy rests. He emphasized the importance of accepting Taiwan, not the mainland, as one's fatherland. Taiwanese have been on the island at least as long as Americans have been in America, and Lin suggested that there is no reason for them to look to a land across the ocean as their home. He implored his compatriots to reject the idea that their fatherland is elsewhere and accept the island as home. He upbraided the Mainlanders and exhorted them, too, to accept Taiwan as a homeland instead of longing to be elsewhere. Lin declared that "Taiwanese should take Taiwan as their one and only country and should also take Taiwan as the fatherland of the Taiwanese."[32] "The so-called Mainlanders in Taiwan who came after 1949 have lived here for forty years and have set down roots here and have given birth to offspring here. They don't plan to leave. Why don't they take Taiwan as their own country? Even when they have a chance to visit the so-called fatherland across the Taiwan Strait, they still come back to Taiwan to live. Therefore, they have to take Taiwan as their fatherland. We are not from the mainland anymore, we are Taiwanese. Taiwan is our native place, our country, and our fatherland."[33]

This is a common theme. Hsieh Chang-t'ing wrote that because of the "stalemate between the KMT and the CCP" the people on Taiwan have developed a sense of sharing a common fate. "This new Taiwanese consciousness accommodates all the Mainlanders, Taiwanese, Hakka, and aborigines. It is a new consciousness that will allow all of us to harmonize and become one."[34]

This rich literature is a grave threat to the ideology of the KMT. It denies Taiwan's ties to the mainland, undermines the basis of KMT rule, inspires people to view Taiwan as a distinct polity, contributes to the drumbeat of the Taiwan independence movement, and amplifies the call for democratic reform as a step toward self-determination. The most potent theme in this literature is the appeal to Taiwanese to take pride in who they are and where they live, rather than to continue viewing themselves as orphans who must be returned, someday, to their fatherland.

Legacies of Frustration and Authoritarianism

Taiwanese and Mainlanders have been wracked by frustrations that have reinforced their own senses of cultural and national identity. For first-generation Mainlanders, the gradual realization that they will not be able to recover and return to the mainland—as Chiang Kai-shek led them to expect they would—came as a shattering disappointment. They have become more sensitive to their plight as alien figures in a society in which they do not, nor generally wish to, belong. Taiwan is a cramped, truncated semblance of the China with which many of the older Mainlanders identify. Younger Mainlanders who have known no home other than Taiwan may find disorienting the sudden rise of Taiwanese nationalism, which casts them in the role of political minority.

For Taiwanese, the authoritarian system imposed by the KMT robbed them of dignity in a way that has proven hard to accept. Intense socialization in the schools emphasized Chinese mainland history, heroes, geography, language, literature, and values at the expense of any attention to Taiwan. The KMT exercised complete control over the island and the affairs of its residents according to a set of Temporary Provisions Effective During the Period of Communist Rebellion, which were enacted on May 10, 1948, and essentially suspended constitutional law. KMT officials scrupulously point out that this period was a state of emergency and was temporary; they rankle at the suggestion that what they imposed was a form of martial law.

Ultimately, these provisions were lifted on July 15, 1987, and replaced by a National Security Act, which critics claimed offered the same sweeping, unregulated powers to the government. Finally, in 1991, the state of emergency was ended with a declaration that the period of mobilization to resist communist aggression had passed.

For the thirty-nine years that the provisions were in effect, an elaborate domestic security apparatus—ostensibly to safeguard against communist infiltration—put every citizen within earshot of government agents, informants, or undercover police and effectively strangled all but the boldest critics. Reports of the intimidation, blacklisting, apprehension, torture, imprisonment, and murder of political dissidents and critics of the KMT have punctuated the history of Nationalist rule on Taiwan.[35]

As Taiwanese bore the brunt of this political repression, it is understandable that they came to see themselves as the victims and the KMT, represented by the Mainlanders, as the victimizers, underscoring another apparent difference. In truth, the situation was far more complex and there have been plenty of Mainlander victims as well as Taiwanese beneficiaries of KMT domination. While it appears that the KMT of the late 1980s and 1990s has been eager to distance itself from the abuses and excesses of the past, it has been hard to slip out from under the shadow of suspicion that, even now, former leaders cast from their graves.

Rigid KMT policies directly and indirectly reinforced distinctions between Mainlanders and Taiwanese in a way that undermined the party's goal of social integration. These institutionalized manners of distinction have contributed to the emergence and sustenance of Taiwanese identity. The approach the KMT employed in its attempt to foster national unity on Taiwan was recognized by Arend Lijphart as generally causing the "gravest practical consequences." "Although the replacement of segmental loyalties by a common national allegiance appears to be a logical answer to the problems posed by a plural society, it is extremely dangerous to attempt it. Because of the tenacity of primordial loyalties, any effort to eradicate them not only is quite unlikely to succeed . . . but may well stimulate segmental cohesion and intersegmental violence rather than national cohesion."[36] That Lijphart's depiction—written without reference to the situation on Taiwan—so accurately describes what occurred on Taiwan suggests that the pattern into which the KMT fell is one into which other regimes have fallen before. Among the policies that highlighted the distinctions between Mainlanders and Taiwanese were those affecting the use of Mandarin versus Taiwanese—probably the irritant that Taiwanese most often spoke of when explaining their sense of frustration and their flagging sense of self. Another way in which the KMT effort to create a sense of unity backfired was the official attitude toward Taiwan.

Attitudes toward Language

Contemporary life on Taiwan bustles without many visible clues of the divisions that seethe beneath the surface or the memories of harsher times, not long in the past. One source of frustration that resulted from KMT cultural policies and continually reinforced the Taiwanese sense of group identity is the issue of dialect.

In Chinese, some dialects differ as little as English does between New York and Mississippi. Other dialects are mutually incomprehensible, sounding as different as English and Dutch or German. "Taiwanese"— the dialect of Taiwan—and Mandarin are mutually unintelligible. Mainlanders came to Taiwan from various provinces of China speaking different regional dialects. Few spoke the dialect of Taiwan, which is a variant of the dialect spoken in a region of Fukien Province south of the Min River from which most Taiwanese come. Taiwanese from that region are called *Minnan jen* (people from south of the Min) and the dialect they speak a form of *Minnan hua* (south of the Min speech) which is related to the Hokkien spoken in and around Amoy. Contemporary Taiwanese language evolved from this dialect and other southern linguistic influences.[37] To communicate, the Mainlanders used Mandarin, the dialect of the north, which had been selected as the "national language." When the KMT came to Taiwan, few Taiwanese spoke this dialect.

As part of its effort to reintegrate Taiwan into the Chinese fold, the KMT enforced a strict policy that entailed using only Mandarin for official affairs, in schools, on radio, and on television.

> Television was first aired [in Taiwan] in 1962 and Taiwanese shows were most popular, which caused some jealousy. So in 1972 the government ordered that all television stations could not air more than one hour per day of Taiwanese-language programs and that hour had to be broken up into two segments at lunch and at night. During the 6:30 P.M. prime-time hour, only one of the three stations could air a Taiwanese-language program. In 1976, another rule was passed which said that all television shows had to be in Mandarin and the shows in Taiwanese would be gradually phased out over the year.[38]

This contributed to the immense sense of frustration that Taiwanese felt. Having been forced by Japanese to speak Japanese and by Mainlanders to speak Mandarin, the Taiwanese resented the imposition that restricted the use of their own mother tongue.

In time, Taiwanese came to feel that their dialect, literature, poetry, songs, and drama were all inferior to Mandarin and the cultural works of the mainland.[39] One consequence of this sense of inferiority was the acceptance of the notion that Mainlanders' pronunciation of Mandarin was "standard" and the accented Mandarin that Taiwanese spoke was inferior. In a culture that emphasizes heavily the importance of conformity with ideals and in which mastery of language is, by tradition, accorded a very high degree of respect, Taiwanese were often made to feel inferior.

In the very earliest years after the KMT arrived, teachers still used both Mandarin and Taiwanese to explain material in class. In 1953, the government mandated that neither Taiwanese nor Japanese be used as a language of instruction, and in 1964 a law was passed forbidding the use of Taiwanese in schools or official settings. This was accompanied by a campaign that emphasized the grace of Mandarin and the comparative vulgarity of Taiwanese.[40]

In schools, speech contests intended to promote fluency in Mandarin caused many Taiwanese to feel inadequate. Taiwanese, which was still the dialect of the home and marketplace, was forbidden in class. It seems every adult Taiwanese who was educated since the KMT arrived recalls the fines, slaps, and humiliations that were meted out as punishment to students heard speaking Taiwanese at school. Taiwanese were made to feel their dialect was somehow less dignified, dirtier, than Mandarin. Taiwanese who spoke Mandarin encumbered with a Taiwanese accent felt vulnerable each time they opened their mouths and ashamed that culturally—and, perhaps, inherently—they were inferior to Mainlanders.[41]

The fallacy of this assumption is that not all those who came from the mainland spoke with the much-coveted "standard" pronunciation any more than all English speak with the clipped Oxbridge accent to which Americans often attribute intelligence, wit, and erudition. In each region of China, Mandarin is tinged with the accent of the dialect that is spoken there as the primary tongue. The Mandarin taken as "standard" is that which is spoken in the north, particularly in the area surrounding Peking. However, the Mandarin spoken in Peking is not at all like that spoken in Chungking, and that not a bit like the Mandarin spoken in Shanghai. Indeed, even Chiang Kai-shek spoke Mandarin with a thick accent of his native Chekiang Province. From the vantage of pronunciation alone, a laborer or rickshaw puller in Peking may have spoken more standard Mandarin than the president, who spoke it with an accent no less heavy than that of many Mandarin-speaking Taiwanese.

Restrictions on the use of Taiwanese have loosened in recent years, and it has become more acceptable—even fashionable—to speak Taiwanese in certain settings. Taiwanese is now the language of commerce outside of Taipei, has slowly reentered the realm of officialdom—even, for symbolic purposes, in the Legislative Yuan—and is apparently a *sine qua non* in campaigning for elected office. K'ang Ning-hsiang illustrated this change in attitudes by recounting a dinner conversation he had with a U.S. government official who had returned to Taiwan after a long absence. "I asked him 'is there any difference between the time you were in Taiwan [before] and now?' He said, 'When I was in Taiwan before . . . you knew [if someone] was Taiwanese, [even though he tried to] speak Mandarin. Although the Taiwanese spoke Mandarin . . . their Mandarin was very poor. But things are different this time . . . [because] there are also Mainlanders speaking Taiwanese. . . . [E]verybody speaks Taiwanese. Even the Mainlanders . . . try their best. . . . [T]he louder they speak [Taiwanese], the more proud they are.' "[42]

The latitude to speak Taiwanese is itself emblematic of the rise of Taiwanese nationalism. Taiwanese dialect is reclaiming social respectability because Taiwanese have asserted their identity. It is now fashionable for Mainlanders to study Taiwanese. Indeed, it has become a badge of honor for high-ranking KMT officials from the mainland to flout their newfound interest in studying Taiwanese. One report in a government-sponsored popular journal indicated that Taiwanese-language courses are even being offered in certain public schools out of concern that "the dialect could someday vanish, since the number of young people who cannot speak Taiwanese has been increasing." The report continues, a bit disingenuously, "In fact, in the 1950s and early 1960s, when the government was working hard to promote Mandarin, use of the dialect in classrooms was strongly discouraged. . . . Even with increased promoting, Taiwanese still faces a long climb to overall acceptance."[43] It is still the case that most Mainlanders do not speak

Taiwanese, even those who were born on Taiwan. This is a source of great uneasiness in settings where Mainlanders, second-generation Mainlanders, and Taiwanese are expected to mix.

Shaw Yu-ming, in a candid statement about the KMT's language policy, remarked that people should be grateful that the government insisted on teaching Mandarin. He said that fostering a universal dialect is an essential part of nation building and allows Taiwanese entrepreneurs to communicate when conducting business on the mainland. However, he did rue one thing: "[I]f something can be criticized, maybe the Mainlanders should [have been] taught Taiwanese on the side. Then you [would] have [had] a true integration."[44]

Attitude toward Taiwan

When Mainlanders arrived on Taiwan, the Taiwanese saw them as interlopers with little concern for the island and no respect for the Taiwanese. For decades, all Mainlanders spoke of was their desire—and intent—to return *home* to the mainland. This attitude was bolstered by official government pronouncements and, therefore, provided a measure of legitimacy that affected notions of identification.

Mainlanders sensed that they were not welcome, felt uneasy about being uprooted and deposited on the distant island, hoped only that they would soon return home, and felt alienated from the Taiwanese. One second-generation Mainlander spoke of her father's attitude toward Taiwan saying that for the first decade after their arrival

> [h]e still thought we were going back there [to the mainland], so we didn't buy anything. We didn't buy a house, we didn't buy anything. We were poor ... but we still could have managed to have some real estate, but he didn't do that [buy any]. And that made us ... relatively poor compared with other Mainlanders, [not to mention] with indigenous people because they owned land, they owned houses, they [had] been here many, many generations. So, my dad was ... very disillusioned when he knew that he was going to settle down here and organize his family here probably all his life. .... [He said,] "I planned not to stay here very long, but now I'm doomed to stay here the rest of my life; even my children will probably stay here the rest of their lives."[45]

Even Hau Pei-tsun made this point when he said that Mainlanders have not benefited personally from all the years during which they have been in leadership positions: "I have been premier. . . . [T]oday, many of us [who have been in important positions] do not even have our own house. We have never thought of our own interests."[46]

For Taiwanese, who had only recently been freed from a half century of colonial administration, Taiwan was home. They expected to be integrated into the Chinese community. Instead, they were viewed with hostility, suspicion, or indifference. Many claim they felt like second-class citizens in their own home. Chiang Chun-nan recalled with some bitterness the sense he got from his KMT-regimented education, which ignored Taiwanese culture.

> Under KMT indoctrination . . . we not only don't know much about Taiwan . . . we learn[ed] to despise Taiwaneseness, Taiwanese language. They said Taiwan has no language, no culture. Taiwanese history started from the day the KMT arrived in Taiwan. Taiwan has no purpose in itself. The purpose of Taiwan is to be a stepping stone to go back to China. It is a transition. It is like a hotel. So, the only hope for Taiwanese is the mainland. The ultimate goal is in the mainland. Everything here is so small. Mountains are small, rivers are so short. [There are] volcanoes, earthquakes. "So, how can we stay here?" [Mainlanders asked.] The KMT brought that kind of philosophy, that kind of view to Taiwan and imposed that . . . view on Taiwanese. So, we feel humiliated. . . downgraded. . . . We have no hope because we are too small. We have no culture.[47]

There are myriad small signals that it is China, not Taiwan, that has significance. City streets on Taiwan were renamed by the KMT for cities on the mainland, for Nationalist ideals, and for Confucian virtues. The vast plaza on which a grandiose monument to Chiang Kai-shek was built is surrounded by four major roads: Chung-shan South Road on the west, named for Sun Yat-sen; Hang-chow South Road on the east, named for the Southern Sung dynasty capital of China; Hsin-i Road on the north, a reference to the Confucian virtue of living up to one's word to manifest significance; and Ai-kuo East Road on the south, literally, "love the country," or Patriotism Road.

As Chiang Chun-nan commented, "The map of Taipei is a map of China; it is easy for [Mainlanders] to go back to visit the mainland, from Chungking to Heilungkiang in just twenty minutes. From Nanking to Hsinkiang, from Canton to Shanghai is two blocks."[48] Another source pointed out that the entire environment created by the KMT and the

Mainlanders reinforced the idea that everything of importance was on the mainland and nothing on Taiwan was of significance. "You live in Taiwan yet you do not see any reference to Taiwan, only to China, Chung-kuo, Chung-hwa. Even restaurants and company names very seldom used local names. All the famous restaurant names from mainland China were used. Even the laundries or the provincial assemblies were all intended to remind citizens of China. 'You do not belong here, you are only passing through. Do not ever forget your motherland. And Taiwan is not your country. . . . Taiwan is not a country, it is only a place.' "[49]

There's No Place Like Home

Attitudes toward the mainland and Taiwan have changed since the government lifted the ban on travel from Taiwan to the mainland in 1987. Since that time, Mainlanders have had an opportunity to return to see relatives and homes left behind forty years ago, their children have had a chance to get a glimpse of the place that their parents had primed them to regard as their true home, and Taiwanese have had the chance to see the land and people with whom they have been told they shall unite. Reactions of people who have made the trip across the Taiwan Strait, predictably, differ according to their identity and have affected people's views of Taiwan and themselves.[50]

Many Mainlanders have found the return visit a disheartening ordeal. They were deeply affected by the sense of deprivation in the PRC, often gave voice to a form of "survivor's guilt," and seemed thoroughly disabused of any residual illusions of ever moving home again. Beyond the shock of revisiting loved ones and sights not seen for four decades is the realization of how terribly far apart Taiwan and the PRC have grown in that time. Mainlanders spent much of the past forty years on Taiwan yearning to return home, upholding the dream of a unified Chinese state, and belittling the value of Taiwan; however, they have discovered that homes they left have vanished and that, after forty years of communism, the China and Chinese culture they value has been better preserved on Taiwan than on the mainland.

As compared to the PRC, Taiwan has a highly developed infrastructure, economic vitality, elevated standard of living, and relatively free social milieu. Initially, people on Taiwan perceived the PRC as backward, politically repressed, and depressing. Relatives who lived through the vicissitudes of Communist rule also bear scars from past campaigns—some the result of denunciations that were based on family ties to Taiwan and the KMT. The most prevalent comment heard from embittered Mainlanders who return to Taiwan after a visit to the PRC is that family members still living in the PRC ply guilt to drain their Taiwan relatives of money and gifts of consumer products.

For the most part, Taiwanese who traveled to the mainland for the first time were taken by the similarity between themselves and their brethren across the strait. While people are highly sensitive to the economic disparity that separates Taiwan from the PRC, they seem impressed that—despite KMT propaganda to the contrary—their "Communist" cousins are just as "Chinese" as they are.

Ma Ying-cheou summed up the different reactions to the mainland, saying that Taiwanese returning from the PRC are "quite fascinated by the mainland; the vast land, the rich resources, everything is fascinating. Cheap labor. Everything. But . . . Mainlanders, particularly those who have lived in the mainland [before], are very frustrated. Very disappointed. Many of them say, 'I don't want to go back again.' "[51]

Shaw Yu-ming pointed out that most of those from Taiwan who have invested in the mainland in recent years are not Mainlanders, but Taiwanese.

> It's the Taiwanese businessmen who are most directly involved in the indirect trade [with the PRC]. It's not the Mainlanders. If we [Mainlanders] go back to the mainland, [we] mostly just look at the Great Wall . . . look at the relatives. Not much else to do. And most of the old soldiers, after a few trips, they don't want to go back to their roots . . . spend all their money. They're not that welcome. They pretty much satisfy their homesickness and they want to stay here [in Taiwan]. Mainland, to them, is more sentimental, or cultural. . . . But mainland to many Taiwanese businessmen is a market. They are the ones who . . . crashed down the door of the mainland. They are the ones who are active [there], not the Mainlanders.[52]

Indeed, there is a lot of anecdotal evidence about Taiwanese rediscovering their roots in the mainland. In addition to the buildup of the economy of coastal, southeastern China, there are temples, hospitals, and schools being built with money donated by wealthy Taiwanese. Religious pilgrimages from Taiwan to the mainland add to the sense that many Taiwanese, secure in their political identity as Taiwanese, find fulfillment in the reestablishment of cultural contact with their origins.

Ma Ying-cheou told of a place in northeastern Taiwan where there was a rivalry between two temple communities whose primary deity of worship is Matsu, a benevolent, female protector of seafarers. Worshipers at one temple went on a pilgrimage back to Mei-chou Island off the coast of Fukien, where the cult of Matsu originated, and brought back with them to Taiwan a statue of Matsu. When the statue was installed, the temple became a popular center of worship because people attributed to it a heightened degree of spiritual authenticity. Not to be outdone, worshipers from the rival temple that also revered Matsu went on a pilgrimage to the same island off the Fukien coast and returned to Taiwan with religious icons. Ma recounted how he visited the temple and, on seeing the newly installed icons, asked " 'Who are they?' 'Those are Matsu's parents.' I said, 'How come Matsu's parents and not Matsu herself?' They say, 'Look, Matsu is a very filial person. [She] always obey[s] what the parents say. So, to worship the parents may be even more effective than if you worship Matsu.' "[53]

The newly formed attitudes of Taiwanese and Mainlanders toward the PRC suggest that the policies of the KMT, which tried to associate cultural and political identity with a unified China, have not fully succeeded. Mainlanders, who one assumed would naturally identify with the place from which they came, now find themselves repulsed by poverty, backwardness, and greed on the mainland, or are just indifferent. Taiwanese, who have not had a political affinity for the mainland, are comfortable looking to Fukien as the touchstone that reinforces their cultural identity, as long as they can look at it from Taiwan. Taiwanese and Mainlanders are equally comfortable pointing to economic disparities and experiential differences that divide the PRC from Taiwan, and, in the eyes of most, this justifies keeping Taiwan politically separate from the mainland as long as the Communists remain in charge.

The ravages of the past four decades in the PRC have done more to accentuate economic and social differences than to cultivate a commonality between the mainland and Taiwan. Although the KMT endeavored to foster the sense that unifying China was critical to the glory of Chinese civilization and the betterment of all Chinese, the strategy it adopted for this task ended up alienating the Taiwanese from this vision. The KMT tried to persuade those it forced to listen that there is only one China and China means unity. Over the years, the

KMT has worked hard to promote itself as a more credible source of leadership than the CCP. It has done this, in part, by extolling the glories of Taiwan's economic development, cultural renaissance, and political liberalization that have evolved under its guidance on Taiwan. At the same time, to discredit the CCP, the KMT ranted about the depravity, oppression, and hopelessness of life under Communist rule in the PRC.

Whereas this dual appeal was intended to bolster the party's image as better suited to being the "sole legitimate government" of all China, the KMT succeeded only in persuading residents of the island that they are better off living on Taiwan than on the mainland and that self-rule would be infinitely preferable to rule from Peking. The KMT expected people to take from this the message that it would lead China and all Chinese to flourish, but the CCP could only cause China to perish. What people heard, however, was not what the KMT had hoped.

The incessant comparison of Taiwan to the mainland caused many to identify success and modernity with autonomy, and deprivation with reunification. For both Mainlanders and Taiwanese, there is a palpable sense that Taiwan is successful, prosperous, and increasingly open politically. People gripe about the cost of living, the stench of pollution, the unrelenting traffic congestion, and other social ills on the island, but they have no interest in trading any of that for life on the mainland. Disgruntled residents of Taiwan might seek an opportunity to relocate to Vancouver or Los Angeles, but few would see any advantage at all in moving to the mainland or forming a union with the mainland that would be likely to dilute the riches Taiwan has earned for itself.

Taiwanese have been particularly attentive to the woes of what used to be West Germany. Reflecting on the way the new Germany must absorb the impoverished, undisciplined, disorderly, and demanding population of the former East Germany, Taiwanese opposed to reunification see the German case as a strong incentive to maintain Taiwan's autonomy. If Taiwan and the mainland are reunified anytime soon under KMT control, the frustrations and cost to the former West Germans will be dwarfed by the costs Taiwanese will incur. What Taiwanese fear even more is that in the hubristic desire for historical significance, leading figures in the KMT will work to reunify Taiwan with the mainland, but will end up "selling out" Taiwan for their personal aggrandizement. The greatest fear is that the Communists will end up taking control of Taiwan. In this regard, residents of Taiwan take note of the increasing tensions generated by Sino-British negotiations in the early 1990s concerning the transfer of sovereignty of Hong Kong and are more determined than ever that Taiwan not be subjected to comparable pressures.

KMT officials vehemently deny any intention to reunify with the mainland as long as the CCP is in control. The whole point of the newly articulated National Unification Guidelines is to map out a policy that appears to be moving toward reunification but that is dependent on political reforms and economic development in the PRC that will not be likely to occur under CCP rule. In effect, it is a plan that allows the KMT to say that it is still determined to reunify, but a plan that cannot be effected as long as the current system in the PRC prevails.

The fear that Taiwan will be sold out is an anxiety that comes from a historical consciousness of being treated like chattel by self-serving political regimes over several centuries. Taiwanese elite have cultivated a sense that, in the past, Taiwan and its people have been treated as objects of exchange—political booty—in machinations effected by alien governments too powerful for the island's residents to resist. Taiwanese have been betrayed before and, therefore, have severe misgivings about any deals that would lead to a political arrangement in which Taiwan is governed from Peking.

Uneasiness about reunification affects Mainlanders, too. While the KMT continues to promulgate reunification as a national goal, it is getting increasingly difficult to believe that many people on Taiwan genuinely expect reunification to benefit them as long as the CCP remains in Peking. Surely, people are happy to fantasize about a time in the future when the CCP falls and there is an opportunity for reunification with a new form of Chinese government. Until the Communists are eliminated from the political stage, however, even Mainlanders on Taiwan are wary of moving too quickly to reunify.

There are different perspectives about these matters, but they seem to lead to the same conclusions. It is difficult to imagine the aging Mainlander elite having a pressing desire to live in the mainland as it is today. They have become too accustomed to the comforts and liberties of life on Taiwan. Even though the standard of living has been improving on the mainland, access to goods and opportunities still extends much farther down into society on Taiwan than on the mainland.

For the elderly KMT soldiers who were pressed into military service as young men, brought to Taiwan in the aftermath of the KMT defeat, and consigned to depressing retirement villages or clusters of ramshackle public housing, there is nothing for them any longer in the PRC. Family they left behind may resent the old soldiers for having "had it so good" on Taiwan while their kin in the PRC suffered the fate that the CCP visited on its citizenry. Those who were married before they left the mainland may have married and sired again on Taiwan. Even those who would like to return to be with their family fear they may be regarded as politically undesirable or worse by the Communists, against whom they once fought.

As to those generations that were born and raised on Taiwan, the only home they have known is the island, and if they cannot identify with that home, they are unlikely to find the mainland more hospitable. The generations that have been raised on Taiwan since the KMT arrived have been influenced by American and Japanese popular culture in a way that their cousins in the PRC have not. The material advantages and political liberties to which they have become increasingly accustomed would not be as readily available in their "home province." To their misfortune, the growth of Taiwanese identity on the island is decreasing the psychic "space" for Mainlanders. Politically, the KMT has been far more welcoming to Taiwanese than has the opposition to Mainlanders. For many, this disturbing turn of events is cause to reevaluate their relationship to Taiwan and their cultural and national identity.

Soong Chu-yu, former secretary-general of the KMT (now governor of Taiwan), on the other hand, said that many people confuse Taiwanese consciousness with democratization. Although there are a lot of Taiwanese who are eager to promote democracy, he said it is important to note that many advocates of Taiwan independence are not really advocates of democracy, and many who advocate democracy, KMT leaders in particular, are not supportive of the independence movement. He recalled that the first democratic movement on the island was led by Lei Chen and other Mainlander intellectuals who had little interest in independence. Likewise, Taiwanization is not the same as seeking independence. Simply because a person has cultivated a Taiwanese consciousness does not mean that he supports the idea of independence.

Soong observed that the Taiwan independence movement is based on a foundation of Taiwanese consciousness compounded by frustration. Originally, Taiwanese consciousness itself was a politically neutral sentiment. Indeed, Soong credited Chiang Ching-kuo for being the first to recognize its importance and to promote Taiwanization. Obviously Chiang opposed Taiwan independence.[54]

Lin Cheng-chieh endorsed this view and said that state (*kuo-chia*) identity and native (*pen-ti*) identity are not the same. "[I]t is not necessarily the case that those who identify themselves as Taiwanese support Taiwan independence. . . . I know a lot of socialists who advocate reunification. But they speak Taiwanese. They are not willing to speak Mandarin."[55] He pointed out that Yu Teng-fa, an opposition leader who was the patriarch of a political dynasty in Kaohsiung, advocated reunification despite his identity as a Taiwanese.[56] Lin maintained that a lot of the older Taiwanese feel this way.[57] Conversely, there is an association on Taiwan of Mainlanders who advocate that Taiwan be independent. So, Lin's point is that one's notion of national identity cannot always be determined on the basis of where one comes from.

Lin advanced the thesis that Taiwanese consciousness was not always synonymous with independence and in theory should not be opposed to reunification. He claimed that during the period of land reform, the big Taiwanese landowners whose property was confiscated by the KMT sent their children overseas to the United States or Japan to study and developed a fatalistic attitude about the Mainlanders who had come from outside Taiwan, taken over the island, and alienated the formerly well-to-do Taiwanese gentry. Lin said that this group was particularly disaffected from the KMT and felt that they did not want to associate themselves any longer with the Chinese. They ceased to be *Chung-kuo jen* and came to see themselves as Taiwanese. Many of this group, the Taiwanese elite, were killed during the period of white terror in 1947.

Lin observed that in the 1980s the Taiwanese overseas began to return to Taiwan and agitate for independence. The movement gradually took root within the *tang-wai* and then in the DPP. Now, there are some who take national identity, Taiwanese consciousness, and independence to be the same thing.[58] It is interesting that Soong Chu-yu offered a similar explanation for the emergence of the independence issue. He indicated that this issue deserved more scholarly attention. The essence of his remarks is that wealthy Taiwanese landowners had been snubbed by Chiang Kai-shek when they went to see him in 1945. Apparently, the late president viewed them as having collaborated with the Japanese during the period of occupation. Once the KMT took

Taiwan, that group suffered the most and was primarily responsible for pushing the idea of Taiwan independence later on.[59]

Taiwan's Identity Crisis

The cultural identity of Taiwanese appears to have been "invented" in reaction to the efforts of the mainland elite to make residents of Taiwan cleave to the Chinese motherland, its culture, and its people. From Benedict Anderson's view, however, even the idea of the Chinese nation must be challenged. Indeed, what the Mainlander elite refer to as Chinese culture and their view of the Chinese nation may itself be as much an imagined community as the Taiwanese nation they so vigorously oppose. Anderson's proposition leads one to question whether there is in fact a Chinese nation, a Chinese culture, or a Chinese state. If all communities are simply imagined, it is possible that the political and cultural elite have established intellectual constructs to promote a vision of a unified nation, one they alone have the bureaucratic and political power to enforce on others.

Anderson speculated that the vision Chinese elite wanted to promote was not the "Chineseness" of their civilization. "The Middle Kingdom . . . though we think of it today as Chinese, imagined itself not as Chinese, but as central." It is the visceral conviction that this centrality is real and that there is a cultural elite whose responsibility it is to perpetuate it and keep it vital that informs the cultural policies of the KMT.[60]

The KMT endeavored to reinforce—or establish—a sense of nationality by intense socialization in the schools, in public places, and through the media on Taiwan as it did elsewhere on the mainland prior to 1949. At the time the KMT arrived on the island in the late 1940s, the Taiwanese-speaking portion of the population outnumbered the non–Taiwanese-speaking segment at a ratio of more than 5 to 1. It is understandable that antipathy for the KMT's attitude of linguistic and cultural superiority developed. When the state acts in this way to assimilate a segment of the population under its jurisdiction, the process is often "forcible, involving the repression of [the] language and culture of subordinate groups."[61] Surely, by viewing the Taiwanese as a group that needed to be assimilated forcibly, the KMT inadvertently nourished the Taiwanese sense of distinctiveness that was the seed of the Taiwan independence movement.

Two contextual factors affected the emergence of this Taiwanese sense of national identity. The defeat of Japan in 1945 ended fifty years during which the residents of Taiwan were subjected to the Japanese system of rule. The arrival of the KMT from the mainland shortly thereafter made for a highly disruptive transitional period. This period may be characterized as one in which there was (1) a sudden disruption in the preexisting sense of security people had in their insular community, and (2) a recognition of sharp contrasts between the indigenous community and the rulers, who were seen as alien to that community.[62] Disruptions may come about because of economic forces, as with industrialization, or because of political forces, as with decolonization and conquest. In the case of Taiwan, the disruptions were caused by decolonization and effects analogous to conquest.

Even though there had been a sharp contrast between the Taiwanese and their Japanese rulers, these were to be expected, as Japanese were aliens. Residents of Taiwan were surprised by the sharp contrast they detected between themselves and the Chinese from the mainland who had come to restore China's sovereignty over the island. The most tangible divisions between the rulers and the ruled were political and cultural. The KMT constrained Taiwanese from meaningful political participation and caused them to feel that the manifestations of their own vernacular, regional, cultural forms were less valued than the state-sponsored manifestations of high Chinese culture.

Mainlanders tend to dismiss the sincerity of those who promote Taiwanese cultural distinctiveness. For Mainlanders of this school, those who promote the notion of a Taiwan culture are either seriously misguided or merely seeking personal aggrandizement. Gellner defended the birth of nationalist sentiments. "It would be genuinely wrong to . . . reduce these sentiments to calculations of material advantage or of social mobility. . . . [T]his is a misrepresentation. In the old days it made no sense to ask whether the peasants loved their own culture: they took it for granted . . . [but] they soon learned the difference between dealing with a co-national, one understanding and sympathizing with their culture, and someone hostile to it."[63] Yet it is common to hear Mainlanders proclaim, as Hau Pei-tsun did, that "[t]hose who advocate independence are a minority. . . . you can say that their personal political ambition overrides their sense of the country's history."[64]

Some Taiwanese opponents of the government dismiss the determination of the Mainlander elite to promote Chinese culture as an effort calculated to smother Taiwanese and stymie would-be challengers to KMT supremacy. They question the sincerity of Mainlanders and denounce the focus on Chinese unity as a shield for political expedience. To denigrate the Mainlanders' view of China as solely instrumental is as cynical as denouncing Taiwanese nationality as a fabrication concocted for the personal gain of the Taiwanese elite.

One must take quite seriously the sense of threat the Mainlander elite must have felt in 1949 and the devotion they felt both to their notions of cultural norms and to political unity. The deep commitment of the Mainlander elite to their vision of China and Chinese culture—coupled with a habitual and unexamined reliance on authoritarian mechanisms of governance—is the most likely source of the cultural repression that the KMT visited on the Taiwanese.

Even this allegiance to Chinese culture, though, is not an unassailable explanation for what happened. Despite the rhetoric of devotion to Sun Yat-sen's Three Principles of the People and an apparent sense of mission to perpetuate the civilization of China, there are reasons to question whether these concepts are manipulated in an instrumental fashion for the purposes of political expedience. It is not really clear that the KMT has an ideology that goes much beyond restoring the unity of China.

When the KMT arrived on Taiwan, it did not fully accommodate to its new role or use its position on the island to develop the island according to any particular ideological goal. The stigma of having "lost" China and the determination to recover the mainland focused the party's attentions beyond the island, not on it. It was only with the stunning economic prosperity of the 1980s that political liberalization was finally undertaken and justified in terms of the regime's fundamental commitment to democracy; a commitment that seemed to elude the KMT for the first forty years of its rule.

Apart from offering scant ideological direction, the KMT has sent contradictory signals about its interest in preserving Chinese culture and restoring the grandeur of Chinese civilization. While defending their role as the guardians of China's civilization, many Mainlanders in the upper echelon of the KMT, including the last three ROC presidents, are Christians. Even though Christianity may be adopted by Chinese without utterly eclipsing underlying Chinese sensibilities, this religious duality casts doubt on the leaders' claims to be devoted to cultural renaissance. It lends credence to the view often stated by opponents of the regime that the KMT has, in fact, given voice to the importance of Chineseness as a way to subdue Taiwaneseness.[65]

By favoring the culture of China's elite the KMT intended to promote what it took to be the genuine culture of the Chinese nation but ended up imposing a "high culture" on a society "where previously low cultures had taken up the lives of the majority, and in some cases the totality, of the population."[66] KMT leaders do not believe that they have imposed a foreign culture on Taiwan. However, the regime made clear that the Taiwanese differed from the cultural standard the authorities endorsed. By reinforcing Taiwanese notions of distinctiveness, the KMT inadvertently boosted people's identity as Taiwanese rather than fostering a deeper identity as Chinese.

Taiwanese tend to recognize the Chinese origin of their own culture, but also sense that beyond sharing in the national culture manifested by the Mainlander elite, they have ties to a more compelling, more immediate set of cultural impulses. These they share with other Taiwanese in a manner that differentiates them from the Mainlanders who —while ruling—are seen as alien.[67]

It is not surprising that these two groups also hold different views of the link between culture and nationhood. The Mainlanders are wont to see culture as coterminous with nationhood. This is part ideological, stemming from the ideological influence of Sun Yat-sen, part political expediency, and part desperation. Former premier Hau Pei-tsun, for example, explained, "There is no reason for Taiwan to be independent. The people [on Taiwan] are all Han. They all came from the mainland. Their culture is entirely Chinese, that is the Han culture." So, in Hau's view, "Taiwan does not have the conditions necessary for independence. Neither culturally nor historically is there a justification for Taiwan's independence. In terms of political realities, it just does not have the necessary conditions for independence."[68]

P'eng Ming-min is correct, though, that this hardly constitutes a "concrete reason why Taiwan should be reunited with China." He derided the scheme that has been advanced by the leaders of the PRC that Taiwan and the mainland should coexist as one country with two systems. That plan would permit Taiwan to maintain its own armed forces, economic system, and political system, except that Taiwan will be considered a part of China.

P'eng asked, "What's the purpose of reunification under those terms? What advantage comes from that? It is a form of racial vanity that leads to this attitude. Basically, it is a very feudal way of Chinese thinking."[69] Indeed, it is this kind of sentimentality about the unity of China that appeals to even the Mainlanders on Taiwan. P'eng elaborated about the implications of this attitude: "The most fundamental basis of the modern state is not ethnic, religious, or linguistic heritage but a sense of commonality—having the same destiny regardless of the ethnic identity. This is the most fundamental aspect of modern nationality, not one's ethnic group, but a common destiny. Even if different ethnic groups are together, people can be of the same nation because they share a common destiny. But, without it, even if the people are of the same ethnic group, they cannot have that commonality."[70] After four hundred years, P'eng added, "the unique history of Taiwan has led to a sense of common experience. How can we have the same experience as the people in Peking?" Chen Shui-pian articulated much the same view:

> Some people consider that the Taiwanese people are different than the Chinese people so the people of Taiwan should establish a Taiwanese nation. There are also those who claim that "The culture of Taiwan is different from the culture of China. This is an oceanic culture, it is a melting pot. Therefore, since the culture of Taiwan is different from Chinese culture or mainland culture, we ought to establish our own country."
>
> Personally, I feel that a nation can be composed of several races. Conversely, a race of people can also establish several countries. . . . China does not have to be one nation. Before we achieve the great unity (*ta i-t'ung*) we can exist as many different countries. One Chinese people can exist as many different countries. So, are the Chinese in Singapore Chinese? Yes, they are Chinese. But, they are of a different country which is not China. Chinese people do not all have to live in one country which is called China. . . . Similarly, just because there are different cultures does not mean that each culture must become its own country. One country can comprise a multitude of peoples and a multitude of cultures.[71]

From the perspective of the process of democratization on Taiwan, it is not the different cultural identities per se that are of significance, but the different conceptions of the Chinese nation to which these identities give rise. The continued political status of the Mainlanders is wrapped up with the preservation of one vision of China. The political status of the Taiwanese depends on another. Those Taiwanese who support independence hope to replace the KMT with a different party, perhaps the DPP, which will promote the Taiwan nation, not the Chinese nation. Those Taiwanese who continue to support the KMT have either been persuaded by the logic of the Nationalist ideology or hope gradually to redirect the policies of the KMT while preserving the social order and economic prosperity that is associated with continued KMT rule.

Notes

1. See George Kerr, *Formosa: Licensed Revolution and the Home Rule Movement, 1895–1945* (Honolulu: University Press of Hawaii, 1974); Lai Tse-han, Ramon H. Myers, and Wei Wou, *A Tragic Beginning: The Taiwan Uprising of February 28, 1947* (Stanford: Stanford University Press, 1991); Douglas Mendel, *The Politics of Formosan Nationalism* (Berkeley: University of California Press, 1970).

2. Interview with Chang Chun-hung, Taipei, May 28, 1991.

3. James W. Davidson, *The Island of Formosa: Past and Present* (London: Macmillan, 1903. Reprint. Oxford: Oxford University Press, 1988).

4. Hungdah Chiu, *China and the Taiwan Issue* (New York: Praeger, 1979), pp.16 ff., 214.

5. W.G. Goddard, *Formosa: A Study in Chinese History* (London: Macmillan, 1966), pp. 164–66.

6. Ibid., pp. 262–63.

7. See John F. Copper, *Taiwan: Nation-State or Province?* (Boulder, CO: Westview Press, 1990), p. 24.

8. See, for example, Goddard, *Formosa: A Study in Chinese History*, chapter 9; Thomas B. Gold, *State and Society in the Taiwan Miracle* (Armonk, NY: M.E. Sharpe, 1986), chapter 3; Kerr, *Formosa: Licensed Revolution and the Home Rule Movement, 1895–1945*; Lai, Myers, and Wei, *A Tragic Beginning,* chapter 2; and Mendel, *The Politics of Formosan Nationalism*, pp. 16–25.

9. Goddard, *Formosa: A Study in Chinese History*, p. 163.

10. Mendel, *The Politics of Formosan Nationalism*, p. 25.

11. P'eng Ming-min, *A Taste of Freedom: Memoirs of a Formosan Independence Leader* (New York: Holt, Rinehart and Winston, 1972), pp. 51–52.

12. Li-li Ch'en, "When Jackals Rule: A Defiant Year Under Chiang Kai-shek," *Mother Jones*, vol. 3 (July 1983), p. 12.

13. Interview with Chang Chun-hung, Taipei, May 28, 1991.

14. Liu Fang, "As People of Integrity, Taiwanese Should Refuse to Watch the Excesses of the TV Series 'Love,' " *Tzu-li Wan-pao* (Independence Evening Post), March 11, 1991, in JPRS-CAR–91–028, May 22, 1991, p. 109.

15. See George Kerr, *Formosa Betrayed* (Boston: Houghton Mifflin Company, 1965); Lai, Myers, and Wei, *A Tragic Beginning;* and Mendel, *The Politics of Formosan Nationalism.*

16. Interview with Chang Chun-hung, Taipei, May 28, 1991. See also Mendel, *The Politics of Formosan Nationalism*, p. 25.

17. This story was told to me several times in interviews with Taiwanese. I challenged one subject, a responsible figure in the DPP, asking him whether this had really happened. He stated that it had; that people of his era witnessed the encounter with their own eyes. While interviewing two Taiwanese women, one told the same story, which she attributed to her father. The second woman objected saying that her family did not have running water for many years after the Mainlanders came in the late 1940s. After a discussion, they concluded that there was running water in most cities in 1947, but not in most rural homes. When I expressed to another Taiwanese friend my amusement at the frequency with which I heard this running water story, my friend advised me with some gravity that this story was just one of several illustrations of how much more advanced the Taiwanese were compared to the Mainlanders—implying that this friend, too, abided by the tale. The story is also recounted in the autobiography of P'eng Ming-min. See P'eng, *A Taste of Freedom*, p. 53.

18. Shih Hua, "Huang Hsin-chieh: 'I am the Youngest Among the Old Rascals'—A Chairman of the Democratic Progressive Party Discusses Developments on Taiwan," *Chiu-shih Nien-tai* (The Nineties), no. 261, October 1, 1991, in JPRS-CAR–92–010, February 28, 1992, p. 75.

19. See Edwin Winckler, "National, Regional, and Local Politics," in *The Anthropology of Taiwanese Society*, ed. Emily Martin Ahern and Hill Gates (Stanford: Stanford University Press, 1981), p. 15.

20. Lai, Myers, and Wei, *A Tragic Beginning*, p. 160.

21. Ibid., pp. 155–64.

22. Linda Chao and Ramon H. Myers, "The First Chinese Democracy: Political Development of the Republic of China on Taiwan, 1986–1994," *Asian Survey*, vol. 34, no. 3 (March 1994), p. 255.

23. Interview with Chang Chun-hung, Taipei, May 28, 1991.

24. Interview with Chu Chi-ying, Taipei, July 4, 1991.

25. Hsieh Chang-t'ing, "T'ai-wan ming-yun Kung-t'ung-t'i ti chung-chi kuan-huai," (The Ultimate Concerns of Taiwan's "Body of Common Destiny"), *Hsin Wen-hua* (New Culture), February 1989, p. 5.

26. Interview with Chiu I-jen, Taipei, March 21, 1991.

27. Interview with Chang Chun-hung, Taipei, May 28, 1991.

28. Interview with Li I-yuan, Taipei, July 2, 1991.

29. Ch'en Li-li, unpublished manuscript, "When Jackals Ruled," pp. 18–19. This passage was among those edited out of the version of this story that appeared in *Mother Jones* in July 1983.

30. Ch'en Yung-hsing, *Cheng-chiu T'ai-wan-jen ti hsin-ling* (Saving the Heart of the Taiwanese) (Taipei: Vanguard Press, 1988); Li Ch'iao, *T'ai-wan-jen ti chou-lou mien* (The Ugly Side of the Taiwanese) (Taipei: Vanguard Press, 1988); Lin Yang-min, *T'ai-wan-jen ti lien-hua tsai-sheng* (The Lotus Rebirth of the Taiwanese) (Taipei: Vanguard Press, 1988); and Sung Tz'o-lai, *T'ai-wan-jen ti tzu-wo chui-hsun* (The Taiwanese Pursuit of the Self) (Taipei: Vanguard Press, 1988).

31. Lin, *T'ai-wan-jen ti lien-hua tsai-sheng* (The Lotus Rebirth of the Taiwanese), p. 5.

32. Ibid., p. 6.

33. Ibid.

34. Hsieh, "T'ai-wan ming-yun Kung-t'ung-t'i ti chung-chi kuan-huai" (The Ultimate Concerns of Taiwan's "Body of Common Destiny"), p. 4.

35. For a sense of this sordid side, see Marc J. Cohen, *Taiwan at the Crossroads: Human Rights, Political Development and Social Change on the Beautiful Island* (Washington, DC: Asia Resource Center, 1988). Cohen's research is presented in a more polemical style than is customary in academic works but nonetheless provides much valuable information.

36. Arend Lijphart, *Democracy in Plural Societies: A Comparative Exploration* (New Haven: Yale University Press, 1977), p. 24.

37. Copper, *Taiwan: Nation-State or Province?* p. 39. See also, Leo J. Moser, *The Chinese Mosaic: The Peoples and Provinces of China* (Boulder, CO: Westview, 1985), chapter 13, especially pp. 191–94.

38. Lin Yu-t'i, *T'ai-wan chiao-yu mien-mu 40 nien* (Faces of Taiwan's Education Over 40 Years) (Taipei: Cultural Division of *Tzu-li Wan-pao* [Independence Evening Post], 1987), p. 114. In September 1991, it was announced that there would be television news broadcasts in the Hakka dialect. *China Post*, September 2, 1991, p. 4.

39. Interview with Chiu I-jen, Taipei, March 21, 1991.

40. Lin, *T'ai-wan chiao-yu mien-mu 40 nien* (Faces of Taiwan's Education Over 40 Years), p. 114.

41. Ibid.

42. Interview with K'ang Ning-hsiang, Taipei, July 1, 1991.

43. See Julian Baum, "Vernacular Vogue," *Far Eastern Economic Review*, August 30, 1990, p. 32; Yu Shiao-min, "Acceptance of Taiwanese Gaining Impetus," *Free China Journal*, January 28, 1991, p. 1.

44. Interview with Shaw Yu-ming, Taipei, June 15, 1991.

45. Interview with Kao Hui-yu, Taipei, May 24, 1991.

46. Interview with Hau Pei-tsun, Taipei, August 27, 1993.

47. Interview with Chiang Chun-nan, Taipei, May 20, 1991.

48. Ibid.

49. Lin, *T'ai-wan chiao-yu mien-mu 40 nien* (Faces of Taiwan Education Over 40 Years), p. 117.

50. Hu Chang, "Impressions of Mainland China Carried Back by Taiwan Visitors," in *Two Societies in Opposition: The Republic of China and the People's Republic of China After Forty Years*, ed. Ramon H. Myers (Stanford: Hoover Institution Press, 1991), pp. 141–58.

51. Interview with Ma Ying-cheou, Taipei, July 3, 1991.

52. Interview with Shaw Yu-ming, Taipei, June 15, 1991.

53. Interview with Ma Ying-cheou, Taipei, July 3, 1991.

54. Interview with Soong Chu-yu, Taipei, June 28, 1991.

55. Interview with Lin Cheng-chieh, Taipei, July 8, 1991.

56. For a brief profile of Yu and his family's influence, see Alexander Ya-li Lu, "Political Opposition in Taiwan," in *Political Change in Taiwan*, ed. Tun-jen Cheng and Stephan Haggard (Boulder, CO: Lynne Rienner, 1992), p. 134, n. 22.

57. Interview with Lin Cheng-chieh, Taipei, July 8, 1991.

58. Ibid.

59. Interview with Soong Chu-yu, Taipei, June 28, 1991.

60. Benedict Anderson, *Imagined Communities: Reflections on the Origin and*

Spread of Nationalism (London: Verso, 1983), pp. 12–13.

61. Rod Hague and Martin Harrop, *Comparative Government and Politics: An Introduction*, 2d ed. (Atlantic Highlands, NJ: Humanities Press International, 1987), p. 32.

62. See Gellner's description of transformation in the fictitious state of Ruritania in Ernest Gellner, *Nations and Nationalism* (Ithaca: Cornell University Press, 1983), pp. 58–62.

63. Ibid., p. 61.

64. Interview with Hau Pei-tsun, Taipei, August 27, 1993.

65. I am grateful to Professor Tu Wei-ming of Harvard University for making the significance of these matters clear.

66. Gellner, *Nations and Nationalism*, p. 57.

67. Ibid., p. 1.

68. Interview with Hau Pei-tsun, Taipei, August 27, 1993.

69. Interview with P'eng Ming-min, Taipei, August 23, 1993.

70. Ibid.

71. Interview with Chen Shui-pian, Taipei, August 25, 1993.

5

Opposition and the Course of Reform

We don't mind being pushed by our people to do more for them —in a democratic system, we view such "push" as trust and support.

—Tsiang Yien-si, secretary-general, Office of the President

Opposition Prior to Liberalization

Introduction

Dankwart Rustow reasoned that "the dynamic process of democratization ... is set off by a prolonged and inconclusive political struggle" that "is likely to force the protagonists to rally around two banners." Often, democracy itself is not what people aim to achieve when reform is initiated, but some way to resolve the prolonged political struggle that divides them. Democracy may be regarded as a means to settle the underlying conflict in the community and may come about "as a fortuitous byproduct of the struggle" to do so.[1] On Taiwan, democratization emerged as a reflection of the "inconclusive political struggle" between Taiwanese and Mainlanders over the question of national identity and, in turn, affected that conflict.

In the early years of KMT rule on Taiwan, opposition to the regime did not arise solely from the tension between Mainlanders and Taiwanese, nor was it exclusively about national identity. A multidimensional opposition emerged from different segments of society arrayed against the authoritarian regime and was transformed by the interaction between the regime and its opponents into something quite different. The polarization of views around the reunification and independence banners took place over time. The demand for self-determination, always a component of Taiwanese opposition—increased in prominence as a reaction to the authoritarianism of the KMT.

Although the most dramatic political reforms have occurred on Taiwan since 1987 with the lifting of martial law, the process began much earlier. One can trace the origins of political dissent on Taiwan back to the period of Japanese occupation and even before that.[2]

Disposition of the KMT

From the start, the KMT was organized to prevent or repress opposition and to invest every social and political organization on the island with a bond to the party that could be regulated and monitored by the political center. Like the CCP on the mainland, the KMT was organized with a Leninist party structure.[3] In other words, the KMT operated with "selective membership recruitment, a revolutionary and nationalist ideology, a centralized decision-making structure under a Central Committee, a policy-making Central Standing Committee and a policy implementing secretariat with organization, intelligence, and propaganda departments, control of the army through a political cadre system, maintenance of a youth league, leadership over the policies and personnel of the state apparatus, and—until recently—intolerance for the existence of any opposition party."[4] The party structure established by Sun Yat-sen under the tutelage of the Comintern in the 1920s remained for most of the past seventy years much as it was then. Like authoritarian regimes elsewhere, the KMT prior to reform was inflexible, moralistic, self-righteous, chauvinistic, jingoistic, paternalistic, repressive, arbitrary, and occasionally brutal.

Unlike the CCP though, the KMT proclaimed an ambition to establish constitutional democracy and therefore expressed a devotion to a style of governance utterly unlike that which it imposed on the populace of Taiwan. The party held itself up as embodying the wisdom and moral rectitude needed to guide the people of the ROC to those ends. However, in accordance with Sun Yat-sen's view that democracy could not be introduced to an inexperienced citizenry all at once, the KMT practiced a form of tutelary democracy. Party leaders claimed to respect constitutional democracy, but they offered little evidence of having much commitment to it. They maintained that only when conditions were appropriate would they implement a fully functioning constitutional democracy in the ROC.

In an address to the National Assembly on Constitution Day, December 25, 1984, President Chiang Ching-kuo reiterated these themes. He explained, in what was a recitation of a commonly cited catechism, that Sun Yat-sen was devoted to revolution "to secure liberty and equality in China" and that the Three Principles of the People were envisaged as a way to create a strong and prosperous China on the basis of those political ideals. He recounted how, since its founding, the ROC suffered many adversities from within and from abroad. He praised his father, Chiang Kai-shek, saying that, even in the midst of misery brought on by war, the elder Chiang recognized the need to promulgate a constitution "as the unshakable foundation for this country's dedication to constitutional democracy."

Chiang Ching-kuo asserted that "constitutional democracy involves a winding path of exploration, dedication, adjustment, and adaptation. Many obstacles must be surmounted before patterns suitable for this nation may be fully developed." He sought to deflect critics of the slow pace of political development by pointing out that, by that time, only thirty-seven years had passed since the constitution was inaugurated. Other states, he said, had taken much longer to develop a functioning democratic system.

To reinforce this message, Chiang explained that "[j]ust as we were beginning to implement constitutional rule, we were confronted with a chaotic situation involving Communist rebellion and usurpation on the mainland." In spite of the obstacles, he said, "the results we have achieved on this bastion of national revival over the last thirty odd years, through prudent, well-planned programs, demonstrate the appropriateness and superior content of our constitutional rule." In one of those classic contradictions that political leaders the world over seem particularly adept at uttering, Chiang proclaimed that because of the "uncompleted efforts for the eradication of Chinese Communism, we are forced to adopt certain expedient measures dictated by time and circumstance. However, we will not deviate from constitutional rule; that is our unchangeable principle."[5]

Indeed, in 1948 the Temporary Provisions Effective During the Period of Communist Rebellion strengthened the hand of the president to enable him to rule with wide latitude. Technically, the provisions were enacted as an amendment in accordance with Article 174 of the 1946 constitution. This enabled the government to maintain that the ROC was ruled by constitutional means, not martial law.[6] Rhetoric to the contrary notwithstanding, this initiated a period of martial law and one-party authoritarianism that lasted until 1987.[7]

Even though the ROC was not communist, it had a one-party system with an authoritarian regime more similar to the communist states it claimed to oppose than the democratic ones it claimed to emulate. Two other such states emerged at about the same time: the Republican People's party (RPP) in Turkey and the Institutional Revolutionary party (PRI) in Mexico. In each of these three polities the "identity of the state was defined by the ideology of the party."[8] Opposition to the way in which the founding party of these states formulated the notion of national identity has given rise to a political movement that challenges the legitimacy of the party. According to Huntington, "Challenging the founding myth propagated by the single dominant party poses a central question for democratization. If the identity of the state is defined by the ideology of the dominant party, how can opposition to the party, which in a democratic system is legitimate, be distinguished from treason to the state, which is illegitimate?"[9] By challenging the "founding myth" propagated by the KMT that Taiwan is a part of China, those who advocated Taiwan's independence were seen to violate laws of sedition. As the KMT had constructed an entire political system designed around its role as the sole legitimate government of China, advocates of independence posed a threat to the idea of a unified China. Challenging reunification was the equivalent of challenging the KMT.

Until recently, the KMT regime did not tolerate much criticism of itself or the policy of reunification. It maintained a political climate that was hostile toward dissent and ruthless toward dissenters. Until 1992 it was illegal to advocate independence, and for most of the first four decades of KMT rule, people were certainly intimidated from openly expressing their views about the party or the status of the island.

Not long after they arrived on Taiwan, the party's top leadership must have begun to realize that their plan to recover the mainland was not going to occur any time soon, if it happened in their lifetime at all. Still, the hubris that comes with unregulated power and the sense of mission the KMT felt about its role as the guardian of China's fate contributed to a dismissive approach to the population of Taiwan. Given the KMT's disposition toward its own power and scope of responsibility to China, it is possible to understand how it might have regarded dissent with such suspicion. In retrospect, one can see that the disposition of the party toward dissent and the high-handed manner in which it wielded power contributed to the intensification of the hostilities opponents of the regime felt toward it. This, in turn, led to a radicalization of dissent that pitted advocates of Taiwan independence against advocates of reunification.

Sources of Early Dissent

Opposition to the KMT in the first several decades of Nationalist party rule on Taiwan reflected the ideals of two very different interest groups: Mainlander intellectuals (who were often assumed or accused by the KMT's security apparatus to be Communist infiltrators) and Taiwanese nationalists. These two groups had distinct grievances about the regime of Chiang Kai-shek, but both were persecuted simply for their opposition. The intellectuals from the mainland advocated political reform and constitutional democracy. This group, epitomized by Lei Chen, editor of the journal *Free China*, was deeply affected by Anglo-American liberalism.[10]

Another group, Taiwanese opponents of the KMT, were not as interested in reforming the ruling party as they were in taking power from it. They tried to loosen the KMT's stranglehold on the political life of the island by chipping away at it through local elections. This was the only feasible strategy they could implement in the 1950s, under a system that restricted contestation to local-level elections as a way to prevent the coalition of an islandwide opposition.[11] This emphasis on elections had at least one positive effect, because as democratization "started at the local level ... local units of government became prototypes for democratization nationwide."[12]

In 1960, these two groups endeavored to join forces by proposing to form the China Democratic party. Before the movement got off the ground, however, Lei Chen was arrested on "a highly questionable charge of associating with communist agents." After a military court tried him, Lei was given a ten-year prison sentence. Harsh practices were evidently used to deal with dissidents during that period, including arrest, imprisonment, and a range of mental and physical means of torture. It is not surprising that such brutality had its desired repressive effect. It left the KMT's opponents sufficiently intimidated that they abandoned their scheme.[13]

Thinking that it had squelched the initiative to dissent, the KMT may have contributed inadvertently to the radicalization of the Taiwanese opposition movement by denying the nascent opposition a legitimate way to express its grievances.[14] One can only speculate about how differently Taiwan might have developed if the KMT had been sufficiently confident to allow the growth of an opposition party that was not exclusively based on Taiwanese nationalism. The frustration, hostility, and considerable distrust that has characterized the opposition's attitude toward the KMT may be ascribed, in part, to forty years of repression.

Several years after the aborted effort to form a union of opposition interests, P'eng Ming-min, then a professor at National Taiwan University, and two former students were arrested on September 20, 1964, for having printed "10,000 copies of 'examination papers' which the printers discovered to be political tracts urging Formosans to unite against the regime." The printers informed the Garrison Command, the quasi-military organ of the party that was responsible for internal security, and the three were arrested.[15] P'eng himself wrote "Paradoxically we had been trapped by our own underestimation of the police-state organization under which we lived and against which we were in protest. As campus intellectuals we had not truly realized to what extent Formosan life had been corrupted to serve the Chiangs' purposes. Every petty informer knew he would be rewarded."[16] In the late 1960s and early 1970s, several opposition journals emerged for brief periods and more intellectuals were arrested and imprisoned for contributing articles that expressed dissent, including writers Li Ao and Po Yang.[17] Although the intellectuals may not have posed a great threat to the KMT, they were dealt with severely as affronts to Chiang Kai-shek himself and the ruling party, which feared that opposition to the KMT would lead to instability.[18]

Political and Diplomatic Causes of Agitation

One facet of KMT rule that intensely irritated Taiwanese activists was that certain officials elected on the mainland in 1947 and 1948 before the KMT came to Taiwan remained in office after the KMT arrived on the island to represent those constituencies from which they had originally been chosen. Viewing itself as the government of all China (although temporarily in exile) rather than simply the government of the island of Taiwan, the KMT preserved three bodies that were created by the constitution of 1946: the National Assembly (a large parliamentary body that is empowered to adopt or amend the constitution and elect the president of the republic), the Legislative Yuan (a national legislature), and the Control Yuan (a smaller body charged with government oversight).

At first, those who were elected to these three bodies in the late 1940s were kept in office because the KMT genuinely planned to return to the mainland. Later, once the prospects of recapturing the mainland became remote, the elected officials were retained to reinforce the idea that *eventually* the KMT would recapture the mainland. Gradually, when dreams of recovery began to dissipate, the KMT had to maintain the three bodies as a way to ensure its own grip on power over the island of Taiwan. Naturally, Taiwanese activists became increasingly angered that none of those charged with governing the island were elected there. As elderly representatives from the mainland began to die, they were replaced by individuals the KMT claimed were "runners up" in the original election.[19] Eventually, critics of the regime demanded that elections be held to fill the spots left vacant by the deaths of the incumbents.

In 1966, the National Assembly amended the constitution to allow the president to call "supplementary elections" to fill seats in the National Assembly, the Legislative Yuan, and the Control Yuan. Consequently, elections were held to fill vacant seats in 1969, 1972, and 1973.[20] Still, the KMT managed to regulate the influx of new blood so that its power to govern was not threatened.

While the KMT was able to control events on the island, it had very little influence on the international political environment. A series of "diplomatic setbacks" in the early 1970s disoriented the regime, as the KMT "found its world of diplomatic make-believe disintegrating about it."[21] This assault on the KMT's international legitimacy created additional incentives for Taiwan's dissident intellectuals to resume their expressions of opposition.[22]

After the United States negotiated the restoration of Okinawa to Japanese sovereignty, a conflict erupted in August 1970 about whether Japan, the PRC, or the ROC had sovereignty over "a cluster of rock . . . islands and lonely reefs lying some 120 miles northeast of Taiwan and 570 miles southwest of Japan" (known as the Tiao-yu-t'ai) that the U.S. had administered along with the larger island.[23] It seemed to

Taiwan's intelligentsia that in response to Japan's claims the government of the ROC buckled under. This revived memories of how an earlier administration had failed to defend China's sovereignty against Japanese claims in 1915 and 1919, contributing to the nationalistic May Fourth Incident.

In the early 1970s, a movement of considerable proportions was aroused among Taiwanese students studying abroad. The movement began among Chinese students on the campuses of universities in Hong Kong and the United States and eventually enveloped Taiwan's universities as well. With strikes, demonstrations, and the posting of broadsides, students and intellectuals urged the government of the ROC to take a firmer stance against Japanese aggression and American complicity in the affront to ROC sovereignty.[24] The KMT was alarmed about the student protests because it had such a long-standing distrust of student demonstrations, a distrust stemming from its experience with such protests during the May Fourth demonstrations of 1919.[25]

The prestige and the legitimacy of the KMT—and Chiang Kai-shek, who embodied it—was damaged twice again. The second time was when President Nixon announced, on July 16, 1971, his intention to visit the PRC and seek a normalization of relations between Peking and Washington. Finally, in October of the same year, the ROC was expelled from the United Nations and replaced by the PRC. This was followed by the disappointment of watching former allies negotiate recognition agreements with the PRC.[26]

These diplomatic setbacks represented massive disturbances to the credibility of a regime that had boasted at home and announced abroad that it was the sole legitimate government of China. Understandably, the opposition saw these slights as additional indications that the legitimacy of the KMT was waning. If Chiang Kai-shek and the ruling party could not uphold the status of China in the eyes of the world community, there was no reason to place credence in the justification offered by the KMT for its continued domination of Taiwan.

Responses of the Intellectual Elite

Young professors and university students on Taiwan responded to the perceived loss of KMT credibility by intensifying their political activities, which, at first, were not repressed.[27] One consequence of the emerging intellectual dissident movement was a shift away from the radical perspective that the KMT be ousted from power so that Taiwan could be independent. A more moderate view gained ground, calling for the establishment of a separate state with a political status distinct from that of the PRC. Opponents also called on the KMT to reform the manner in which it governed.[28] The intelligentsia began to address itself not only to matters of political reform but to liberalization in general. It argued for academic freedom and a reassessment of economic development. Writing individually and in groups, academics beseeched the KMT authorities to shift priorities from planning the recapture of the mainland to the development of Taiwan as an alternative to the PRC system (which both the ruling party and the intellectual elite detested).

In October 1971, a group of fifteen prominent intellectuals—Mainlanders and Taiwanese—published a startlingly frank proposal for sweeping reforms in *Ta-hsueh tsa-chih* (The Intellectual).[29] They maintained that although the KMT's goal of reuniting China was laudable, the first step should be the creation of a genuinely prosperous, open society on the island. Writers for the journal began to challenge the legitimacy of the KMT and the way society was developing under the guidance of the Nationalists. They called on the ruling party to grant basic political liberties—freedom of speech and association, for example—and demanded that greater attention be given to human rights and social welfare.[30]

The publication of this proposal sparked a vast upsurge of support from the island's intelligentsia. Counterproposals and treatises about specific dimensions of reform began to appear with regularity. The liberalism of the intellectuals was itself a cause for concern in the KMT because the ruling elite "tended to equate liberalism with selfishness and lack of discipline, regarding it as an alien ideology not suitable for China. Worse still, they saw liberalism as a Trojan horse employed by the Chinese Communists for the destruction of traditional culture."[31]

There was a palpable change in the nature of demands, too. The intellectuals' aims were carefully reasoned and specific. Their entreaties of the KMT were not just the restatement of grand political ideals—such as demands for independence or democracy—but addressed particular needs in the realm of social and economic welfare. In short, the professors and students called for national rejuvenation where the nation was limited to Taiwan.[32]

Growth of Taiwanese Consciousness

Beginning in the early 1970s, Taiwan's intellectuals moved from a position in which political reform was seen as an abstraction expressed in terms of moral principles to the advocacy of specific reforms for the benefit of the island of Taiwan and the welfare of its residents. Although the goals espoused by the reform-minded intellectuals did not foreclose the possibility of pursuing Taiwanese nationalism, that was not the primary focus at that stage. Indeed, many of the key figures speaking out against the KMT at that time were Mainlanders who were concerned to a great extent with making Taiwan open and democratic, not necessarily independent. Perhaps this increased attention to Taiwan itself contributed to the rise of Taiwanese nationalism and the current friction between Taiwanese and Chinese nationalists. This was a period—perhaps the first— when the immediate and tangible problems of Taiwan and the people who resided there, rather than the elusive ideological ambition to reunite China, came to the fore.

Just as the focus of dissent was changing to reflect a new era, so too was the nature of the dissidents. A new breed of activists emerged at that time who were largely Taiwanese raised during a period of greater prosperity, who identified with middle-class ideals, and who, unlike the earlier generation of critics, had had the opportunity to study such things as sociology, political science, and law.[33] Moreover, this generation "adapted political techniques, specific democratic procedures, institutional designs, and legal frameworks from the West." It became increasingly clear as the decade wore on that "[i]n comparison with earlier dissidents, this new democratic leadership was equipped with organizational skills and was more prone to adopt mobilization tactics."[34]

In May 1972, Chiang Ching-kuo was made premier.[35] For the next year, the government did undertake some moderate reforms, but nothing so extensive as the intellectuals had envisaged. The Tiao-yu-t'ai movement subsided in the summer of 1972 and the agitation for reform was quieted a year later as the academics and students who had been most involved were silenced by intimidation or were encouraged to recognize that working with and within the KMT offered tangible rewards.[36]

Until the mid-1970s, most advocates of reform were writers and intellectuals—many of them Mainlanders—attached to journals that advocated democratic reform of the government, not independence. These publications served as surrogates for political parties. They enabled the chief sponsors and officers to disseminate their point of view and to generate support during a period when the formation of political organizations was prohibited.[37] This all changed in the middle of the decade.

Opposition activists played a cat-and-mouse game with the authorities. The activists established dissident journals, published for a while, were censored, were shut down by the authorities, and eventually reestablished other journals with different names to repeat the process. For example, in 1975 Taiwanese activist K'ang Ning-hsiang and intellectual Chang Chun-hung started *T'ai-wan Cheng-lun* (Taiwan Political Review). After the authorities closed it down some months later, K'ang and Chang went on to publish a magazine entitled *Pa-shih Nien-tai* (The Eighties).

Another consequence of the awakening interest in the welfare and lives of the common people of Taiwan that occurred in the mid- to late 1970s was the development of a new form of literature. At about that time a new breed of vernacular writing called nativist literature (*hsiang-t'u wen-hsueh*) began to flourish. Traditionally, literature available on Taiwan dealt with melodramatic romances of the elite, historical fiction, and kung-fu adventure tales of China's past. Nativist literature, by contrast, focused on the life experiences of common, native Taiwanese. It was also a highly politicized style of writing.[38] Chiang Chun-nan recounted its emergence.

> Suddenly, a young group, a small group of Taiwanese writers came to write about Taiwan. These people also used some kind of slogans associated with communism: "the farmers," "the workers," and that was the time of the last stage of the Cultural Revolution. So, one or two of them even used Cultural Revolution slogans ... "theory of the third world," or "colonialism," "imperialism" and these kinds of new terms. These were new on Taiwan. They made people very worried. At that time, the political warfare section in the Ministry of Defense tried their best to scare or to suppress that kind of Taiwanese literature.[39]

There have been other manifestations of Taiwanese culture in the world of the arts. A modern dance company, *Yun-men* (Cloud Gate), was also formed to express feelings about Taiwanese legends, history, and tales of migration. In recent years, a rock group named *Hei Ming-dai* (Blacklist) has taken to singing only in Taiwanese dialect.[40] These and other developments demonstrate that Taiwanese intellectuals had moved beyond merely opposing the KMT to express a new consciousness. This Taiwanese consciousness was the basis for political opposition framed in terms of a distinct national identity and aimed at ending the KMT's monopoly of power.

Origins of an Opposition Party

In 1977, it was still illegal to form a political party, hold marches, or stage rallies. In spite of regulations that prohibited these activities, a coalition was formed by independent, Taiwanese, non-KMT politicians that was "outside the party" (*tang-wai*). In local elections, candidates affiliated with the *tang-wai* coalition won twenty-two seats in the Taiwan Provincial Assembly and four posts as either county magistrate (county executive) or mayor, in what was perceived as a victory at the expense of the KMT.[41]

One sign of Taiwanese frustration with the KMT's tight grasp on the electoral process was a violent protest in November in the city of Chung-li in T'ao-yuan County. Hsu Hsin-liang, later the chairman of the DPP, had been a "rising star" in the KMT. He had been given a government scholarship to study in England and, when he returned, he served in the Provincial Assembly. During the course of the protests of the early 1970s, Hsu "defected" from the KMT and wrote a critical memoir of his time in the assembly. He was not nominated by the party to run for the post of county magistrate of T'ao-yuan County, but did so anyway as an independent.

In the course of the election day, a crowd of ten thousand gathered to object to the use of paper ballots and demand that voting machines be used.[42] A riot ensued that was the largest and most violent political event on Taiwan in the thirty years since the 2–28 Incident of 1947. In the end, Hsu won and the confrontation came to be called the Chung-li Incident. Mild by subsequent standards, the Chung-li Incident rattled the KMT, for it was the first overt act of political protest against the government since the 1940s.[43]

Flush with excitement about their newly discovered power, the *tang-wai* activists planned a campaign for the Legislative Yuan election slated for 1978. To their dismay, the elections were canceled several days before the scheduled vote in the wake of President Carter's announcement, on December 15, 1978, that the United States was severing formal ties to the ROC to recognize the PRC.

The Kaohsiung Incident

In the spring of 1979, the *tang-wai* held a series of lectures and rallies across the island. In August 1979, a group of Taiwanese opposition activists that was "later to emerge as the precursor of the avowedly pro-independence 'New Tide' faction" of the DPP organized a journal entitled *Mei-li Tao* (Formosa).[44] As a way to get around the prohibition against organizing a political party, the *tang-wai* opened "service offices" for *Mei-li Tao* magazine that served as local headquarters for *tang-wai* activists.[45]

On December 10, the *Mei-li Tao* office in Kaohsiung held a rally to mark "International Human Rights Day."[46] The rally degenerated into a riot in which 183 policemen were injured. Apparently, "few demonstrators were hurt because the police were under instructions not to react with force."[47] Stories about how many people were involved and what happened at the incident differ widely, each side blaming the other for provoking the violence.[48] The following day, fourteen opposition leaders were arrested as well as more than one hundred of the magazine's supporters. Of these, some were released soon thereafter, thirty-three were tried in civilian courts, but eight of the more prominent leaders of the magazine and *tang-wai* activities were singled out to be tried by court martial on charges of sedition.[49] In the end, the eight were convicted and given prison sentences ranging from twelve years to life despite considerable indications that their confessions had been extracted by improper means, including sleep deprivation and, in one case, beating.[50]

The Kaohsiung Incident—or *Mei-li Tao* Incident—may well have been a trap for opposition leaders.[51] It effectively and abruptly halted the intellectual movement, but it did not end the demands for reform. The elections that originally had been scheduled for December 1978 were eventually held in December 1980, a year after the Kaohsiung Incident. After crushing the opposition and jailing its leaders, the KMT may have been surprised that the attorneys and relatives of the eight Kaohsiung defendants were then elected to office.[52]

According to one observer, the election results made a deep impression on President Chiang Ching-kuo, who realized that despite the effort to purge the opposition of its key leaders, the voters were willing to support the purge victims—if only symbolically—by electing their relatives and attorneys.[53] It is unlikely that Chiang Ching-kuo viewed himself as a ruthless autocrat, and he probably did not wish that to be his legacy. Subsequent events tend to support the notion that Chiang began to reassess the attitude of the party and its practices and policies. Although Chiang must be credited for seizing the opportunity to initiate reform, if he felt he could have continued to suppress the opposition, he probably would have done so. Chiang's recognition of the need to reform was a reaction to the vitality of the opposition and the strong show of public support for those against whom the government had built an elaborate—if exaggerated—case.[54]

Whatever Chiang may have been thinking or planning, what followed the Kaohsiung Incident and the end of the *Mei-li Tao* period of intellectual ferment was a period of relative suppression that afforded no opportunity for vocal expression of dissident views. Although the incident had a chilling effect on public discussion of politics, it ultimately ended up strengthening, rather than weakening, the opposition movement. The ruling authorities may have hoped that by jailing the leadership of the *Mei-li Tao* movement and those accused of planning the Kaohsiung demonstration (allegedly part of a plot to overthrow the government) they would decapitate the opposition. Instead, the movement turned out rather like an earthworm. Once beheaded, the body sprouted a new head, as a second generation of opposition leaders emerged to fill the roles of the senior leaders who had been jailed.[55]

The Henry Liu Incident

The government's primary means of discrediting the opposition was to link it in people's minds with communism. Whether the KMT actually believed it or not, official propaganda about the *tang-wai* decried it as a "three-in-one" enemy comprised of communists, hoodlums, and advocates of Taiwan independence.[56] This appeal may have caught the attention of the Mainlander criminal underworld, especially the Bamboo Union Gang (*Chu-lien-pang*) which "began in the 1950s as an organization of Mainlander juvenile delinquents."[57] In the aftermath of the 1980 elections, this gang of second-generation Mainlanders, reputed to have close ties to the KMT, became concerned with the burgeoning independence movement and what ramifications it had for the future of Taiwan.

In October 1984, Bamboo Union Gang members assassinated Liu I-liang (Henry Liu), a Taiwan-born U.S. citizen living in Daly City, California, who had written an unflattering and unauthorized biography of President Chiang Ching-kuo.[58] In the subsequent investigations by the FBI and local police, it became evident that the assassins had acted in collusion with Taiwan's military intelligence organs and "possibly under the direct influence of Chiang Ching-kuo's supposedly ambitious son, Chiang Hsiao-wu."[59] This brought to light how the state intelligence apparatus and the ruling party made use of the underworld as part of its effort to quell dissidence and how widespread its networks of agents was even within the United States.

According to one analyst on Taiwan, Chiang Ching-kuo reacted to the Henry Liu murder in an unexpected fashion. In some ways, this event was the watershed after which Chiang may have become more accepting of the need for reform. In the immediate wake of the murder, Wang Hsi-ling, the head of military intelligence, and two Bamboo Union Gang leaders, Chen Chi-li and Wu Tun, were sentenced to life imprisonment even though they had acted in accordance with what they took to be Chiang's program of suppression. Chiang's son, Hsiao-wu, was sent off to Singapore to head up Taiwan's trade office there. This was a move calculated to dispel rumors that there would be another generation in the Chiang line of succession. In addition, the military-intelligence group responsible for masterminding the slaying was disbanded and its functions merged with another unit under the command of the chief of general staff to ensure greater control over security affairs.[60] According to Yang Hsien-hung, "Henry Liu was the silver lining of a black cloud."[61]

At about the time of the Henry Liu Incident the government was in the midst of a campaign to crack down on the criminal underworld, and the Bamboo Union Gang may have "offered its services to the intelligence agencies in return for protection."[62] After the Henry Liu debacle, the KMT turned its back on those criminal elements who had previously cooperated with the party authorities. Yang Hsien-hung commented that "to be a crony of the KMT was to go to jail, so it changed the minds of a lot of gangsters who had earlier been in the substructure of the KMT."[63] This led to a realignment in which gangsters who had been loyal to the KMT began to support the anti-KMT opposition.

Yang concluded that members of the "black societies" who had worked surreptitiously with the ruling authorities to suppress the opposition found themselves in the same prisons with opposition leaders and others who had been jailed for political crimes. Both groups shared an antipathy for the KMT and, in Yang's view, allied to form an anti-KMT bond in a manifestation of the principle that the enemy of my enemy is my friend. The implication of Yang's argument is that Chiang Ching-kuo may have initiated reform, but only because he realized that the forces stacked against him were formidable.

President Chiang Ching-kuo, like Belshazzar, saw the handwriting on the wall.[64] Unlike the Babylonian king, though, Chiang understood the signs. He saw the need to redistribute power to include Taiwanese and to redirect the KMT's energy from recovering the mainland to making Taiwan flourish. Although he may not have envisaged that the reform process would extend as deeply into the political and social fabric of Taiwan as it now has, he undoubtedly expected that by offering to increase the proportion of public officials who were Taiwanese and by liberalizing at the margins, the Mainlander-dominated KMT could retain its grip on power over the island.[65]

The Onset of Liberalization

From Tang-wai *to DPP*

The process of liberalization has proceeded rapidly since the mid-1980s. As indicated earlier, the sequence of events that Huntington described as a "transformation" fairly accurately depicts the interaction between the ruling party and opposition forces that has led to the establishment of democratic practices on Taiwan. As Huntington suggested about such processes, Chiang Ching-kuo's initiation of reforms was probably motivated by the sense that it would be possible to liberalize without sacrificing power. Chiang may also have realized that to do so would bolster the legitimacy of the KMT in the eyes of the international community. Consequently, at the Third Plenum of the Central Committee of the KMT in March 1986, President Chiang told the assemblage that the time for constitutional democracy had arrived. A twelve-man task force was established to put together a plan for the party's transition.

In April 1986, the *tang-wai* expressed an interest in setting up the Taiwan Research Association for Public Policy (TRAPP) with branches throughout the island as a way to extend its political influence. In May, the KMT entered into a dialogue with *tang-wai* representatives. The first meeting, which took place on May 10 at the Lai Lai Sheraton Hotel in Taipei, determined that the TRAPP could be established. Meetings continued erratically throughout the summer.[66]

In June, the task force offered a six-point proposal advocating that large-scale elections be held to fill posts in the Legislative Yuan, Control Yuan, and National Assembly to address the problems caused by the deaths of officials elected on the mainland.[67] The task force also recommended that there be increased opportunity for local self-government, including the direct popular election of the mayors of Taiwan's two largest cities, Taipei and Kaohsiung—posts that the KMT had filled by appointment. The president was particularly interested in two other suggestions of the task force and instructed its members to continue working out a plan to simplify the national security laws by which the country had been governed under martial law and to permit the formation of "civic associations." This was a step that Chiang must have suspected would lead to the formation of an opposition party.[68]

Against the backdrop of the fall of Ferdinand Marcos to the forces of "people power" in the Philippines in February 1986 and a series of violent student-led riots that ultimately forced out Chun Doo Hwan in South Korea in 1987, the *tang-wai* reorganized itself as a political party before it was legal to do so. On September 28, 1986, *tang-wai* representatives announced at a press conference at Taipei's Grand Hotel that they intended to form the Democratic Progressive party and appointed a seven-man committee to draft the platform and party rules.[69] Chiang did not recognize the illicit party, but did urge his twelve-man task force to expedite the drafting of a new law to replace the Emergency Decree so that martial law could be lifted and the DPP legalized retroactively.[70] On October 7, Katharine Graham of the *Washington Post* visited Taiwan and interviewed the president, who told her that martial law would soon be lifted and new parties would soon be permitted as long as they abided by three conditions: (1) to uphold the 1946 Constitution of the ROC, (2) to oppose communism, and (3) to oppose Taiwan independence.[71] By October 15, Chiang was able to push plans to liberalize these regulations through the party's Central Committee.[72]

Once the direction of events became clear, barriers began to fall and changes began to occur more rapidly than anyone planned or could control. On November 8, the DPP's platform and articles appeared in the press. Significantly, the DPP documents never referred to the Republic of China, but to Taiwan.[73] Two days later, Chiang Peng-chen, a representative in the Legislative Yuan, was elected chairman of the new party.

In a dramatic confrontation that evoked memories of Benigno Aquino's return to the Philippines and Kim Dae Jung's return to Korea, Hsu Hsin-liang, who had essentially been in exile in the United States since the Kaohsiung Incident in 1979, attempted to return to Taiwan. On November 30, 1986, approximately ten thousand Taiwanese supporters of Hsu clogged the road to the Chiang Kai-shek International Airport outside of Taipei where they were locked in a nine-hour standoff with police that ultimately turned violent.[74] In the course of the melee, twenty-six police vehicles, as well as those of two television stations (China Broadcasting Corporation [CBC] and China Television System [CTS]), were overturned and damaged, and there were scores of injuries on both sides.[75]

Hsu was not permitted to board a Taipei-bound plane in New York that day, but he did manage to fly to Tokyo and from there to Manila. On December 2, Hsu and three Japanese newspaper reporters flew to Taiwan on a Philippines Airlines flight but upon landing in Taipei were forced to return to Manila on the same aircraft.[76] Again, demonstrators at the airport clashed with police, leading the DPP to condemn the violence and call on the government to identify and prosecute the perpetrators; the DPP evidently believed the violence was begun by government agent–provocateurs planted in the crowd. Elections were held on December 6, 1986, and the DPP won 22 percent of the popular vote and took twelve seats. Another two seats went to independent opposition candidates so that a total of fourteen seats and 33 percent of the votes were earned by the opposition. In elections for the National Assembly, the DPP took eleven seats and 13 percent of the popular vote. It also won several county magistrate and mayoral posts.[77]

Hsu ultimately made it back to Taiwan in September 1989, arriving illegally by boat. He was arrested, convicted on charges of sedition stemming from the Kaohsiung Incident, and sentenced to ten years in prison. In January 1990, President Lee Teng-hui pardoned him.[78]

The Pace of Liberalization Accelerates

Since 1986, Taiwan has successfully, though at times fitfully, passed through the opening phase of liberalization in which the authoritarian regime loosened the legal and institutional bonds that had enabled it to restrain contestation and dominate political institutions operating islandwide and within county and urban settings. During this phase, "civil society" was allowed to expand its scope, and some effort was made by the regime to codify new rights and privileges commensurate with the relaxation of controls that had limited personal and political liberties. Residents of Taiwan enjoyed newly provided freedoms of speech, press, assembly, travel, and association.

On May 12, 1986, the KMT Central Standing Committee began to consider the possibility of political reforms, and on October 15 it decided to lift martial law and replace it with a National Security Law.[79] On July 15, 1987, the Emergency Decree that had effectively suspended constitutional process in 1948 was lifted and replaced by a new National Security Law. Although some complained that the changes were no more than "old wine in new bottles," the sense of imminent calamity justifying the extraordinary security measures had passed and the new law was intended to operate within the context of a normal, constitutional system.

There was an amnesty for many—not all—political prisoners. For example, in May 1987, six of the eight Kaohsiung defendants were released. In July, twenty-three political prisoners were freed to coincide with the lifting of martial law. The government asserted that it had released 144 political prisoners in the past several years and that it had shortened the sentences of the seventy remaining in jail. In 1988, thirty-one more were released.[80]

A law was passed in September 1987 regulating political marches and assemblies. Although prospective demonstrators had to request a permit at least three days prior to the planned event and were somewhat constrained in what they could do at the demonstrations, this did offer a legal channel for public political expression, which had, up until that time, been forbidden. As part of the accelerated process of reform, the ban on political parties was lifted, the ban on establishing new newspapers and expanding the page length of those that already existed was lifted, and the ban on visiting the mainland was also repealed.[81]

Effects of Liberalization on the KMT and DPP

Throughout the opening phase of liberalization, the opposition focused on two related issues: the illegitimacy of both the Legislative Yuan and the National Assembly and the need for independence. Both matters impinged on the legitimacy of the KMT. The ruling party gradually moderated its stance on these matters and accepted the rationale of the opposition that National Assemblymen and Legislative Yuan representatives elected on the mainland in 1947 and 1948 should retire. Their slots, and a range of other positions, were ultimately opened to popular election.[82] Getting the elderly National Assemblymen and Legislative Yuan representatives to retire has been a major effort of the reform wing of the KMT. After a ruling by the Council of Grand Justices (the tribunal responsible for interpreting disputes pertaining to the constitution), the 81 representatives and 472 assemblymen were forced to retire by the end of 1991. One report stated that each of the retiring members of the National Assembly received a pension of NT $5.3 million (about U.S. $200,000).[83]

By 1988 the complexion of the KMT representatives in the Legislative Yuan had changed. Many of the representatives had been nominated by the KMT and ran—often unopposed—in designated constituencies. Younger members of the party were nearly all second-generation Mainlanders born on Taiwan who could legitimately claim to share with the opposition a sense that the political system of the island and the mainland policy of the KMT were in need of reform. Newly elected, second-generation Mainlanders formed the core of the critical "young Turks" who were openly hostile to the hierarchical practices of the KMT and the manner in which the party did its political business.[84]

In addition to changing the political system on Taiwan, political reform has transformed the opposition. Considering that the DPP was formed out of the *tang-wai* coalition, it is understandable that it did not cohere under a single set of policy objectives. This disunity has been reflected in the party's Central Committee membership, in disputes over policy objectives, and in the selection of party leadership.

During 1987–1988, the party chairman, Yao Chia-wen—recently released from prison—was associated with the more extreme New Tide faction. The DPP's approach to opposition at that time was to emphasize the importance of "self-determination" as a means to create a democratic Taiwan and to realize the party's nationalistic goals. Still, it was clear that democracy and self-determination were a means to another end: Taiwan independence. For this reason, the party advocated visible street protests as a way to shake up the people of Taiwan and disabuse them of the "false consciousness" of viewing Taiwan as a part of China with which they had all been so thoroughly indoctrinated by the KMT.[85]

This tactic seemed to work, but only at the start. After a while, people began to accept the government's view of these protests as contributing to disorder that threatened the stability and security of the nation. More important, people feared that the unrest might disrupt Taiwan's steady drive for greater prosperity by frightening away the business and trading partners from abroad on whom Taiwan depends. Also, Taiwan still has a "security first" mentality in which "democratization has always had a lower priority than national security," and the populace seems to endorse some restriction on the degree to which disorder is allowed to persist in society at large.[86]

In October 1988, Huang Hsin-chieh, associated with the more moderate Formosa faction, won the DPP chairmanship. Huang led a faction that favored steady democratization, rather than independence, as the opposition's primary goal. He was interested in demonstrating that the DPP could become a credible, responsible alternative to the KMT. An uneasy balance existed in the Central Committee of the DPP between the two factions, and the result was that the image of the party often emerged as contradictory and self-defeating as the two sides of the party competed for dominance. The rift between the two factions continues to be a factor not only in DPP internal politics but also in intraparty posturing.[87]

Contributing to the appearance of fragility and ineffectiveness were occasional hints that the party that called itself the Democratic Progressive party was not itself particularly democratic. In September 1988, Lin Cheng-chieh, a highly respected, young second-generation Mainlander, wrote an open letter to Yao Chia-wen, who was then the chairman of the DPP, complaining that the Taiwanese in the DPP discriminated against Mainlanders. Three months later, in December, Fei Hsi-p'ing—a mainland-elected Legislative Yuan member and one of the founding members of the DPP—quit the party and accused the DPP leaders of being "fascists." Fei is reported as having said that the more time he spent in the DPP, "the more I felt I was an outsider."[88]

In 1991, Lin Cheng-chieh also resigned from the DPP, citing as a cause for his disaffection the DPP's intolerance of anyone who was not fully supportive of Taiwan independence.[89] Lin declared, "I hope my withdrawal can cause other party officials to think that the direction they are leading in is not too good for the party, because only when the DPP becomes more broad based will it be able to become the ruling party on Taiwan."[90]

Early on, the DPP developed a reputation for causing disruptions in the Legislative Yuan chambers, when some of its representatives traded blows and invectives with the lawmakers from the ruling party. The bombastic behavior was calculated to call attention to what the opposition regarded as the ludicrous irrationality and illegitimacy of the legislature and National Assembly that preserved in power men who had been elected in 1947 and 1948 to represent constituencies on the mainland. Coupled with the popular impression of the DPP as a party of brawlers, the constant internal bickering and revelations of intolerance toward Mainlanders supportive of political reform but unsympathetic to calls for independence did little to bolster the DPP's potential to serve as a credible alternative to the KMT in the late 1980s.

Moreover, once reform began, the KMT pulled the tactical rug out from beneath the feet of the DPP by lifting martial law and agreeing to electoral reform. Rather than bolster the moderates in the Formosa faction, who emphasized the desirability of democratization as a primary goal, the KMT's acceptance of the need for Taiwanization and significant reform provoked the more radical elements in the DPP to make even more extravagant demands. Ultimately, this led to open calls for Taiwan independence.[91]

The status of the DPP improved with the December 2, 1989, elections. For one thing, the elections were the first after the lifting of martial law and the first in which a legal opposition party was able to compete. At stake were the largest number of contested positions in the Legislative Yuan, Taiwan's Provincial Assembly, the city councils of both Taipei and Kaohsiung, and various local posts since the KMT came to Taiwan.[92] All told, the KMT won about 60 percent of the vote and the DPP about 31 percent. This was taken as an enormous victory for the DPP even though it was still a sweep for the ruling party, which easily retained control of all the legislative bodies.[93]

Within the DPP, the Formosa faction was able to claim that its gradualist approach to democratization had been successful in spite of the knowledge that the elections may not have been entirely fair. The New Tide faction, on the other hand, was able to claim that twenty-three of thirty-two candidates who advocated independence under the banner of a New Nation Alliance received substantial popular support at the polls and, therefore, that the more extreme road had been vindicated.[94] Two consequences of the election were the institutionalization of a two-party system and the lesson that the quest for democracy and the quest for national identity were linked.

Another shift that was detected in the 1989 campaign was the growing acceptance of Taiwanese, not Mandarin, as the language of politics. Evidently, much of the campaign leading up to the election had been conducted in Taiwanese, and leading KMT figures readily admit the need to communicate in the native language of the electorate in order to garner support. Even General Chiang Wei-kuo, the son of the late President Chiang Kai-shek, and other "prominent first-generation Mainlanders are belatedly boning up on the language they have spurned since 1949." A new text has been developed using Chinese characters, rather than romanized forms of Taiwanese, indicating a shift in emphasis from teaching Taiwanese language to Western missionaries to training Chinese-reading Mandarin speakers.[95]

One question that stemmed from the success of the DPP in the 1989 elections was how enthusiastically the voters felt about the issue of independence. If one listened to the KMT and read polls presented in the pro-KMT newspapers and journals, it appeared that

> this polarization around the issue of the Taiwan-mainland divide and independence now seemed at odds with the concerns of the electorate. Public opinion polls (of dubious reliability, but nonetheless indicative of an undoubted social phenomenon) suggested that only 15 percent of the electorate positively supported independence. Voters were more concerned with candidates' personalities and attributes, and with "pocket-book" issues like pollution, traffic congestion, the stock market, corruption and street crime. On many of these issues, it was hard to distinguish the two parties.[96]

However, the issue of national identity and the question of Taiwan's independence remained the focus of subsequent election campaigns in the early 1990s.

As to the viability of the DPP to capture an even greater share of votes or to head a government, the deep divisions and factional strife within the party have limited its effectiveness and, inadvertently, kept the brakes on the process of reform. This division within the opposition has undoubtedly frustrated each faction in its effort to promote its cause and may detract from the party's potential to unseat the KMT. Had the KMT felt that the DPP was genuinely capable of replacing it in office, though, the ruling party may have responded to the demands for reform in a much less obliging fashion. Paradoxically, the weakness of the opposition may have given moderate reformers within the KMT an opportunity to make adjustments to the system that they would not have made without any opposition (particularly from the vocal proponents of independence), but which they could afford to make while the DPP was divided and under the leadership of moderates in the Formosa faction.

The Influence of Lee Teng-hui

With the death of President Chiang Ching-kuo in January 1988, power was transferred to Chiang's vice-president, Lee Teng-hui, who served out the remaining two years of Chiang's term. By 1990, the term was over and the National Assembly was charged with electing a president for the following six years. In the days before March 21, when the National Assembly was expected to settle the matter, thousands of students camped out in the Chiang Kai-shek Memorial plaza in central Taipei to demand democratic reforms. They opposed the idea that the president was to be selected by a body composed of assemblymen who did not represent the island's population.

In an event that self-consciously recalled symbols of the student demonstrations and sit-in in Peking in 1989, students in Taipei congregated on the grounds of the Chiang Kai-shek Memorial, went on hunger strikes, wore headbands inscribed with political slogans, and demanded that the political system of Taiwan be reformed. Unlike their cousins in Peking, the students on Taiwan had a narrowly focused agenda that included "the disbanding of the electoral college [National Assembly], the suspension of the Temporary Provisions that freeze aging Mainlanders in office, a timetable for full democratization, and a complete revamp of the Constitution."[97]

In a gesture that was also reminiscent of Chao Tzu-yang's emotional visit to Tiananmen Square, President Lee went to the Chiang Kai-shek Memorial to meet with the students on the afternoon of the day he was elected by the National Assembly to a new six-year term. He pledged to convene a broad-based, high-level conference to study the needs of the nation. That pledge resulted in a National Affairs Conference that drew together a host of Taiwan's political and academic leaders who met from June 28 to July 4 to consider Taiwan's political development and offer recommendations for democratization.[98]

Lee's election had tremendous symbolic, as well as practical, significance. He was by no means universally supported within his party and was elected only after a vicious battle with the conservative KMT hard-liners. While President Lee is very much a product of the KMT, he is also Taiwanese and of Hakka heritage. He may be viewed by many Taiwanese as one of their own, but to Mainlanders his identity marks him as one of "them" rather than one of "us." Those who supported Lee were generally Taiwanese members of the KMT who became known as the "mainstream" faction during Lee's term in office. A "nonmainstream" faction was composed largely of Mainlanders who—with the encouragement of Madame Chiang Kai-shek herself and other prominent figures of that generation—opposed Lee's appointment. These two factions, which crystallized at the moment the matter of succession had come to pass, battled during the subsequent years for dominance over the direction the party and the state would take.

This created a situation on Taiwan from 1987 to 1992 that is precisely the sort that Huntington identified as the next stage of a transformation. As he suggested, a faction within the regime that favors democratization acquires greater power vis-à-vis the hard-liners, who are resistant to reform. This ushers in a period of "liberalized authoritarianism" and ultimately leads to the subjugation of the hard-liners by those in the ruling elite who favor democratization. As this process unfolded, it became evident that on Taiwan the division between reformers and hard-liners within the ruling party reflected the Taiwanese/Mainlander divide.

Chiang Chun-nan observed that the shift within the KMT was sensed by the Taiwanese population of the ROC. He suggested that, in this regard, the Republic of Korea has an advantage over Taiwan because Park Chung Hee and Chun Doo Hwan are both from the same community as the Korean opposition, so the two sides of the political spectrum can relate to each other "on equal footing." He said that on Taiwan, it was only when Lee Teng-hui became president that people began to feel their leader came from their own society. Before that time, rulers were "from outside so we never feel we are equal . . . we are different, you know, we are kind of inferior." He said that Taiwanese were always fighting for their rights from a position of inferiority, not from a position of equality.[99]

Chiang illustrated the importance of this sense of equality by telling a story about the late president, Chiang Ching-kuo. He said the president was known to have had eleven Taiwanese friends. He made a great effort to befriend "ordinary people," most of whom were owners of small shops, such as the owner of an ice cream shop in Nantou and the owner of a fish restaurant in Penghu. Chiang Chun-nan said it was ridiculous that the president tried so hard to demonstrate that he was a friend of the people when it was so obvious that he had little actual contact with Taiwanese.

The same was true for Premier Yu Kuo-hua. Yu was from Chekiang and spoke Mandarin with a heavy accent. His English, however, learned in London where he was educated, was quite good. Chiang said that Yu was always going abroad to attend international meetings and that he knew New York, Tokyo, and London better than he knew Taiwan. "If he took a train from Taipei to Kaohsiung, I bet he would not remember more than four stations—the names of the stations on that line." By contrast, he said, everybody knows Lee Teng-hui, and Lee has many friends. "Now the leadership is [of the] same background, same lands, same education, we can communicate with each other. That's new for us; [a] new experience."[100]

As president, Lee Teng-hui has been consistently supportive of the process of democratization, yet he has not sold the shop to his Taiwanese brethren. While the staunchest conservatives in the KMT did not fully trust him because he is Taiwanese, the moderate reformers may have seen Lee's provincial origins as an asset. Lee's identity has allowed him to speak to the Taiwanese majority—as one of them—with credibility that a Mainlander could not muster. To retain his credibility with the old guard in the KMT, though, Lee had to tread delicately around the sensitive question of national identity.

Throughout the first several years of his presidency, Lee steered a fairly unobjectionable course through the choppy waters of the reunification/independence debate. He has also used his prestige to persuade doubters that the government is serious about democratization. His public view is that

> Taiwan's separation from mainland China is an unfortunate political fact. This has caused Chinese people on both sides of the Straits to live under two different political systems and lifestyles, and has resulted in a great disparity in living standards between people on the two sides. However, "blood is thicker than water"—the identical ethnic, cultural, and historical background of the Chinese is an undeniable fact. Though I was born in Taiwan, I am president of the Republic of China. Faced with a small group of people advocating secessionism, I am naturally concerned. I will do my best to dispel the doubts of these people and help them believe in the government's determination to promote democracy, and have faith that all actions taken by the government will respect the rights of the people in Taiwan and safeguard their security and welfare. I firmly believe the government will ultimately win the trust and support of dissidents and dissolve their differences.[101]

In a spring 1991 press conference, Lee stated, "I have on many occasions stressed there are no 'Mainlanders' or 'Taiwanese' and there are no so-called 'conservatives' [in the KMT]. To talk about the 'second generation' and 'conservatives' is just silly. We are united and harmonious."[102] On another occasion, the president said that the residents of Taiwan were all in the same boat and that their mutual concern should be focused on how to keep that vessel afloat. He said that no one would benefit if the boat sank while everyone was fighting for better seats.[103]

Moreover, Lee has expressed the view that Taiwan must stay afloat politically so that it can serve as a guide for the development of the rest of China. Speaking of the successes of Taiwan's development in a National Day speech in 1992, Lee said that the people of Taiwan "have the ability and ambition to extend (their) experience to the whole of the Chinese mainland so that all Chinese may share it." He endorsed the view, which is most often heard from Mainlanders in the KMT, that "[A]s Chinese, we must view China's future and the freedom and welfare of the Chinese people as our personal concern. . . ."[104]

Lee Teng-hui may have intended to shore up his *bona fides* in this transitional era by appealing to the "nonmainstream" faction in selecting as premier Hau Pei-tsun. Where Lee spoke with credibility to Taiwanese and was suspect in the eyes of many Mainlanders, Hau Pei-tsun had precisely the opposite difficulty. Hau is a Mainlander who had most recently served as defense minister and, before that, chief of the general staff of the armed forces. Ideologically, Hau was deeply anxious about the pace and direction of political reforms and viscerally opposed to the notion of Taiwan independence. His tenure in office as premier was marked by sharp and biting conflicts with members of the Legislative Yuan and all too frequent denials that he and President Lee were working at cross-purposes.[105]

As premier, Hau Pei-tsun was quite outspoken about the question of national identity. During a general interpolation session at the Legislative Yuan, DPP legislator Chiu Lien-hui said that the Taiwan people are not under any "obligation to make sacrifices for the sake of reunification." Hau obviously disagreed, saying that reunifying with China "will not sacrifice [the interests of the people]. On the contrary, it is for the protection of all existing things here. . . . But an independent Taiwan will sacrifice [local interests] . . . and bring immediate destruction." Hau believes that reunification under democracy would be good for the country, but that "[a] plebiscite to decide the status of the nation will only bring disaster to Taiwan." He asked whether the PRC would tolerate the results if the people of Taiwan decided to vote for independence and added, "The world [democratic] trend is good, and rational development of democracy will be good [for the island], but [you people] just want a plebiscite to change the national title. . . . If [you] established a Taiwan republic and other people established their own republics in Penghu and Kinmen and Taipei, don't you think it would be chaotic? And chaos is detrimental to the interests of the nation and the public."[106]

On November 19, 1991, Hau cudgeled the advocates of independence, saying that "Taiwan independence is like a cancer which destroys a person's life, then perishes with it." He defended the government's one China policy and said that the government does not aim to reunify immediately, that it will wait until both sides have reached a comparable level of economic and democratic development.[107]

In an address given at the opening of a conference about democracy, Premier Hau said that he had three worries about Taiwan's future development: "identifying with the country, . . . democratic temperament, . . . [and] the meaning of public opinion." Hau said that democracy can only thrive in a place where citizens all identify with the country. To him, the country is the Republic of China, not Taiwan.[108] He urged people to stop debating the issue of reunification or independence and to devote themselves to the matter of national economic development. According to Hau, "If you want to talk about Taiwan independence, we are already a sovereign, independent nation . . . and if you want to talk about a leadership headed by a native Taiwanese, our President is from Taiwan, so is the governor here [at that time, it was Lien Chan]." He added that more than half the heads of government offices are Taiwanese.[109] He also said that it was foolish for Taiwan to look to Japan, England, and the United States as models for democratic development because "none of the democratic countries have a national identity problem. . . . This is a fact we must face."[110] So while the president was viewed by Taiwanese as a potential ally in their effort to promote political reform and to secure the independence of Taiwan, the premier clearly was not. Mainlanders and all those concerned with the maintenance of social order and national security took comfort from Hau Pei-tsun's firm stance. This division of views, a division based largely on national identity, led to an intensification of political conflict between the KMT and DPP and advocates of reunification on the one hand and advocates of independence on the other.

The Uncertain Loyalties of the Military

During the presidencies of the two Chiangs, there was a triangular relationship of power among the military, the KMT, and the government that reflected an "emergency" mentality. Once Chiang Ching-kuo died and Lee Teng-hui succeeded him, the charismatic power of the president was no longer as great as it once had been and the sense of emergency significantly diminished. Taiwan entered a new phase in which there was a "dual presidential-parliamentary logic" that has lent itself far better to constitutional rule.[111]

As to the military, for obvious reasons it is difficult to find reliable information about it or its role behind the scenes of the political dramas played out in public. Certainly Lee Teng-hui's appointment of Hau Pei-tsun was taken as an effort to reach out to the hard-liners in the military. It is worth bearing in mind that the military was formed as a revolutionary force and a branch of the KMT. The party has, historically, exercised control over its military services, but with the effort to separate the party and the state in the political sphere, one must assume that the transformation of the military from a politicized to a professional force will be the source of continuing concern.[112] The disentanglement of the party from the military also raises questions about which entity it is that the military is intended to defend. It is hard to know, for example, what the military would do if the KMT were a minority party.

Even after the electoral successes of the DPP in the late 1980s and early 1990s, this was still a significant source of anxiety. Chen Shuipian spoke forcefully about the need for the armed forces to be nationalized. He ruminated about what might happen otherwise. If the people decided that Taiwan should remain independent, he said, but the army refused to support this notion and staged a coup, that would mean there is no democracy on Taiwan.[113]

Hau Pei-tsun opposed the suggestion that the military on Taiwan was the army of the KMT. He said it was the army of the Republic of China.

> Of course, this is the army which the KMT has, for seventy years, established, managed, and trained, but basically, now it is the army of the ROC. The army of the ROC is loyal to the ROC constitution and the ROC president, but is not exclusively dedicated to the KMT. Any political party which is the ruling party must be loyal to the ROC and to the ROC constitution.
>
> Conversely, if any political party becomes the ruling party and invalidates the name of the Republic of China terminating the ROC, I do not think that the army will agree to go along with this. The army's responsibility is to protect the ROC. If there is a political party which is not loyal to the ROC, I do not think the army will sit by and watch.[114]

Hau's attitude, if representative of the armed forces, certainly would not relieve the anxieties of the opposition. What the former minister of defense and premier has asserted, in essence, is that the armed forces would, if pushed to it, overrule the mandate of the populace. This is a startling admission and one that bodes ill for the development of a democratic state. It is not clear, though, how widespread Hau's view about this is and how seriously proponents of independence need to take Hau's stark assessment.

Reform from Above

During the period 1987–1992, liberalization was a process controlled by the ruling party. The KMT opened in ways it chose to, albeit under some public pressure, and granted liberties it deemed acceptable. While genuine changes occurred, and although many were made in response to demands by the increasingly vociferous opposition, it is probably true that the regime maintained the power to regulate which demands it would meet and which it would deny. This was a transformation, to recall Huntington's term, and up to the end of the 1980s, the KMT-as-state remained in control. The cost of suppression may have risen steadily, but the regime was still capable of suppressing. What happened on Taiwan up through the end of the 1980s was a centrally managed release of pressure, although it was more controlled some times than at others. Still, one should bear in mind that for the first few years of liberalization, the reforms were enacted from above.

This equation shifted. Although it is probably not possible to identify a particular date on which the KMT lost control of the process, in the early 1990s the KMT seemed far less capable of controlling political outcomes than it had been a few years before. The increasingly responsible role played by opposition lawmakers and the competitive struggles within the KMT for domination of the party contributed to a sense that the KMT was no longer in control of the process of reform. With the election of a new National Assembly in 1991 and a new Legislative Yuan in 1992 and the prospect of a popularly elected president (either by direct or indirect balloting), the KMT increasingly found itself at the mercy of a competitive system it had allowed to emerge but was unable to control.

The liberalization of society and politics that has occurred since 1987 has been eased by an extraordinary rate of economic growth and widespread prosperity. The growing cosmopolitan and consumerist tendencies of Taiwan's population are noticeable in the proliferation of middle-class tastes and values. Economic growth has brought with it a flood of ideas, styles, and commercial reasons for communication with the rest of the world. All this has enhanced the degree of pluralism and impelled authorities to tolerate what would have been intolerable only a few years before.

One conclusion Hu Fo and Chu Yun-han came to after an extensive series of surveys following the 1983 and 1986 elections is that "elections for national lawmakers not only have increasingly acquired the normal function of popular accountability and system legitimization in a representative democracy, but in the transition they actually functioned as a catalyst of democratization."[115] This conclusion comports with the notion that, to transform a nondemocratic system into a democracy, one must be prepared to use democratic means, and that elections are the most significant component of the democratic process. Since the surveys were conducted, electoral competition on Taiwan has only become more intense and the offices affected even more powerful. When Chiang Ching-kuo died in 1988, few would have been bold enough to suggest that within a decade the president would be selected by popular vote, and yet, by the early 1990s, that was seeming ever more possible.[116]

Still, Taiwan is not yet at a stage where democracy as a system of decision making pervades every level of society. Harry Eckstein pointed out that "a government will tend to be stable if its authority pattern is congruent with the other authority patterns of the society of which it is a part."[117] By no means are democratic patterns of authority common in other arenas on Taiwan, although there is a certain amount of percolation occurring from the political sphere to other spheres. Still, democratic values are not well ingrained. There is a sense that Taiwan is still learning how to be democratic.

Moving Beyond Liberalization

Disparate views of national identity held by Taiwanese and Mainlanders predate the onset of liberalization. Of course, other strains beset the relations between the KMT regime, which for years was dominated by Mainlanders, and its critics—most of whom are Taiwanese. None is as divisive or arouses as much raw animus as does the dispute about national identity. Indeed, expanding political participation engendered more open debate and increased the scope of genuine contestation. In this fashion, the process of liberalization has accentuated the conflict—so long repressed between those who champion the virtues of reunification and those who endorse Taiwan independence—and has contributed to the consolidation of their views.

By resisting calls early in its tenure on Taiwan for genuine reform, and by discrediting the motives of its critics, the KMT induced frustration and hostility among Taiwanese that mounted with time. This resulted in an ever-widening gulf between the ruling elite and the Taiwanese populace that eroded the party's legitimacy in the eyes of its citizenry. To bolster its sagging legitimacy, the KMT clung to the threadbare mantle of Chinese unity, long after any reasonable observer could see that the KMT was not going to take back the mainland by force. This gradually galvanized the opposition against KMT rule and led opponents to see their struggle in terms of competing visions of national identity. That central-level politics on Taiwan has been divided about no other issues as sharply as it is on the matters of national identity and Taiwan's political status has noteworthy implications for the prospects of democracy.

Expectations of Democracy

Beyond feeling that the system is unfair, those who promote democracy seem to have specific expectations of what it will bring. One set of expectations pertains to the form of government Taiwan should have and another set concerns the way that form of government will influence the question of Taiwan's political status. For many people, the objective of democratization was to make politics on the island more reasonable by transforming the system into one in which those who govern do so fairly and with popular consent.

This expectation may have changed. Lu Ya-li observed that in the 1960s when people spoke of reform, their primary objectives were freedom and liberty, not democracy. Now, he said, liberty is no longer a big problem for most people and the central demand is for democracy.[118] However, even though people often talk about how unfair the system is, it is not at all clear how many of them completely appreciate how a democracy actually functions or what would have to change to create a democratic system on Taiwan.

On Taiwan, democracy has been held up by the opposition in a way characterized by one student of democracy "as simply the reverse of absolutism, a polemical notion whose function is to oppose, not propose. The utterance of 'democracy' is a way of saying no to inequality, injustice, and coercion."[119] For the KMT, which itself is divided in terms of how it wants to navigate the current of reform, democracy has been viewed as a way to reestablish the party's sagging legitimacy. Many party leaders apparently understood the need to reaffirm their mandate to continue bearing the standard for Taiwan and to press ahead with the KMT's modified vision of reunification. Their ambition for democracy has been linked to their search for legitimacy and so has focused somewhat narrowly on efforts to secure the consent of the governed. They have seemed willing to compromise a bit of their authority for the possibility of gaining popular confirmation of their legitimacy, but have been reticent about a thoroughgoing democratization for fear that they will lose power entirely.

The opposition, by contrast, has not been interested in a bounded program of electoral reform. It exploited every opportunity to restructure the rules of Taiwan's political game so that a genuine sounding of popular views is possible. The aim of the opposition seemed to be to unseat the KMT and allow the populace to determine the political status of Taiwan and the form of government it wishes to have. The opposition apparently expected that most residents of Taiwan would prefer to abandon the idea of reunification, and, if given the opportunity to do so, some might support an outright declaration of independence. These ambitions for reform notwithstanding, it is not entirely clear that what the opposition has in mind is any more democratic than the status quo, with the singular exception that the government's right to rule would be established by consent of a majority of the governed.

For one thing, it is not clear that the DPP was set up primarily to be an opposition party in a two-party democratic system. There seems to be some tension among the party leadership itself about what the party's objectives are. In 1991, Yao Chia-wen, past chairman of the DPP, said that the "DPP is a very strange organization. It is an organization to protest [against the] KMT and . . . promote reform, an organization to teach people to participate in political activities, an organization to study and to solicit the idea of Taiwan[ese] identification. This is not a simple political party [because it is composed of people] who try to protest KMT rule, try to talk about Taiwan history, try to talk about Taiwan language and Taiwan independence and also to organize the people to go to the demonstrations. So this is not a common political party."[120] Hsu Hsin-liang, speaking several months before he was elected party chairman, offered a more hopeful view of his party's ambitions. He claimed that the DPP is more interested in democracy than in independence or in the expression of national consciousness. He said the focus of DPP endeavors is to establish democratic institutions, such as a legislature elected by the people of Taiwan and a president selected by popular election.[121]

It certainly seems that many on Taiwan believe that by designing a system that appears more democratic, they will turn Taiwan into a democracy even if the habits and values associated with democracy have not yet been well established. Democracy is almost always discussed as a way to alter the balance of power among the political elite. However, there is good reason to believe that many Taiwanese concur with what Chen Shui-pian stated rather explicitly, "[D]emocracy is the process and independence is the goal."[122]

Notes

1. Dankwart Rustow, "Transitions to Democracy: Toward a Dynamic Model," *Comparative Politics*, no. 2 (April 1970), pp. 352–54.

2. See George H. Kerr, *Formosa: Licensed Revolution and the Home Rule Movement, 1895–1945* (Honolulu: University Press of Hawaii, 1974); and Douglas Mendel, *The Politics of Formosan Nationalism* (Berkeley: University of California Press, 1970). For additional accounts of the history of reform since the KMT took control of Taiwan, see Cal Clark, *Taiwan's Development: Implications for Contending Political Economy Paradigms* (New York: Greenwood Press, 1989); Thomas B. Gold, *State and Society in the Taiwan Miracle* (Armonk, NY: M.E. Sharpe, 1986); Simon Long, *Taiwan: China's Last Frontier* (New York: St. Martin's Press, 1991); Peter W. Moody, *Political Change on Taiwan: A Study of Ruling Party Adaptability* (New York: Praeger, 1992); and Tien Hung-mao, *The Great Transition: Political and Social Change in the Republic of China* (Stanford: Hoover Institution Press, 1988).

3. Tien, *The Great Transition,* p. 1.

4. Andrew Nathan, *China's Crisis: Dilemmas of Reform and Prospects for Democracy* (New York: Columbia University Press, 1990), pp. 129–30; and Constance Squires Meaney, "Liberalization, Democratization, and the Role of the KMT," in *Political Change in Taiwan*, ed. Tun-jen Cheng and Stephan Haggard (Boulder, CO: Lynne Rienner, 1992), chapter 5.

5. Chiang Ching-kuo, "President Chiang's Address to the National Assembly at the 1984 Constitution Day Ceremony," in *Republic of China: A Reference Book, 1986,* ed. Dixson D.S. Sung and Lawrence C. Ho. (New York and Taipei: Highlight International, 1986), p. 455.

6. *Republic of China Handbook, 1990* (Taipei: Kwang Hwa, 1990), p. 720. For a detailed summary of the content of this emergency decree, see Fei-lung Lui, "The Electoral System and Voting Behavior in Taiwan," in *Political Change in Taiwan*, ed. Cheng and Haggard, pp. 173–75, n. 2.

7. Hsu Chi-ming, deputy chairman of the Research and Planning Board of the Ministry of Foreign Affairs, said, "Taiwan was under a state of emergency. Foreigners called it martial law. We consider it a 'Decree of Emergency.' The implications are not the same." Interview with Hsu Chi-ming (Steve), Taipei, June 16, 1991.

8. Samuel Huntington, "Foreword," in *Political Change in Taiwan,* ed. Cheng and Haggard, p. xii. See also Cheng and Haggard's more elaborate discussion of these similarities in their "Regime Transformation in Taiwan," ibid., pp. 18–21.

9. Huntington, "Foreword," p. xii.

10. Tien, *The Great Transition*, p. 93.

11. Ibid., p. 94.

12. John F. Copper, *A Quiet Revolution: Political Development in the Republic of China* (Washington, DC: Ethics and Public Policy Center, 1988), p. xii.

13. Mendel, *The Politics of Formosan Nationalism*, pp. 114–21.

14. Tien, *The Great Transition*, p. 94.

15. Mendel, *The Politics of Formosan Nationalism*, pp. 117–18.

16. P'eng Ming-min, *A Taste of Freedom: Memoirs of a Formosan Independence Leader* (New York: Holt, Rinehart and Winston, 1972), p. 135.

17. Marc J. Cohen, *Taiwan at the Crossroads: Human Rights, Political Development and Social Change on the Beautiful Island* (Washington, DC: Asia Resource Center, 1988); Mab Huang, *Intellectual Ferment for Political Reforms in Taiwan, 1971–1973* (Ann Arbor: Center for Chinese Studies, University of Michigan, 1976); Mendel, *The Politics of Formosan Nationalism*; and Tien, *The Great Transition*.

18. Long, *Taiwan: China's Last Frontier*, p. 66.

19. Ibid., p. 189.

20. Ibid.

21. Ibid., p. 67.

22. Huang, *Intellectual Ferment for Political Reforms in Taiwan*.

23. Ibid., p. 5.

24. Ibid., pp. 5–12. The issue was revived on October 21, 1990, when a band of sportsmen and political activists from Taiwan attempted to land on one of the islands and was intercepted by Japanese forces. This drew an official, albeit conciliatory, response from Japan and reignited the unresolved controversy. See Tai Ming Cheung and Charles Smith, "Rocks of Contention," *Far Eastern Economic Review*, November 1, 1990, p. 19.

25. Interview with Yang Hsien-hung, Taipei, November 7, 1990.

26. Huang, *Intellectual Ferment for Political Reforms in Taiwan*, pp. 12–19.

27. Ibid., p. 18.

28. Clark, *Taiwan's Development*, p. 130.

29. This journal was first published in 1968 by a group of intellectuals (Taiwanese, Mainlanders, and Hong Kong Chinese) and was devoted during its early years to theoretical discussions pertaining to modernization and expositions about the humanities. In the aftermath of the Tiao-yu-t'ai protest movement in 1971, two other groups of intellectuals—including many Mainlanders—helped to reorganize *The Intellectual*, and it became a leading forum for expressions of dissent by the intellectual community. The KMT's tolerance for open debate was brief, however, and the journal lasted no longer than the two years during which intellectuals were permitted to air their views.

30. Gold, *State and Society*, pp. 93–94.

31. Huang, *Intellectual Ferment for Political Reforms in Taiwan*, p. 3.

32. Ibid., p. 59.

33. Cheng and Haggard, "Regime Transformation in Taiwan," p. 10.

34. Ibid., p. 11.

35. Gold, *State and Society*, p. 92.

36. Tien, *The Great Transition*, p. 95. See also Huang, *Intellectual Ferment for Political Reforms in Taiwan*, pp. 103–8 passim.

37. See Ya-li Lu, "Political Opposition in Taiwan: The Development of the

Democratic Progressive Party," in *Political Change in Taiwan,* ed. Cheng and Haggard, p. 124.

38. Gold, *State and Society*, p. 114.

39. Interview with Chiang Chun-nan, Taipei, May 20, 1991.

40. Andrew Leonard, "Finding a Voice: Hokkien Rock Group Probes Taiwan's Cultural Identity," *Far Eastern Economic Review*, August 30, 1990, pp. 32–33.

41. Chou Yangsun and Andrew Nathan, "Democratizing Transition in Taiwan," *Asian Survey*, vol. 27, no. 3 (March 1987), p. 280.

42. Cohen, *Taiwan at the Crossroads*, p. 35.

43. See Long, *Taiwan: China's Last Frontier*, p. 70.

44. Ibid., p. 71.

45. See Tien, *The Great Transition*, p. 96.

46. The December 10 rally was intended as a prelude for a larger demonstration scheduled to occur in Taipei on December 16. Ibid.

47. Lu, "Political Opposition in Taiwan," p. 125.

48. See John Kaplan, *The Court-Martial of the Kaohsiung Defendants* (Berkeley: Institute of East Asian Studies, University of California, 1981), pp. 16–17.

49. Ibid., p. 18. The eight were Huang Hsin-chieh, Shih Ming-teh, Yao Chia-wen, Chang Chun-hung, Lin Yi-hsiung, Chen Chu, Lin Hung-hsuan, and Lu Hsiu-lien.

50. Ibid., p. 46. For a more extensive discussion of the aftermath of the riot, see Cohen, *Taiwan at the Crossroads*, pp. 38–43.

51. See Cohen, *Taiwan at the Crossroads*, p. 40. See also Kaplan, *The Court-Martial of the Kaohsiung Defendants*, for a more balanced account.

52. Those elected to seats in the Legislative Yuan included: K'ang Ning-hsiang (an activist who had been in Kaohsiung during the riot but was not arrested), Huang Hsin-chieh's brother (Huang Tien-fu), Chang Chun-hung's wife (Hsu Jung-shu), one of the lawyers working for the defendants (Chang Teh-min), and a *tang-wai* academic (Huang Huang-hsiung). Yao Chia-wen's wife, Chou Ching-yu, was elected to the National Assembly with the highest number of votes of any candidate in either election. Cohen, *Taiwan at the Crossroads*, p. 41.

53. Interview with Yang Hsien-hung, Taipei, November 7, 1990.

54. Ibid.

55. Tien, *The Great Transition*, p. 98.

56. Interview with Yang Hsien-hung, Taipei, November 7, 1990.

57. Moody, *Political Change on Taiwan*, p. 52.

58. See David E. Kaplan, *Fires of the Dragon: Politics, Murder, and the Kuomintang* (New York: Atheneum, 1992). Liu is better known in Chinese by his pen name, Chiang Nan.

59. Moody, *Political Change on Taiwan*, p. 52.

60. *Free China Journal*, July 7, 1985, p. 1.

61. Interview with Yang Hsien-hung, Taipei, November 7, 1990.

62. *Free China Journal*, December 9, 1984, p. 2; Moody, *Political Change on Taiwan*, p. 88.

63. Interview with Yang Hsien-hung, Taipei, November 7, 1990.

64. Dan. 5: 1–30.

65. See Long, *Taiwan: China's Last Frontier*, p. 67. Tien Hung-mao defined

"Taiwanization" as "the creation of a more pluralistic KMT power structure and parliamentary reforms to enhance native Taiwanese participation in the legislative process." See Tien Hung-mao, "Transformation of an Authoritarian Party State: Taiwan's Development Experience," in *Political Change in Taiwan*, ed. Cheng and Haggard, p. 34. See also Linda Chao and Ramon H. Myers, "The First Chinese Democracy: Political Development of the Republic of China on Taiwan, 1986–1994," *Asian Survey*, vol. 34, no. 3 (March 1994), pp. 218–19.

66. See Ramon H. Myers, "Political Theory and Recent Political Development in the Republic of China," *Asian Survey*, vol. 27, no. 9 (September 1987), p. 1010.

67. Chou and Nathan, "Democratizing Transition in Taiwan," pp. 285–86.

68. Ibid., p. 286. The task force also suggested that the KMT find ways to improve public order and strengthen party work.

69. Myers, "Political Theory and Recent Political Development in the Republic of China," p. 1010.

70. Chou and Nathan, "Democratizing Transition in Taiwan," p. 288.

71. Myers, "Political Theory and Recent Political Development in the Republic of China," p. 1006.

72. Mah Soo-lay, the secretary-general of the KMT at that time, denied that the KMT was forced into these concessions by domestic or international pressures. Ibid.

73. Ibid., p. 1011.

74. Ramon Myers reported there were two thousand supporters, but Chou and Nathan claimed there were ten thousand. Myers, "Political Theory and Recent Political Development in the Republic of China," p. 1013; Chou and Nathan, "Democratizing Transition in Taiwan," p. 291.

75. This event occurred after seven opposition figures tried to return from the United States on November 14. At that time, approximately eighty supporters staged a sit-in at the airport when six of the seven were barred from entering because they did not have the appropriate visa. The incident turned nasty and several police officers and protesters were injured. Myers, "Political Theory and Recent Political Development in the Republic of China," p. 1013.

76. Ibid.

77. Martin Lasater, *A Step Toward Democracy: The December 1989 Elections in Taiwan, Republic of China* (Washington, DC: American Enterprise Institute Press, 1990), pp. 79–84; Tien, *The Great Transition*, pp. 183–90; Tien, "Transformation of an Authoritarian Party State," p. 45; and Lu, "Political Opposition in Taiwan," p. 131.

78. See Lincoln Kaye, "Prison Before Pardon," *Far Eastern Economic Review*, January 4, 1990.

79. Tien, *The Great Transition*, pp. 2, 13; Long, *Taiwan: China's Last Frontier*, p. 183.

80. See Long, *Taiwan: China's Last Frontier*, p. 185.

81. Long reported that "[s]ince 1951, the number of newspapers granted publication licenses had been frozen at 31, and the number of pages had also been restricted. In 1955, pages were limited to six per newspaper, and only increased to twelve in 1974." See Long, *Taiwan: China's Last Frontier*, p. 184. See also Tien, *The Great Transition*, chapter 8.

82. See Leo Y. Liu, "Self-Determination, Independence, and the Process of Democratization in Taiwan," *Asian Profile*, vol. 19, no. 3 (June 1991), p. 197.

83. *China Post*, December 12, 1991, p. 1.

84. Long, *Taiwan: China's Last Frontier*, p. 190.

85. Ibid., p. 196.

86. Copper, *A Quiet Revolution*, pp. xii–xiii.

87. Long, *Taiwan: China's Last Frontier*, p. 196.

88. See ibid., p. 195; Lu, "Political Opposition in Taiwan," pp. 132–33; and *China Post*, June 6, 1991, p. 1.

89. Lu, "Political Opposition in Taiwan," p. 132.

90. It is interesting that Chang Chun-hung, then secretary-general of the DPP, admitted that his party was full of prejudice, but said that the mood within the party was a reflection of the tensions that had been caused by continuous repression and political persecution under KMT rule. *China Post*, June 10, 1991, p. 1.

91. See Long, *Taiwan: China's Last Frontier*, p. 194.

92. Lasater, *A Step Toward Democracy*, p. 2.

93. Ibid., p. 4.

94. Long, *Taiwan: China's Last Frontier*, p. 198.

95. Ibid. See Julian Baum, "Vernacular Vogue," *Far Eastern Economic Review*, August 30, 1990, p. 32.

96. Long, *Taiwan: China's Last Frontier*, p. 198; Hu Fo and Chu Yun-han, "Electoral Competition and Political Democratization," in *Political Change in Taiwan*, ed. Cheng and Haggard, pp. 177–98, especially the conclusions of their survey research that support the notion that voters do not necessarily select candidates on the basis of the Taiwanese/Mainlander issue.

97. Lincoln Kaye, "The Old and the Restless," *Far Eastern Economic Review*, March 29, 1990, pp. 10–11.

98. The controversies leading up to and the proceedings of the conference are described in some detail in Ts'ai Ling and Ramon H. Myers, "Achieving Consensus Amidst Adversity: The Conference to Decide the Republic of China's Destiny," *American-Asian Review*, vol. 9, no. 2 (Summer 1991); and vol. 9, no. 3 (Fall 1991).

99. Interview with Chiang Chun-nan, Taipei, May 20, 1991.

100. Ibid.

101. *Free China Journal*, July 5, 1991, p. 7.

102. *China Post*, May 1, 1991, p. 3.

103. *Free China Journal*, October 1, 1991, p. 1.

104. "Lee Teng-hui on National Day," Foreign Broadcast Information Service: China (FBIS-CHI) 92–198, October 13, 1992, p. 33.

105. See Tien, "Transformation of an Authoritarian Party State," in *Political Change in Taiwan*, ed. Cheng and Haggard, p. 52.

106. *China Post*, November 9, 1991, p. 1.

107. *China Post*, November 20, 1991, p. 1.

108. *China Post*, March 30, 1991, p. 1.

109. Interview with Hau Pei-tsun, Taipei, August 27, 1993; *China Post*, June 14, 1991, p. 4. Some Taiwanese politicians and intellectuals took issue with the premier's claim that Taiwanese had "made it" by reaching the top posts in more

than half of the government offices. A report in *Hsin Hsin-wen* (The Journalist), June 30, 1991, pp. 31–32, was unsympathetic to the premier's claim. It suggested that the premier was only correct if a small group of offices was taken into account. Reviewing the complete list of ministerial and agency heads, the publication demonstrated that seventy-seven heads are Mainlanders and only forty-three heads are Taiwanese. See JPRS-CAR–91–057, October 18, 1991, pp. 40–42.

110. *China Post*, June 4, 1991, p. 1. This statement prompted an editorial in the *China Times Express* that stated, "Before Taiwan can become a democratic example of a Chinese society, ideological struggles over unification and independence claims must be put to rest. What Taiwan should do now is to further implement democracy and continue national development. For this we need a cease fire in the ideological wars." *China Post*, June 6, 1991, p. 2.

111. See Edwin Winckler, "Taiwan: Changing Dynamics," in *China Briefing, 1991*, ed. William A. Joseph (Boulder, CO: Westview Press in cooperation with the Asia Society, 1992), p. 148.

112. Lu, "Political Modernization in the ROC," in *Two Societies in Opposition: The Republic of China and the People's Republic of China After Forty Years*, ed. Ramon Myers (Stanford: Hoover Institution Press, 1991), p. 126.

113. Interview with Chen Shui-pian, Taipei, August 25, 1993.

114. Interview with Hau Pei-tsun, Taipei, August 27, 1993.

115. Hu and Chu, "Electoral Competition and Political Democratization," p. 197.

116. In 1994, it was determined that the president would be selected by popular vote starting in 1996.

117. Harry Eckstein, *Division and Cohesion in Democracy: A Study of Norway* (Princeton: Princeton University Press, 1966), pp. 225ff.

118. Interview with Lu Ya-li, Taipei, February 26, 1991.

119. Giovanni Sartori, "Democracy,"in *International Encyclopedia of the Social Sciences*, vol. 4, ed. David Sills (New York: Macmillan and The Free Press, 1968), p. 116.

120. Interview with Yao Chia-wen, Taipei, June 7, 1991.

121. Interview with Hsu Hsin-liang, Taipei, June 3, 1991.

122. Interview with Chen Shui-pian, Taipei, August 25, 1993.

6

The Rhetoric and Symbolism of Politics

A Combative Year in Review

On Taiwan during the period of rapid reform, the unresolved questions about national identity infused politics at the central level with rhetoric and symbols that dominated public exchanges concerning policy options. Tension generated by conflicting attitudes toward the political status of Taiwan and the national identity of its people affected discourse about other political matters that ordinarily might have been viewed as minor or procedural. The passions aroused by fears and ambitions pertaining to the status of Taiwan were manifested in the behavior of political figures individually, as well as by political parties, as they interacted on the public stage.

This is not to suggest that every policy discussion that took place in the public realm should be interpreted as having had some bearing on the question of national identity. There were, quite naturally, matters that were discussed simply to keep the proverbial trains running on time or to ensure that the mail was delivered. What is of interest here is the extent to which the question of national identity affected the discussion of other issues, particularly issues pertaining to the redistribution of power.

In the effort to dismantle an authoritarian system by which a state has been governed and construct a democracy in its stead, political actors bargain—explicitly and implicitly—about the redistribution of power. On Taiwan, this negotiation about the division of political goods has been expressed in terms of national identity and Taiwan's political status.

One might get the impression that determining the national identity was itself the fundamental source of conflict among the political actors. While this was sometimes true, the objective of the negotiations among political figures or parties was often aimed at something else. That is, the question of national identity subsumed a more basic conflict about who would retain and who would acquire power in the system that is under construction. The eagerness to stake a claim for power in the evolving new system was cloaked in moralistic arguments about the victimization of Taiwanese or the grandiose cultural destiny of the Han people.

Although people care about the matter of national identity, obviously some are more exercised about the matter than others. The shift from authoritarian rule to democracy would entail a redistribution of power even if there were consensus about Taiwan's political status and its people's national identity. That is what democratization is all about. The course of democratization on Taiwan, however, has been shaped by the conflict about national identity, and the rhetoric of national identity has dominated the struggle for power.

Conflict about identity may no longer be a concern for the majority of Taiwan's population. Indeed, public opinion surveys conducted by Academia Sinica suggest that, in general, people are not particularly affected by an "ethnic" problem in their daily affairs. When considering such things as their professional life, their marriage, and their interaction with neighbors and friends, very few felt that their behavior was shaped by concerns about ethnic identity. In terms of politics at the central level, however, 24.2 percent of those surveyed in 1990 viewed the ethnic problem as either serious or very serious.[1] A survey conducted by *Hsin Hsin-wen* (The Journalist) the same year found that 36.3 percent of respondents believed that the ethnic problem was worsening while only 8.1 percent saw it improving.[2]

Statistics such as these undoubtedly raise more questions than they answer. For instance, what is more significant: that 24.2 percent of the respondents to the Academia Sinica poll felt that politics at the central level was affected by ethnic tensions or that the other respondents did not indicate such concern? What is the relationship between an individual's perception that there are tensions between Mainlanders and Taiwanese in central-level politics and the question about national identity? Regarding the poll conducted by *Hsin Hsin-wen* (The Journalist), one wonders what factors people were thinking of when they agreed that the ethnic problem is worsening or improving? Perhaps the most significant finding in these polls is that many more people detected the effects of ethnic tension in central-level politics than in the rest of their lives and that far more people saw the situation worsening than improving.

To appreciate how the issue of national identity has influenced the course of democratization, one must consider the context in which this debate occurs. Although the KMT maintains its view that Taiwan is part of China and that the two must ultimately be rejoined, it has moderated its approach to reunification and has staked out a less provocative, more pragmatic scheme for reunifying the parts of China. The KMT's view is expressed in the National Unification Guidelines, which have been adopted as official government policy and which stipulate a multi-stage process of liberalizing relations with the mainland leading to an eventual reunification. This plan differs significantly from the jingoistic mentality that prevailed for much of the past forty years.

Within the KMT, there has been some division about this matter. The mainstream faction, or the Taiwan faction, associated with President Lee Teng-hui, has been content for this process to unfold over the long term. Those in the "nonmainstream" faction, the China faction, have been interested in accelerating the pace of reunification for fear that, unless the process is sped up while they still have influence, the Taiwanese in the party may not pursue this goal vigorously enough to realize it.

The DPP as an organization has assumed the mantle of the Taiwan independence movement, although the drive for independence is taken up more avidly by those in the New Tide faction of the DPP than by those who are associated with the Formosa faction. Still, the strength of the DPP as an opposition party is derived from its role as a party of Taiwanese defending the island against the continued rule of Mainlanders who, by dominating the KMT for most of the past four decades, clung to the notion that Taiwan's political autonomy is temporary. Although DPP leaders and their supporters may disagree about the best way to achieve equity for Taiwanese on Taiwan, it is probably true that most oppose the idea that the island should eventually be governed as part of a greater polity: China.

This question regarding the identity of the island, and the manifold ways in which uncertainty about national identity touches an individual's sense of identity, is the force that has driven political reform on Taiwan. Even if there were no question about identity, there might still be opposition to the ruling party and other sources of friction between the ruling elite and the ruled masses. There is also no reason to assume that the KMT has ruled Taiwan in an authoritarian manner only because of its interest in suppressing challenges to its view of Taiwan's status. Indeed, one need only consider how the PRC and Singapore have been governed to realize that even in Chinese communities where there is greater consensus about national identity, authoritarian rule is not exceptional.

However, one may fairly state that because of the polarized view of national identity on Taiwan, every step in the process of reform has been viewed in terms of balancing the forces of reunification against the forces of independence. Every political compromise has been evaluated in terms of the conflict between not only a ruling elite and an opposition but between reunification and independence as well.

In this light, the question of national identity may be seen to have influenced both the pace and direction of democratic reforms; however, it has also been the most evident impediment to reforms. The extent to which daily political life is a reflection of the competition between opposing views of national identity cannot be measured in any absolute way. Public opinion polls have been trotted out both by the KMT and by its opponents to demonstrate the actual sentiment of the population. In the end, these polls tend to cancel each other out and are overshadowed by the effects of the only polls that matter—elections.

If one is alert to the pervasive presence of the dispute about national identity, it is possible to see its manifestations in the rhetoric and symbols of political interaction as well as in the less explicit signals that political figures use to communicate with one another and with the populace. For most of the time since the KMT arrived on Taiwan, the pervasive mood of political suppression checked the open expression of views other than those of the KMT. Since the onset of reforms, however, political and social change proceeded with such rapidity that each day brought new challenges to the standards that were up to that point unshakable. With each year, as taboos were dismissed and restraints undone, the language and symbols of politics become more and more explicit. The dramatic way in which political change evolved on Taiwan, unfolding day after day, offers abundant illustrations of the central role identity plays in the process of democratization.

As a way to illustrate the permeation of central-level politics with the question of identity and to appreciate how the question of national identity has affected the process of democratization, it is helpful to consider the events of 1991. In some respects, 1991 was an exceptional year for politics on Taiwan. Relations between legislators in the Legislative Yuan were combative, tense, ugly, and violent. This contentiousness was compounded in relations between the executive and legislative branches. Popular dissatisfaction with the rate of reform and its apparent inequities was also vividly demonstrated.

Throughout the year, civility was undermined by hostility, and the language of rationality was subverted by symbolism. Emotions about politics on the island were raw and exposed in 1991, and, by reviewing what happened that year, one gets a sense of the tensions that lay beneath the surface before and that have been channeled in other ways since.

Clemency for Political Prisoners

In the early decades of its rule on the island, the KMT felt no compunction about locking its most vocal opponents behind bars. In May 1990, a career dissident named Huang Hua violated the election law by declaring his candidacy for the presidency on the DPP ticket.[3] Huang was arrested on charges of sedition and, in December 1990, was sentenced to prison for ten years. The next month, in January 1991, the government granted clemency to 4,705 prison inmates to mark the eightieth anniversary of the founding of the ROC in 1911. Fourteen people imprisoned for promoting independence had their sentences commuted, and by May 1991 all political prisoners other than Huang Hua were released.

While Huang Hua remained in prison for promoting independence, the government reduced the sentences of an additional 10,000 convicted criminals by either one-half or one-third. Three of those who benefited from this sentence reduction were men incarcerated for killing Henry Liu in California seven years earlier. The men who plotted Henry Liu's murder had already been granted one sentence reduction in 1988; the clemency arrangements of 1990 made these men eligible for release. They served only five years of what were once life sentences.

The release of the three responsible for having schemed to assassi-
nate Henry Liu after five years in prison while Huang Hua remained
behind bars for advocating that Taiwan be independent is a situation
rich in political symbolism. Although the two cases were entirely un-
connected, the appearance of a double standard of justice reinforced
the impression that those affiliated with the KMT who intended to
safeguard the Nationalists' image would be protected by legal fictions
crafted to appear legitimate, while those who promoted Taiwanese
national identity would be held to stricter readings of the law. Huang
Hua was eventually released on May 18, 1992.[4]

A Year of Legislating Dangerously

The most exaggerated rhetoric and flamboyant displays of political
symbolism occur in the legislative chambers in full view of Taiwan's
journalists, their cameras, and hence the entire population. On December 28, 1990, after the vote was taken in the Legislative Yuan on the
clemency bill that resulted in the early release of the three who con-
spired to murder Henry Liu, the legislature erupted in mayhem. A DPP
legislator, Chen Shui-pian, accused the secretariat of the legislature of
engaging in procedural irregularities that deprived the DPP of the opportunity to oppose the bill. Chen and the DPP believed that the clemency bill should be extended to all those who were convicted of
sedition more than once—a group that included many who advocated
Taiwan independence.[5] As an expression of its frustration and disre-
spect for the ruling authorities, who had exploited their power to deny
the DPP representatives of what they viewed as their right to speak, the
DPP members in the Legislative Yuan threw oranges at the KMT
legislative leaders.

What began as a protest against the secretariat's misapplication of
legislative rules devolved into a more general venting of hostility by
the DPP. Chief among its grievances was the resentment it felt about
the continued presence in the legislature of aged, mainland-elected
deputies. The DPP charged that the ruling party governed the island
through a tyranny of the majority within the legislature, even though
its legislators represented the interests of the Mainlander minority on
Taiwan.

The aged lawmakers were elected to represent constituencies on the
mainland and were initially allowed to remain in office for ideological

reasons. Their continued tenure reinforced the KMT's claim to be a national government in exile that was prepared to return to the mainland and resume its earlier role as the government of all China. Obviously, this objective became less credible with the passage of years, just as the legislators themselves became more feeble. Still, the KMT clung to the idea that the legislators could not be replaced until elections could be held again among their constituencies on the mainland.

Not only the DPP, but also the younger Taiwan-born members of the KMT, pushed to have the elderly lawmakers retire so that the legislature could function efficiently with statesmen elected from among those over whom the government of Taiwan had de facto dominion. At first, the KMT leadership balked at the idea of edging the elderly representatives out of office because with the replacement of legislators born and elected on the mainland with those born and elected on Taiwan, the legislature would be transformed from one that could claim to represent all China to one that would be a legislature of Taiwan only.

This argument is an example of the conflict over power masquerading as a concern for national identity. Even the staunchest members of the KMT elite understood that the geriatric members of the legislature had outlived their ideological value. The KMT would not be able to recover the mainland before these legislators died. The KMT stuck with its story as long as possible, however, because the presence of the mainland-elected legislators gave the KMT an ironclad voting bloc of support in a legislature that had become increasingly pluralistic.

Eventually, the KMT leaders accepted the need to replace the old legislators, but during the drawn-out process of persuading the senior lawmakers to retire the opposition exploited the anachronisms of the system to underscore how the KMT had "stacked the deck" against the Taiwanese. One observer described the proceedings in the legislative chambers during this period as follows:

> Debates often seemed dominated by histrionic performances by DPP members. One fiery orator, Chu Kao-cheng, although a moderate in DPP terms, had acquired a reputation as a firebrand, and the nickname "Rambo" because of his at times quite literally pugnacious approach to political debate. Meanwhile, the KMT was able to field equally passionate debaters from among its "young Turks." But the seats in the Legislative Yuan would often be almost deserted. A sprinkling of an-

cient-looking gentlemen, some of them in traditional Chinese dress, could be seen on the benches, sometimes snoozing.[6]

The issue of the legislature's composition was a dominant theme in legislative politics during 1991. It often came to the fore in violent confrontations between the KMT and the opposition about the rate at which those politely referred to as "senior deputies," but more derisively labeled the "old thieves," would be replaced. The KMT party leaders officially acknowledged that they could not sustain indefinitely the policy that allowed the senior deputies to remain in office and agreed in principle that the elders would have to be eased out of power. The Council of Grand Justices ruled that thirty-two such representatives were to retire by the end of 1990, but by year's end only three had retired; three others had died. No amount of cajoling, retirement compensation, or public abuse could force the seniors to abandon their posts.

This led some observers to accuse the KMT of foul play. It spurred discussion about the likelihood that there was a division in the KMT between the "young Turks," who agreed that the seniors should be replaced, and the more conservative party loyalists, who evidently saw great advantage in holding on to the party's overwhelming legislative majority by allowing the senior deputies to remain in office until the very last minute.

On the first day of the legislative session after the New Year holiday of 1991, the senior mainland-elected deputies boycotted the session to protest the disruption that had occurred in the last session of 1990 and to demonstrate the power they wielded. Without their presence in the chambers, the seniors essentially prevented the legislature from beginning because the requisite quorum of eighty-one could not be met. Wu Yung-hsiung of the DPP tried to offer a motion of protest, but the vice-speaker, Liu Sung-fan, stopped him, saying that, lacking a quorum, the legislature was not officially in session and therefore there was no forum in which to offer a motion.[7]

DPP legislator Lu Hsiu-yi—a member of the New Tide faction who had developed a reputation for disrupting legislative proceedings—blamed the frequent breakdown of order in the chambers on the senior legislators. "[T]he old thieves are the root of the chaos in the Legislative Yuan. . . . [T]hey have no right to vote. . . . [T]heir constituencies have either died or become the enemy [Communists] a long time ago."

Lu complained that the KMT's tolerance of the senior legislators reinforced the alienation between the legislature and the people of Taiwan. The Legislative Yuan was maintained to preserve the fiction that the ROC governed all of China. Lu Hsiu-yi explained his opposition to the senior deputies by declaring, "I'm not a Chinese. I'm a Taiwanese. This is the Legislative Yuan of your China, not the Legislative Yuan of Taiwan."[8]

Although many of the senior deputies were already too infirm to attend regular sessions of the legislature, and those who attended often spent their time reading, napping, playing chess, sipping tea, and talking, rather than participating fully in the deliberations of the session, their commitment to remain in office reflected their sense of mission. A senior deputy was quoted as saying, "[W]ithout us, the Legislative Yuan would be composed of wholly Taiwan-elected legislators and this would be tantamount to an independent state." In February 1989, the KMT had offered each of the senior legislators NT $4 million (U.S. $147,000) in pensions to encourage retirement. By 1991, only 35 percent had taken the party up on its offer.[9]

For several years, the floor of the Legislative Yuan was the scene of acts of violence and physical confrontation between legislators. These frequent and chaotic interruptions reflected the highly emotional state of political conflict between the opposition and the KMT. At one level, this was a conflict between advocates of democracy and those in power who resisted change. It was often expressed, however, as a conflict between those who claimed to represent Taiwan and those who claimed to represent China.

When the legislature officially reconvened on January 3, 1991, a scuffle broke out in which KMT senior legislator Chang Hung-hsueh punched DPP legislator Lu Hsiu-yi. Lu responded by throwing a book in Chang's face and splashing him with tea before Lu was subdued by his KMT counterparts.[10] Frank Hsieh, another DPP legislator, demanded the immediate retirement of five mainland deputies born during the Ch'ing dynasty, who were already over ninety years old.[11] Several days later, Hsieh spray-painted a large "#1" on the desk of a senior deputy whom he designated as the first of the lot who should retire.

The senselessness and uncivil nature of legislative politics attracted the attention of domestic and foreign journalists. Each outrageous event was covered with the begrudgingly ghoulish enthusiasm of American sportscasters reporting on ritualistic hockey-rink brawls. After the first volley of punches of 1991, the mass-circulation *Lien-ho pao* (United Daily News) published an editorial acknowledging the flaws in the legal framework that preserved the senior deputies in power, but criticizing the legislators for failing to deal with the deficiencies of the system in a more constructive fashion. "It is a fact that the structure of the Legislature is not reasonable, with aging legislators reluctant to retire yet failing to attend meetings. But as a legislature guided by supplementary [Taiwan-elected] lawmakers, why can't these people work out a set of rules of order and invent different kinds of measures to prevent embarrassing scuffles from occurring?"[12]

The government and many of Taiwan's elite were gravely embarrassed by a January report in *Newsweek* magazine about the combative legislature. In a story entitled "Fighting for Democracy: In Taiwan's Parliament, Chairs and Fists Fly," *Newsweek* reported that Liang Su-yung, former speaker of the Legislative Yuan, repeatedly bore the brunt of his frustrated colleagues' assaults. During 1990, the article reported, Liang's colleagues broke "six of his ribs, squirted him with a watergun, ripped away his podium, and [threw] him from his ceremonial chair." In one incident during December 1990, "police had to escort him through a hail of oranges, wastebaskets, and teacups" hurled at him by angered legislators. The story explained that other representatives also were assaulted and out-and-out brawls were common. Occasionally, police had to be called into the legislative chambers to restore order.

The report concluded by stating that by the end of the year, only twelve bills had been passed, but the legislature had to shell out U.S. $16,000 to replace microphones and furniture. In response, the *China Post* reported that the *Newsweek* article contained a number of inaccuracies. For instance, Liang Su-yung had only been the speaker since 1989, even though he had been elected in 1948. His ribs were never broken, but the former speaker, Liu Cheng-tsai, had ribs broken, as had DPP legislator Lin Cheng-chieh. Also, Liang was never thrown from his ceremonial chair, but the chair itself was hurled away from the podium by DPP legislator Wei Chao-chien.[13]

These physical manifestations of the conflict between the opposition and the KMT legislators have probably attracted more attention than they are worth. To begin with, there was a sense among the political and academic elite that these outbreaks were ploys, not spontaneous expressions of hostility, and came to be seen as part of the fabric of parliamentary proceedings. Still, it caused Taiwan some distress to be singled out by the international news media as the legislative boxing capital of the world.

The secretary-general of the Office of the President, Tsiang Yien-si, wrote about these theatrical acts of violence.

> As our political process becomes more pluralistic and democratic, these conflicts receive encouragement and reenforcement and sometimes dominate our political stage. This gives the impression that our politics is more conflictive than harmonious. When these conflicts become at times violent and law-breaking, people begin to fear that they are detrimental to our more democratic political system. Just imagine, when people see parliamentarians throwing chairs around, tearing down microphones, and even fighting each other, they may say, "If this is democracy, maybe we could do better without it!"[14]

Despite his distaste for the physical conflicts, Tsiang added that he believes that most of those involved "really want to see a more democratic system in the future. Ultimately they would not want to do anything intentionally to harm our hope for democracy."[15]

From the perspective of those in the DPP, the brawls and scuffles were a way to draw attention to the unfairness of allowing aged legislators elected on the mainland to dominate a legislature that governs Taiwan. Regarding the legislators' objections to senior deputies in the National Assembly, Frank Hsieh of the DPP has defended the use of forceful tactics as a mode of protest and has stated that the resistance of the KMT to alter the structure of the Legislative Yuan and National Assembly "insults the people . . . by making obvious the absurd situation of the [two legislative bodies]." According to Hsieh, the DPP hopes that "people throughout the country will be forced to pay closer attention to it and to discuss it. We know, of course, that the current public opinion and media reports have been unfavorable toward us and are likely to cause us to lose people's support."[16]

While the flamboyant displays of hostility continued in the legislative chambers, the "noncombatants" became increasingly disgusted with the trend in Taiwan's political development. Legislator Lin Cheng-chieh, then of the DPP, expressed concern about the dissolution of order in the legislative process and pointed out that the nature of the conflict between the KMT and the opposition threatened the future of democracy. "The common people are fed up with the ugly political struggle in which the two sides are engaged. They are filled with feelings of insecurity. When these feelings become too strong, they can have bad consequences. The common people could prefer a return to the order they had before. If the Legislative Yuan is not equal to the task, everyone will suspect the representational system is no good. They will demand a strongman. We could lose all possibility of experimenting with consultations and democracy. The popularity of Hau Pei-tsun would steadily rise." Lin Cheng-chieh also said "What is actually happening is that both parties are blaming each other. Both are right. The question is, has either of them subjected itself to a self-analysis, asking itself if it is equal to being the ruling party or the party out of power? They can only be persuasive if they have analyzed themselves. Does the ruling party have the capacity to rule as we enter into a democratic period? No, it does not. Does the party out of power have the capability of giving all the people a completely new alternative? No, it does not."[17]

Interviews with other legislators resulted in several humorous comments. When DPP legislator Lu Hsiu-yi was asked why he so often used force in the legislature and was advised that it created a negative impression of him in the public eye, he responded that when the speaker of the Yuan, Liang Su-yung, violated legislative procedures, "I naturally became angry and, as a result, threw a copy of the agenda at him. Nevertheless, I am still a man of propriety. If I threw water at old members or threw objects at them, it was because they refused to retire and because they were still in the Legislative Yuan representing the 'people's will.' As an individual, I certainly do not have hatred for anyone. Several days ago, instead of hitting Lin Tung, I spat on him. This was a symbolic act that showed my humane position."[18] Ting Shou-chung, a young KMT legislator who is a Taiwan-born Mainlander, was asked why he did not partake in the fisticuffs on the floor of the Legislative Yuan. He responded, "It is not that I do not know how to fight. I am qualified in elementary-level Tae Kwon Do. However, as a professor at Taiwan University, engaging in physical violence would only detract from my position."[19]

These tantrums, some feigned, some for real, drew attention to the conviction with which legislators were committed to their point of view. The causes for the outbreaks of violence rarely had to do with substantive policy differences and almost always were incited by conflicts pertaining to national identity. Often, the cause was a procedural slight in which the opposition felt cut out.

As the television-viewing public grew accustomed to seeing its legislators brawling, the power of that technique to draw attention to perceived injustices diminished. Gradually, the frequency of these intramural contests of sincerity also diminished.

The Premier and the Parliament: Hau Dare You!

In 1991, the premier, Hau Pei-tsun, was a central figure in the intermingled conflicts between the KMT and the DPP and between Mainlanders and Taiwanese. The appointment of this powerful Mainlander general was viewed in some circles as a way for Taiwan-born President Lee to substantiate his legitimacy in the eyes of the aging KMT old guard and, in particular, the military. Hau lived up to his reputation for firm, decisive speech and actions. He appeared to be the "bad cop" held in check by KMT moderate "good cops," and his tone often suggested that without restraint he might be inclined to be even more dictatorial. There was also considerable concern about his competition with President Lee over control of the military and of policies pertaining to the pace of reforms.

Taiwanese were, and still seem, reluctant to criticize Lee Teng-hui. One journal explained, "Emotional ties to Lee Teng-hui are a psychological need of Taiwanese who seek self-determination. Therefore, with Lee Teng-hui 'who is in the same camp,' Taiwan's opposition forces have not played the same role as opposition parties in democratic countries. On the contrary, they have gone out of their way to avoid criticizing the KMT chairman."[20] Whereas President Lee is viewed by Taiwanese as one of their own, Hau was fair game for all those disillusioned or angry with the government, with the KMT, and with Mainlanders. Throughout 1991, the premier was the target of scathing barbs from legislators and political cartoonists, but Hau was known to "give as good as he got." Recalling some of his exchanges with members of the opposition in the Legislative Yuan, one gets a palpable sense of the way in which "ethnic" politics came to dominate national affairs and the level to which political discourse sank during some of the fiercest exchanges.

Perhaps the most startling event of the legislative year occurred on the first day of the eighty-seventh legislative session, which began after the Chinese New Year holiday in February 1991. Premier Hau was to deliver his administrative report to the Legislative Yuan. By that time, he had been in office for less than one year and had already been vilified by the opposition as a harsh, arrogant Mainlander. He was seen as more inclined to the militaristic "strongman" politics, away from which the opposition was hoping to move, than to the consultative, democratic system that the KMT claimed an interest in developing. In the days before the premier was scheduled to present his report, legislative leaders began to expect that the opposition might use the occasion of the premier's visit to the legislative chambers as an excuse for some display of hostility.

To preempt the disruptions anticipated from the opposition, the KMT caucus met with the DPP caucus to negotiate an agreement about the premier's visit to the Legislative Yuan. The KMT agreed to announce the names of thirty-five senior KMT deputies and the dates on which they were scheduled to retire in exchange for "safe passage" for the premier's visit. When the seniors failed to retire on the specified dates, the DPP representatives began to wonder what incentive there was to continue negotiating with a KMT that did not keep its promises.

On February 26, the premier arrived at the Legislative Yuan with key members of his cabinet, prepared to present his report. His presentation was originally scheduled for 10:00 A.M. and he had been assured by legislative leaders that he would be able to make his presentation no later than 11:00 A.M. At first, the DPP lawmakers asked for a moment of silence to commemorate the deaths of those killed during the 2–28 Incident. The speaker, Liang Su-yung, acceded to this request, and he, the premier, and the cabinet stood with the legislators in tribute to the victims of an event that had become the focus of the opposition's efforts to shame the KMT for having suppressed the Taiwanese for forty years. This was an act of considerable contrition on the part of the KMT leaders. Joining in the moment of tribute reflected their understanding of the role the 2–28 Incident plays in the memories of the Taiwanese elite and of the tactic of delegitimization-by-shame employed by the opposition.

Owing to its perception that the KMT had failed to live up to its end of the bargain with regard to the retirement of the senior deputies, the DPP legislators felt no compunction about delaying the premier's presentation by filibustering. DPP legislator Wang Tzung-sung contributed to a chaotic air by bringing to the podium a briefcase that contained a gasoline-soaked overcoat, which he attempted to set on fire. He was stopped by one of his KMT colleagues. Another legislator, Wu Yung-hsiung, tossed at the speaker's podium a handful of "spirit money" (fake bills that are commonly burned in large bundles as offerings to the spirit of one's deceased ancestors or to deities) to symbolize his mourning for the senior legislators.

As 11:00 A.M. neared, the premier was photographed checking his watch and looking about impatiently. At 11:00 A.M., while the DPP legislators were engaged in their obstructionist tactics, the premier abruptly stood up, signaled that the other members of the cabinet should follow him, and walked out of the legislative chambers.

One press report stated, "Both the ruling Kuomintang and the opposition DPP lawmakers were stunned and stood open-mouthed, not believing the premier could have just walked away like that."[21] At a hastily convened press conference, the government spokesman, Shaw Yu-ming, said that the premier did not intend that his action be interpreted as an absence of respect for the legislature, but that the premier had no idea when the Legislative Yuan would be ready for his report. Hau felt that because of the recent outbreak of war in the Persian Gulf and the need for him to attend to the launching of the six-year economic development plan, he and the cabinet had a responsibility to serve the nation and could do that better by getting back to work rather than sitting in the chambers waiting for the legislature. Shaw added that the premier had walked out to "uphold the minimal dignity of the cabinet" and that when the legislature was ready, Hau could return within ten minutes to offer his constitutionally required report.[22]

That afternoon, the premier returned to the Legislative Yuan. He apologized for delaying his report, but not for having walked out. He restated his view that he and his cabinet wanted to get on with the nation's six-year development plan rather than wait around in the legislative chambers. At 5:30 P.M., he finally delivered his report.[23] The DPP members severely criticized the premier, saying that Hau had sparked a constitutional and political crisis.[24] DPP member Lu Hsiu-yi claimed that the premier's behavior demonstrated that Hau viewed himself as a "strongman and the Parliament as merely his rubber stamp." In a statement about the matter in a government-sponsored publication, it was reported that Hau's walkout may have "rubbed a few legislators the wrong way" but that, as far as the government was concerned, the whole incident was no more than a "tempest in a teapot." Still, the report continued, "in the interest of unruffling feathers, everyone has agreed to abide by a new rule that any official summoned must get permission from the speaker and all the legislators before being excused."[25] Even members of the KMT Breakfast Club (otherwise known as the Collective Wisdom Association) said that the premier's action showed his contempt for the legislature.[26]

The premier continued to have stormy relations with the opposition lawmakers, reflecting, in part, the tension between mainland rulers and Taiwanese opponents. On March 1, DPP legislator Chen Ting-nan was questioning Premier Hau during an interpolation session about the premier's postponement of a highway project that would have benefited Ilan County, an opposition stronghold. Ilan County had counted on the NT $56.6 billion (U.S. $2,080,000), 30.8 kilometer highway project as an opportunity to develop its tourism industry. The highway would have cut travel time from Taipei to Ilan from two and a half hours to forty minutes.[27]

Originally, the government had agreed to build the highway from Taipei to Ilan because Formosa Plastics Corporation, one of the nation's largest corporations, had planned to build a naphtha cracker plant in the locality. Popular objections in Ilan to the environmental hazards associated with the chemical plant led Formosa Plastics to abandon its plan to build on that site. When it was announced that the project had been postponed, Chen accused the premier of seeking to punish Ilan County for its objections to the naphtha cracker.[28] In its coverage of the postponement, the government-sponsored publication *Free China Journal* reported that Premier Hau "is known as a man of action and few words, but he sometimes moves too fast for his party." Apparently, he "caught KMT lawmakers by surprise" by announcing the postponement of the highway project and was criticized roundly from both sides. "The premier wasn't exactly called on the carpet by KMT officials, but at a March 18 high-level meeting, he promised . . . that he would seek support of KMT legislators in advance of any further policy changes."[29]

The DPP had been given twenty minutes to question the premier, and Chen had forty seconds left on the clock when a KMT legislator, Huang Ho-ching, tried to force Chen to stop talking. To protest this violation of the regulations, all the DPP legislators stormed out of the legislature.[30]

The level of contempt with which the two sides regarded each other was frequently displayed in exchanges of ad hominem attacks. Several weeks after the exchange about the Taipei–Ilan highway, the premier returned to the Legislative Yuan and engaged legislators in a heated debate about independence, emphasizing his view that it is not feasible for Taiwan to declare its independence. In the course of the exchange, DPP representative Yeh Chu-lan questioned the premier about his connections to the PRC in remarks that suggested Hau may have ulterior motives for supporting the KMT's stance on reunification. Yeh alleged that Hau's younger brother, Hau Po-sen, was elevated to high office in Kweichou Province immediately after Hau Pei-tsun was named premier in June 1990.

Some Taiwanese are concerned that Mainlanders like Hau are planning to "sell out" to the PRC in exchange for elevated positions in the government of a reunified China. The revelation about Hau Pei-tsun's brother was seen as lending credence to the suspicion that the KMT and the CCP might be conducting secret negotiations. Hau denied Yeh's allegations, commenting that they were "entertaining, but a case of turning white to black. . . . I have no ties whatsoever to the Communists. . . . [I]t is the advocacy of Taiwan independence and not the unification of China that is a sell-out of Taiwan."[31]

Throughout the exchange, Yeh addressed the premier as "Mr." Hau and refrained from calling him "Premier" Hau. Hau returned the discourtesy in kind, addressing Yeh using the term "Miss" rather than "Legislator." Hau pledged to kowtow (bow three times) if Yeh renounced her demands for independence. DPP legislator Chiu Lien-hui told the premier that if Hau renounced his desire for reunification, he (Chiu) and Yeh would both kowtow.

Chiu then challenged the premier to acknowledge his own "Taiwaneseness" after having lived on Taiwan for forty years. For a Mainlander, particularly a high-ranking officer of the KMT, this is a trick question of sorts. It had been de rigueur for the KMT to insist that all Taiwanese are Chinese, but unheard of to expect Mainlander Chinese to identify themselves with the island of Taiwan. Hau deftly parried the question: "[O]f course I am a Taiwanese compatriot . . . but Taiwanese compatriots have no right to advocate Taiwan's independence from China because Taiwanese compatriots are Chinese. . . . The word compatriot connotes one country. When Taiwanese compatriots go to the mainland they are not going to a foreign country. Since Taiwanese and Chinese are compatriots, Taiwanese compatriots should not advocate independence from China."[32]

Pursuing the issue from another tack, DPP legislator Chen Shui-pian proposed that there be a referendum among voters on Taiwan to settle the identity matter once and for all. Hau objected, saying that, in view of the PRC's policy toward independence, Chen's notion that a referendum would settle the matter was "wishful thinking." Premier Hau declared that "ballots cannot resist the enemy's bullets."[33]

Later that week, the invectives flew even more furiously. Chen Shui-pian likened the premier to Adolf Hitler. Hau Pei-tsun said that among the acts for which Hitler is known is his attempt to set fire to the Reichstaag. Referring to lawmaker Wang Tzung-sung's effort to set the overcoat in his briefcase on fire when Hau appeared before the Legislative Yuan in February, the premier asked rhetorically, "[W]ho tried to set fire to Parliament? Was it me?"[34]

In response to another question by DPP legislator Frank Hsieh, Premier Hau said that he had a "Chinese heart harboring Taiwan feelings." Hsieh inquired whether Hau's "Chinese heart" differed from that of Teng Hsiao-p'ing. Hau responded that his heart embraced both Chinese traditions and Confucian thoughts, but that Teng Hsiao-p'ing's heart gave rise to little other than despotic egocentric behavior.[35]

In an interview some months after he resigned, the former premier offered a reflective but upbeat response to a question about why the opposition had gone beyond criticizing his policies to attack him personally. Hau said that the DPP criticized him because he opposed Taiwan independence. "I firmly oppose Taiwan independence, but I am not opposed to Taiwanese. Moreover, they [the DPP] often confuse my opposition to Taiwan independence with opposition to Taiwanese. There were a lot of false slander and rumors. So, I do not care about all that. I don't bother with them because a lot of them are just slanderous, there's no truth to what they say." Hau spoke with pride about his record as premier. He said that he worked to end the wild speculation on land that drove up real estate prices and caused a tremendous gap between the rich and poor. He fought to crack down on tax evaders, which made a lot of Taiwan's evaders unhappy. "So, I believe that what I did in the Executive Yuan was supported and endorsed by most of the people. I think that this can be seen in the society. Because the period when I was premier was a very unstable, dangerous time, public security was very bad. Several major entrepreneurs were afraid to drive their Mercedes Benz for fear of kidnapping, extortion, and blackmail by gangsters." Hau admitted that there were many points of disagreement between himself and President Lee Teng-hui. Still, he made it clear that he respects the legal system. "I am not the sort who will become a new kind of dictator today." He concluded by saying, "I oppose the Chinese Communists, not China. I oppose Taiwan independence, not Taiwanese. But the Taiwan independence types take this 'opposition to Taiwan independence as opposition to Taiwanese' which is only propaganda. Most of the people understand things more clearly, and will not be taken in."[36]

One reason why Hau was so easy for the opposition to hate is that he was so closely identified with the interests of the Mainlanders and apparently resistant to rapid democratic reform. The most virulent assaults on Hau were not prompted by disagreements about concrete policy options, but rather on the basis of his attitude toward the question of national identity. In that Taiwanese generally, whether in the KMT or in the opposition, tended to endorse the democratization under way during Hau's tenure, and because democracy was viewed as a necessary step toward Taiwan's self-determination, Hau became identified as hostile to democratic reform.

Strikingly Unruly Behavior

The most violent outburst in the legislature during 1991 occurred in April, when DPP legislator Chang Chun-hsiung stood nose to nose at the podium with speaker Liang Su-yung and accused him of being biased, unfair, and "only knowing how to protect the interest of his party." What happened next is not entirely clear. Chang claims he "feigned" a slap across the face of the elderly speaker to shame him.[37] Whether Chang actually made contact or not, speaker Liang hit back, triggering a response from Chang, who then grappled with the speaker. Liang either fell or was knocked to the floor as the two men continued to struggle. Other legislators threw shoes, ashtrays, and microphones torn from their stands toward the speaker as a free-for-all broke out in the legislative chambers.

As Liang and Chang were pulled apart, police were called in to end the fracas. DPP legislator Lu Hsiu-yi tried to break through the phalanx of police, but the police restrained him and dragged him out of the chambers. In the process Lu was kicked and punched, and eventually he passed out. He and another DPP legislator, Tai Cheng-yao, were hospitalized after the altercation.

In the aftermath of the melee, Lu reported to journalists at the hospital that the police "kicked me, grabbed my hair, and punched me in the stomach. While they dragged me out of the chamber, they let my head and body hit the edge of tables and chairs," which caused Lu to lose consciousness. The police said that Lu was probably injured because he continued to struggle as they attempted to restrain him. In addition, eleven police also sustained injuries in the effort to calm the situation.

Legislator Chang Chun-hsiung said that he did not actually slap the speaker; he only "wanted to wake him up. . . . He is too old. I would never have thought to hit him. What I did was to insult him, to make him know that what he did was wrong." The speaker, on the other hand, declared later that "Taiwan's democracy died today." He blamed the mob mentality of the DPP for the demise of democracy. In response to the unruly legislative behavior, the three television networks announced that they would no longer air footage of scenes such as the one that took place that day because they felt it improper to expose young viewers to the violence in the Legislative Yuan.[38]

Chu Chi-ying, director of the Cultural Affairs Division of the KMT and spokesman for the party, spoke about the public reaction to the feisty legislative sessions.

> At first, the audience enjoyed watching. But now they have become tired of it. At first they believed that the DPP had some reason to do it. Now, maybe they have no reason to do it. I think that is a good sign to indicate that finally people realize that the KMT is the force to provide them with democracy and stability.
>
> You know, one day I received a phone call from a housewife. . . . She said, "Mr. Chu, could you make a phone call to the three [television] stations . . . and tell them not to televise fist fights in the Legislative Yuan?" She said, "[T]his morning my husband was leaving the house, and our two children asked their dad, '[W]hat are you going to do today?' . . . [My husband responded,] 'Well, I'm going to attend a meeting.' . . . [The children asked,] 'Are you going to fight?' "
>
> The children believed that to go to a conference . . . means a fistfight. And this young woman was so frustrated, so sad . . . they learned it from T.V. We don't need this kind of social education. I asked her, "[H]ave you called the three television stations?" She said, "[Y]es, I

did." I said, "I can't help you. If I make a phone call to the T.V. stations, they will say, '[T]he KMT wants to control the T.V.' "[39]

The print journalists had also adapted to the increasing frequency of these disruptions and had dubbed certain legislators with nicknames. In addition to Chu Kao-cheng, who was the first to popularize the use of violent tactics in the legislature and was therefore given the name "Rambo," DPP legislator Lu Hsiu-yi was referred to as the "Naughty Old Boy," Speaker Liang Su-yung was called the "Tough Guy," and KMT senior legislator Yang Pao-lin was referred to as "Big Sister," for sitting on the sidelines, scolding the opposition lawmakers, and occasionally tossing paper cups of water at them.[40]

National Assembly: Old Guard Dissembling

In the spring of 1991, there were several episodes of political drama that overlapped in time and symbolic import. Each sequence of events was sparked by a conflict between the KMT and the opposition concerning the extension of democratic reforms into areas that threatened the ruling elite's capacity to dictate how the nation would be defined.

In April 1992, the National Assembly convened to revise the Constitution of the Republic of China. The National Assembly has served as an electoral college of sorts to select the president and amend the constitution.[41] Before that time, in recognition of the need to legitimize the role of the assembly, the KMT had already agreed that the first assembly would retire and a second assembly would be elected in December 1991.[42] A controversy emerged about whether the first National Assembly would have any role in the revision of the constitution.

The opposition favored a one-stage revision process that would take place only after the second National Assembly was elected in December 1991, so that the only people who could vote to amend the constitution would be those elected on Taiwan. The KMT favored a two-stage process that would enable the first National Assembly to meet before its members retired and to exercise its authority by establishing some framework for the revision of the constitution, then permitting the second National Assembly to convene in 1992 to conduct the actual revisions.[43]

Needless to say, when the first National Assembly was convened for the last time in an extraordinary session, the stage was set for a showdown. Eight DPP deputies who had been elected in supplemental elections were expected to take the oath of office before the assembly began. The oath included the words "the Republic of China" and referred to the date in terms of "the eightieth year of the republic." The DPP representatives refused to legitimize the ROC in that way and used "Republic of Taiwan" and "1991." Grand Justice Ma Han-pao judged the oaths as taken to be invalid and, therefore, the eight were initially barred from participating in the assembly.

Seeing that their scheme had backfired and worked to the advantage of the KMT, the DPP representatives agreed to retake the oath so that they could exert some influence during the proceedings of the assembly. When they took the oath a second time, they did so with only the barest adherence to the legal requirements. One wore a headband emblazoned with a statement of protest, one held the DPP flag as he pledged an oath to the ROC, several drew maps of Taiwan on their pledge statement, and some mumbled inaudibly or read the oath in Taiwanese rather than Mandarin.[44] In the end, the eight were permitted to participate despite their derisive attitude.

Fighting first broke out in the assembly when the meeting chairwoman, Yeh Ching-feng, tried to end discussion about the election of a new presidium for the assembly. The DPP wanted the presidium elected anew, not simply carried over from earlier sessions, so that the DPP might be represented on the body that determined guidelines and procedural matters for the assembly. The chairwoman claimed that it was unnecessary to continue discussion because it was too time-consuming. DPP deputies grabbed the microphone to stop the chairwoman from counting votes and this led to the outbreak of a rather nasty fight. One report commented that, "Unlike other fistfights at the legislature, deputies from the two sides dealt solid blows to each other, also pulling hair and grabbing eyeglasses. . . . [S]ounds from the punches could be heard thirty to forty meters away. Opposition deputies took the worst of it, however, as they were vastly outnumbered."[45] The struggle continued throughout the afternoon, but in the end the KMT prevailed and the presidium was not open to reelection.

Fists flew again when DPP assemblywoman Wong Ching-chu addressed the KMT whip, Hsieh Lung-sheng, about the KMT's failure to live up to its agreement to seat the DPP delegates together. Hsieh said that the KMT did not feel any need to live up to its end of the bargain when the DPP did not keep its promise to allow President Lee to address the assembly without interruption. The DPP members had heckled the president when he gave the opening address to the assemblage. Wong shoved Hsieh and Hsieh shoved back. Another DPP assemblyman, Su Chia-chuan, was outraged to see the KMT whip shove the DPP assemblywoman and rushed to defend her. He punched Hsieh in the eye, cutting his eyebrow, drawing blood, and tearing his cornea. Su was also injured in the skirmish, but both later returned, bandaged, to apologize.[46]

Beyond skirmishes stemming from the questions about identity, the most significant controversy that emerged at the National Assembly mirrors that which has stymied the Legislative Yuan, the issue of elderly, mainland-elected representatives. Initially, there had been some agreement between the KMT and the DPP that no substantive changes would be made to the constitution during the 1991 extraordinary session. The session was called to determine the "form" of the constitutional revisions that would be undertaken the following year, after elections were held to replace mainland-elected with Taiwan-elected deputies.

When it became clear to the eight DPP assembly representatives that the KMT had not kept its word and that the National Assembly was indeed undertaking more than had been agreed to, the eight withdrew from the assembly and declared that they would take their protest to the streets. The DPP sponsored rallies, seminars, and a protest march to demonstrate its opposition to the senior assemblymen having a hand in the actual revision of the constitution.[47] Several days later, seventeen DPP legislators in the Legislative Yuan withdrew from that body in sympathy with the eight DPP National Assembly members of their party. DPP members of city councils in Taipei and Kaohsiung and at the Taiwan Provincial Assembly did likewise. The result was that DPP representatives to the most powerful, influential deliberative bodies on Taiwan joined forces and withdrew from their posts in the hope that they might shame the KMT into restricting the influence of mainland-elected delegates to the National Assembly.[48]

On April 16, 1991, the DPP made known its intention to hold a massive demonstration at the Chiang Kai-shek Memorial in downtown Taipei. In preparation, the police cordoned off the streets around the memorial park and the roads to the presidential palace nearby.

That night, President Lee Teng-hui gave a rare, five-minute-long address, which was televised throughout Taiwan. Judging from its re-action, the government seems to have viewed the DPP walkout and the threatened protest as a potential crisis. President Lee assured his audi-ence that the only purpose of the National Assembly was to reform the constitution, but he cautioned "that constitutional reform is not revolu-tion. The right way to pursue democracy is to follow the procedures set by the constitution." He explained that the objective of the current session of the National Assembly was to "add or revise pertinent con-stitutional stipulations having to do with the exercise of emergency presidential powers, the positioning of the National Security Council and the Central Personnel Administration, and the formulation of a legal basis for the election of central-level representatives." As a way to quell anxiety that the current session of the National Assem-bly would complete the job of revising the constitution before it dis-banded, Lee said that there were many important issues that would not be taken up until the convening of the second National Assembly in 1992.

In a statement aimed at reversing any perception that the KMT was insincere about advancing democratic reforms that the opposition takes credit for promoting, the president added

> It is everyone's hope to pursue democracy. But from the experiences of other countries pursuing democracy, we see both successes and failures that brought agony to the public and society. Success or failure de-pends, on one hand, on the sincerity of the government implementing democracy and, on the other, on the public's democratic discipline and its capacity to distinguish truth from falsehood. And a responsible polit-ical party should follow legal procedures in voicing political views to solicit others' approval rather than resorting to rash acts that would betray the voters' trust and impair the nation's fledgling democracy.[49]

On April 17, ten thousand DPP supporters gathered on the campus of Taiwan University in southern Taipei. At 3:30 P.M., despite failing to obtain the legally required permit from the police, they began a march northward toward the Chiang Kai-shek Memorial. The police had erected barbed-wire barricades to keep the marchers away from the memorial, and so they marched further north to the Taipei train station in central Taipei, where they staged a sit-down protest. Then they continued on, heading toward Yangmingshan in the northern part of the city where the National Assembly was meeting. After eight hours, still short of their destination, they made camp. During their march, there were several confrontations with the police, rocks were hurled at the riot squads, and the protestors failed in their effort to march by the home of Madame Chiang Kai-shek, who epitomized for them the Mainlanders' stranglehold on Taiwan's politics.[50]

That night, most of the protesters rested after the first day of their "long march" and prepared for the next day's second phase. Meanwhile, in a style that has come to typify negotiations between the KMT and the opposition, the protesters' leaders met in a downtown hotel with representatives of the KMT.[51] As a result, the DPP agreed to call off the finale—the planned march to the National Assembly meeting site the next day—and the KMT consented to insert a sunset clause into the constitution pertaining to the control of the security agencies. This diminished the absolute authority of the president and institutionalized greater power for the legislature.

KMT secretary-general Soong Chu-yu balked at the suggestion that the KMT had conceded to the DPP. His comments about the agreement suggest either his sincere interest in reform or a bureaucrat's impulse for "spin control." "[T]his is what the ruling party should be doing. It is not a matter of concession or compromise. We ought to be doing this for [a] better outcome. . . . When working out fundamental policy lines, the ruling party should be hearing not just from inside the party, but must take into consideration the non-government parties' views as well."[52] What happened during this sequence of events accords well with what O'Donnell, Schmitter, and Whitehead wrote about as the negotiation of a "transitional pact" between authoritarian rulers and opposition forces. They described the working out of such pacts as a key step in the movement from an authoritarian government to a nonauthoritarian "something else."

A pact can be defined as an explicit, but not always publicly explicated or justified, agreement among a select set of actors which seeks to define (or, better, to redefine) rules governing the exercise of power on the basis of mutual guarantees for the "vital interests" of those entering into it. Such pacts may be of prescribed duration or merely contingent upon ongoing consent. In any case, they are often initially regarded as temporary solutions intended to avoid certain worrisome outcomes and, perhaps, to pave the way for more permanent arrangements for the resolution of conflicts.[53]

President Lee Teng-hui, reflecting on the whole series of events that week, responded in a news conference on April 30 that the DPP walk-out from the National Assembly was "very regrettable," but acknowledged that "there was a reason for the walkout. The reason was the lack of room for maneuvering. There was no environment for them [the DPP representatives to the assembly] to play their role. They could not win by raising their hands, they could not win by making statements, and they were not respected. They walked out because of this feeling."[54] Although the process of negotiation demonstrated that the moderate leaders within both parties understood they had more to gain by compromising than by allowing the extremists in their ranks take control of the process, the appearance that the DPP had backed down in the face of the KMT led to another round of protests. Throughout, the focus of dissent was the role of the senior National Assembly deputies and the seemingly invidious, impenetrable network of control the KMT had cultivated to stay in power. By disbanding the protest march, the DPP had appeared weakened in the eyes of those who viewed the KMT concessions as marginal and ineffectual in the context of a system that had enabled the mainland elite to dominate for so long.[55]

Republic of Taiwan

One of the most telling controversies between the KMT and the DPP concerning matters of identity is the issue of constitutional reform. The constitution became the field on which advocates of reunification and advocates of independence did battle. It has also been the sphere in which the struggle between conservative and reformist forces has been most conspicuous. That constitutional reform is viewed as the way both to advance the interests of democracy and to affirm national identity makes the negotiation of revisions a momentous undertaking.

For extremists in the DPP, the idea of amending the 1946 constitution is wrongheaded. In their eyes, the entire political system the constitution has been used to justify reflects the interests of Mainlanders, with scant regard for the interests of the Taiwanese. They believe it must be replaced, not revised. Consequently, in August 1991, the DPP held a seminar to draft a new constitution so that when the National Assembly convened in 1992, the DPP could propose that the 1946 constitution be scrapped. The political community was stunned when it became known that the first article of the draft constitution bluntly stated what no one had dared to proclaim before. Article 1 read, "Taiwan is a democratic republic of the people, by the people, and for the people whose name is the Republic of Taiwan."[56]

This was the boldest effort yet by the opposition party to place the national identity issue squarely before the voters as an issue for national debate. With the National Assembly elections in December, the DPP was asking voters to make a decision: Do you want the KMT, which will simply modify the 1946 constitution, which upholds the idea of a unified Chinese state? Or do you want the DPP, which will assert in words what has already been true in fact—that Taiwan is independent?

The announcement of the proposed DPP constitution caused quite a furor, both on the island and beyond. Chen Han, the chief prosecutor of the Taipei High Court, appointed a prosecutor to investigate the legality of the DPP's draft. Almost immediately, though, DPP figures began to back down from the draft constitution. One member of the opposition dismissed the draft and indicated that the public should not pay it much attention—that it was more political than legal.[57] Huang Hsin-chieh, who was then DPP chairman, said that the draft was produced by only some of the members of the DPP and was only intended to draw attention to the need for a new constitution. He confessed that he himself found the draft unsatisfactory. Hsu Hsin-liang, who later succeeded Huang as party chairman, announced that he had voted against the draft and admitted that most DPP members realized that the clause would be impossible to implement.[58]

Chu Chi-ying, the director of the KMT Division of Cultural Affairs and party spokesman, denounced the DPP for claiming to speak on behalf of the will of the people when a *Lien-ho pao* (United Daily News) public opinion poll showed that 60 percent of the 1,494 respondents disapproved of the "Republic of Taiwan" clause in the DPP's draft constitution. He also observed that the DPP was wrong to assume that what had recently occurred in Estonia, Latvia, and Lithuania was a model for Taiwan. He noted that the three Baltic states had declared independence from a political system that had repressed its citizens, but that the Republic of China was a democracy.[59]

Premier Hau blasted the DPP and, commenting about the advisability of Taiwan independence, said, "It would be a pity to pull down the Great Wall on the eve of victory."[60] He declared that revising the constitution is preferable to scrapping and rewriting it, because "[a]fter the house is fixed and refurnished . . . it will be more comfortable. . . . If it is torn down, and everyone wants to rebuild it according to his own plan, it will never be built."[61] Clearly, the premier was angry, but not threatened, by the DPP actions. Hau likened the people of Taiwan to crew members on a boat. "Dissenting ideas are allowed, but the captain has the power to decide which course to follow in a stormy sea. . . ." Hau said the captain would never permit an opinion that would put the ship in danger.[62] Hau cautioned against continued tension between the political parties and between Mainlanders and Taiwanese, warning that the constant friction could divide the nation. He advised that regardless of where people were born, those living in Taiwan needed stability and prosperity, and the DPP call for a Republic of Taiwan jeopardized those objectives.[63]

On September 7, 1991, an article in the PRC's *Jen-min Jih-pao* (People's Daily) angrily denounced the DPP's draft constitution.[64] The continued disturbance caused by the DPP draft constitution prompted President Lee Teng-hui to issue a statement in which he declared:

> On October 13, during its fifth national convention, the Democratic Progressive Party neglected the dissuasion of the government and every segment of the society and passed a resolution to include the so-called "Taiwan independence clause" in its party platform. Such [a] reckless and irresponsible move has completely disregarded the security of the nation, the stability of the society, and the well-being of all people, and makes one feel deeply distressed and regret[ful].
>
> I have emphasized over and over: there is only one China. Every bit of our effort is based on the premise of one China, concentrating on the future and development of all people. I sincerely pointed out . . . that the links uniting the Chinese people cannot be broken, and the entire Chinese people share a common destiny. Anyone advocating the split of the nation's territory shall turn into a sinner who will be [destroyed] by the history and culture of China. Any action taken by the means of such advocacy to create social unrest deserves even more to be punished by the law.[65]

The Central Political Party Screening Committee said that the DPP had to alter the clause to omit the portion about independence and notify the Ministry of the Interior by November 12 according to Article 54 of the Law on the Organization of Civic Groups. Yao Chia-wen, a member of the Standing Committee of the DPP Central Committee, claimed that the clause was not formally a part of the constitution, but only a part of the party's platform. "According to the law ... [only] the constitution and ... changes in leadership should be submitted," not items on the party's political platform.[66]

Tsai Li-hsuen, director of the Civil Affairs Department under the Ministry of the Interior, said that the DPP was playing word games by saying that it would submit its constitution but not its platform for official approval. The Central Political Party Screening Committee warned that if the DPP failed to revise and submit its constitution for approval, it might result in the DPP being forced to disband. In Tsai's view, the platform was a supplement to the constitution.[67]

The compromise over the issue of the independence clause was that the DPP would submit it to the Ministry of the Interior—even though it is not required by law to do so.[68] However, the DPP ultimately did not submit the document as expected. After a month of jousting back and forth about whether the DPP would or would not submit its platform, it was determined that the DPP had violated the government's instructions. One report suggested, "[T]he government might delay meting out the punishment until after the elections, to avoid any political crisis. But they also said many radical DPP members hope the government will dissolve their party before the polls, because this would enhance the DPP's image as a political victim."[69] On November 25, the DPP refused to drop its demands for independence, and Chang Chun-hung declared, "The DPP is ready to face any punishment by the Political Party Screening Committee." He claimed that there was no way for the government to evade the Taiwan independence issue. Almost all of the DPP candidates running in the National Assembly elections had a Taiwan independence platform.[70] The issue was left unresolved until after the December elections.

Conclusion

As one recalls the events of 1991 it is evident that although the issue of national identity was not the actual topic of debate or subject of contention, it flowed as a strong undercurrent that affected discussions and arguments about other matters. It is fair to say that the national identity issue was probably more pervasive in central governmental affairs than at the county, city, or local level of politics, but that occasionally—as with the Taipei–Ilan highway—it also affected central–county relations.

Many of the explosive arguments, debates, and conflicts between the KMT and the opposition forces that have surfaced in the years of struggle for democracy have had less to do with the proximate causes of disagreement and can be more easily understood as surrogates for the debate about Taiwan's identity. The divisiveness is not really motivated by uncertainty about Taiwan's current status—all agree that Taiwan is currently an autonomous polity—but rather about its future status.

It seems evident that the controversy about national identity existed before political reform was initiated in 1987, but it has evidently flourished since then. From that perspective, it is both a by-product of reform and a spur to democratization. During the early 1990s, however, it also appeared that the failure of Taiwan's elite to formulate a consensus about national identity was a threat to the continued development of democracy and to the consolidation of democratic reforms that had been achieved.

Notes

1. See Hsiao Hsin-huang, "The Issue of Ethnicity Revisited," *Tzu-you Shih-pao* (Liberty Times), December 12, 1990, p. 4; and Sun Yat-sen Institute of Social Sciences and Philosophy, Academia Sinica, *Tai-wan ti-chu she-hui i-hsiang tiao-ch'a: Pa-shih-nien pa-yueh ting-chi tiao-ch'a pao-kao* (General Survey of Social Attitudes in Taiwan) (Taipei: Sun Yat-Sen Institute of Social Sciences and Philosophy, Academia Sinica, 1992).

2. *Hsin Hsin-wen* (The Journalist), July 23, 1990, p. 24. I am grateful to Lin Wen-chung for calling these surveys to my attention.

3. Marc J. Cohen, *Taiwan at the Crossroads: Human Rights, Political Development and Social Change on the Beautiful Island* (Washington, DC: Asia Resource Center, 1988), p. 329.

4. Julian Baum, "Easing-up Somewhat: The KMT Government Revises Sedition Law," *Far Eastern Economic Review*, May 28, 1992, p. 18.

5. *China Post*, January 5, 1991, p. 1.

6. See Simon Long, *Taiwan: China's Last Frontier* (New York: St. Martin's Press, 1991), p. 186.

7. *China Post*, January 3, 1991, p. 1.

8. *China Post*, January 11, 1991, p. 1.

9. *China Post*, January 7, 1991, p. 1. By December, 464 National Assembly senior deputies had stepped down; each received NT $5.3 million (about U.S. $200,000). *Free China Journal*, December 13, 1991, p. 1.

10. *China Post*, January 4, 1991, p. 1.

11. *China Post*, January 7, 1991, p. 1.

12. *China Post*, January 10, 1991, p. 2.

13. *Newsweek*, January 14, 1991, p. 31; *China Post*, January 12, 1991, p. 1.

14. See appendix 2: Letter from Tsiang Yien-si, July 8, 1991.

15. Ibid.

16. Tsao I-hui and Lin Chia-chun, "Is There Any Other Way Aside from Fighting," *Hsin Hsin-wen* (The Journalist), January 20, 1991, in JPRS-CAR–91–024, April 30, 1991, p. 100.

17. Ibid., pp. 97–101.

18. Ibid.

19. Ibid.

20. See *Chiu-shih Nien-tai* (The Nineties), November 1, 1990, pp. 66–67, in JPRS-CAR–91–002, January 16, 1991, p. 109.

21. *China Post*, February 27, 1991, p. 1.

22. Ibid.; *China Post*, February 28, 1991, p. 1; March 1, 1991, p. 1.

23. *China Post*, February 27, 1991, p. 1.

24. According to the Constitution of the Republic of China, Article 57, section 1, "The Executive Yuan has the duty to present to the Legislative Yuan a statement of its administrative policies and a report on its administration. While the Legislative Yuan is in session, Members of the Legislative Yuan shall have the right to question the President and the Ministers and Chairmen of Commissions of the Executive Yuan." *Republic of China Yearbook, 1990–1991* (Taipei: Kwang Hwa, 1990), p. 714.

25. *Free China Journal*, March 18, 1991, p. 2.

26. *China Post*, February 27, 1991, p. 1. The Breakfast Club is a coalition of Taiwan-elected KMT legislators who share an eagerness for the internal political reform of the KMT.

27. *China Post*, March 4, 1991, p. 1; March 8, 1991, p. 1.

28. Communications Minister Clement Chang had apparently told Ilan County officials that the highway had been canceled because of the county's efforts to block construction of the naphtha cracker. *China Post*, March 4, 1991, p. 1.

29. *Free China Journal*, March 21, 1991, p. 2.

30. *China Post*, March 2, 1991, p. 1. When Hau Pei-tsun appeared before the Legislative Yuan on March 12, DPP representative Chen Shui-pian tossed papers in the face of the premier and asked him how he could "bounce the check" by reversing his decision about the highway to Ilan. *China Post*, March 13, 1991, p. 1.

31. *China Post*, March 23, 1991, p. 1.

32. Ibid.

33. *Free China Journal*, March 28, 1991, p. 1.

34. In another derogatory reference to Hau's similarity to an unsavory foreign dictator, Chen Ting-nan compared Hau to Idi Amin. Hau said he did not mind that Chen had compared him to the despised former Ugandan leader because he was willing to suffer the criticisms of others as long as he himself did what he thought correct. However, Hau said that by comparing him to Idi Amin, Chen implied that the 21 million people of Taiwan were similar to poor and illiterate Africans.

Frank Hsieh chided Hau for his apparently racist remark, saying that the premier ought not equate social development with race. In addition, Hsieh pointed out that most of the states that recognize the ROC are African and, therefore, Hau may have inadvertently damaged Taiwan's relations with its African allies. Hau thanked Hsieh for his comments and gracefully retracted his statement, stating that he was not a racist. The premier added, "ROC founder Dr. Sun Yat-sen's Three Principles of the People states that all people are equal." *China Post*, March 23, 1991, p. 1.

35. *China Post*, March 27, 1991, p. 1.

36. Interview with Hau Pei-tsun, Taipei, August 27, 1993.

37. Liang was born in 1920.

38. *China Post*, April 13, 1991, p. 1.

39. Interview with Chu Chi-ying, Taipei, July 4, 1991. During a visit to Taiwan a month later, former U.S. President Gerald Ford is quoted as having said that the fights in the Legislative Yuan were "healthy" as long as there was an opportunity for everyone to participate in the legislative business of the Yuan. He applauded the efforts of the KMT to democratize, but underscored the importance of preserving the rights of the minority. *China Post*, May 5, 1991, p. 1.

40. *China Post*, July 23, 1991, p. 1.

41. For a description of the history and function of the National Assembly, see *Republic of China Yearbook, 1990–1991*, pp. 110–14.

42. On January 29, 1954, the Council of Grand Justices ruled that those assemblymen "frozen" in office would retire when the second National Assembly was elected. This ruling was amended in June 1990 to require that senior deputies step down by the end of 1991. Since 1969, there have been several supplementary elections to fill vacant seats left after the deaths of original deputies. Fifteen seats were filled in 1969, fifty-three in 1972, seventy-six in 1980, and eighty-four in 1986. *Free China Journal*, December 3, 1991, p. 7.

43. *China Post*, January 31, 1991, p. 1.

44. *China Post*, April 13, 1991, p. 1.

45. *China Post*, April 10, 1991, p. 1.

46. *China Post*, April 13, 1991, p. 4.

47. *China Post*, April 16, 1991, pp. 1, 3.

48. *China Post*, April 17, 1991, p. 1.

49. *Free China Journal*, April 22, 1991, p. 1.

50. *China Post*, April 18, 1991, p. 1.

51. The meeting on the night of April 17 was attended by DPP secretary-general Chang Chun-hung, former party chairman and adviser Yao Chia-wen, DPP Legislative Yuan party whip Cheng Yu-cheng, National Assemblyman Su Chia-chuan, and New Tide faction representative Wu Nai-jen, and their counterparts from the KMT, including KMT secretary-general Soong Chu-yu, his deputy, Alexander Cheng; the KMT social affairs director, Chung Jung-chi; the director of the KMT Cultural Affairs Department, Chu Chi-ying; and the deputy director of the Policy Coordination Council, Hung Yu-chin. *China Post*, April 19, 1991, p. 1.

52. Taipei, China News Agency (CNA) in English, 0743 GMT, April 17, 1991, in FBIS-CHI–91–076, April 19, 1991, p. 55.

53. Guillermo O'Donnell, Philippe Schmitter, and Laurence Whitehead, eds., *Transitions from Authoritarian Rule: Tentative Conclusions about Uncertain Democracies* (Baltimore: Johns Hopkins University Press, 1986), p. 37.

54. Taipei Domestic Service, 0655 GMT, April 30, 1991, in FBIS-CHI–91–086, May 3, 1991, p. 59.

55. Ibid. The National Assembly did amend the constitution but in ways that were only partially objectionable to the opposition. The assembly voted to end the state of war with the PRC by abrogating the Temporary Provisions, which had enabled the president to govern under emergency regulations; the DPP undoubtedly approved of this. New powers were given to the president to substitute for those he lost under the Temporary Provisions, and these were institutionalized as part of the constitution to be activated at times of national crisis; to this the DPP objected. The National Assembly agreed to reduce its own size from 593 to 327 and to reduce the size of the Legislative Yuan from 230 to 161. Finally, it recognized that all the senior deputies in the Legislative Yuan and senior assemblymen in the National Assembly would retire by the end of 1991, something else the DPP could not have found objectionable. The deliberative bodies of the future would be composed of those elected on Taiwan, who would hold two-thirds of the seats; the remaining one-third would be reserved for representatives of overseas Chinese.

The Constitution of the Republic of China provides that a certain number of seats be set aside for representatives of the overseas Chinese community. The relationship of overseas Chinese to the republic is a reflection of Sun Yat-sen's notion that those Chinese living outside of China had been instrumental in funding the Revolution of 1911 and were therefore to be considered part of the political community. According to ROC law, individuals who are born to Chinese parents are considered citizens of the republic regardless of where they actually were born, or where they reside. Dual citizenship is permissible. See *Free China Journal*, April 4, 1991, p. 4.

56. *Tzu-li Wan-pao* (Independence Evening Post), August 28, 1991, in JPRS-CAR–91–060, October 30, 1991, p. 60.

57. *China Post*, August 27, 1991, p. 1.

58. *China Post*, August 29, 1991, p. 4.

59. *China Post*, September 5, 1991, p. 1.

60. *China Post*, December 18, 1991, p. 1.

61. *China Post*, August 30, 1991, p. 1.

62. *Free China Journal*, October 25, 1991, p. 1.

63. *Free China Journal*, September 27, 1991, p. 1.

64. In the following weeks, the Taiwan stock market dropped 5.57 percent, the greatest fall in three months. The NT dollar, which had been rising in value against the U.S. dollar, also dropped. *China Post*, October 15, 1991, p. 3.

65. *Free China Journal*, October 18, 1991, p. 1.

66. *China Post*, November 7, 1991, p. 1.

67. *China Post*, November 8, 1991, p. 1.

68. *China Post*, November 11, 1991, p. 1.

69. *China Post*, November 21, 1991, p. 4.

70. *China Post*, November 26, 1991, p. 1.

7

The Politics of Elections

The quest for democratization and the controversy about national identity have intermingled most prominently in the occasional, but increasingly frequent, elections. Indeed, one could say that the 1991 elections for the National Assembly and the 1992 elections for the Legislative Yuan were essentially about the question of national identity. By examining the lead-up to and outcome of these two elections, one can appreciate more fully how democratization has been affected by the underlying tension about national identity, even when that is not always made explicit.

Well before the Mainlanders arrived on Taiwan, Taiwanese who lived under Japanese rule were given limited experience with local elections and "home rule," although Japan's administration of the island was certainly not democratic.[1] This experience and the unsuccessful struggle for self-determination that occurred during the period of Japanese occupation helped to shape the political culture of Taiwan. By the time the KMT assumed control of Taiwan, the political experiences of the Taiwanese were already considerably different from those of their Mainlander cousins.

K'ang Ning-hsiang pointed out that the electoral system that was in place for local elections on Taiwan when the KMT arrived did not exist elsewhere in China. Now that there is a certain amount of international attention on Taiwan, he said, the KMT is taking credit for having successfully engineered the political development of the island, but K'ang feels that it is the Taiwanese, not the Mainlanders, who deserve the credit for this, since the practice of holding elections and the expectation that they be held predate the Mainlanders' arrival on Taiwan.[2]

Indeed, the system the KMT brought to the island led to tension, repression, and confrontation between Mainlanders and Taiwanese.

The style of politicking that came into practice on Taiwan featured high levels of mass participation but severely limited contestation, with centrally controlled constraints and widespread social practices diminishing the significance of participation.

During the first four decades, elections were held for certain local offices and for the Taiwan Provincial Assembly, but none of the offices subject to election had significant political power. Real power remained in the hands of the KMT and the central organs of the government, for which competition was restricted. Even in those elections where competition was possible, the KMT was exceptionally well organized for getting out the vote and was quite adept at cultivating the loyalty of supporters by the judicious distribution of tangible benefits. This superior organization has become the hallmark of KMT rule. Although the ruling party has opened more contests to popular participation since it came to the island, its own performance at the polls has remained good.

If one believes that the success of the KMT is ideological, then one must accept that voters choose candidates on the basis of party affiliation or political views. It seems that this is not generally the case. In fact, the KMT's greatest asset is its superb organizational skills and resources, a residue of the more "Leninist" phase of its early command of the island. This rigid control has been manifested in the operation of a gargantuan political machine that reaches down into every residential alley and lane to ensure popular support for the government's candidates. Prior to the onset of liberalization in the mid-1980s, one observer found that "[o]rders are sent out to every KMT member, and word is passed to sympathizers on how they should vote in each election. . . . Among the sympathizers, mainland-born soldiers, their families and the civilian Mainlanders count heavily. The KMT may also be able to deliver the votes of soldiers stationed in a given area, making the political officers responsible for the soldiers voting as the KMT desires."[3] The effectiveness of the KMT machine was enhanced by factors that have remained active ingredients of Taiwan's political life: the susceptibility of the voter to suggestion from local party officials about whom to vote for and the skillful pressure applied by the party to buy votes. Regardless of how one differentiates between mobilization and intimidation, the high levels of voter participation in elections prior to liberalization should not be mistaken for a high quality of contestation. The KMT manipulated with great skill the voting public by designating which candidates were to be supported by which neighborhoods. Under a single-vote, multimember system derived from the Japanese, a candidate needs only to collect enough votes in a specified district to pass over a certain threshold to be elected.[4] The KMT has successfully assigned candidates to districts and apportioned votes for each candidate in such a manner that its candidates receive just enough votes to win, but not so many that they sap strength from others who need to accumulate enough to get over the threshold, too. Since the onset of reforms in the mid-1980s, the KMT's capacity to regulate elections has diminished. Much of the old system remains in practice, but elections have become increasingly competitive; the inclination to manipulate the outcome, however, has been slow to die.

Huntington observed that during the "third wave" of democratization it was fairly common for authoritarian regimes to hold elections and, usually, they lost them. "The confidence of authoritarian rulers that they could win the elections they sponsored was undoubtedly further bolstered by the extent to which they felt they could manipulate electoral procedures."[5] In the case of Taiwan, the KMT held elections after liberalization began. Technically speaking, it won all of them, in that it maintained a majority. In real terms, however, its capacity to command the process to ensure a certain level of representation did diminish.

Elections for National Assembly

For much of 1991, political activity on Taiwan focused on the National Assembly elections, which were held in December. Recognizing the extraordinary power of the National Assembly to determine the course of political development by revising the constitution, the KMT was determined to exercise renewed vigilance to ensure that the new assembly would be dominated by the KMT. It is not surprising that the import of even the smallest procedural controversy pertaining to the rules for the elections was exaggerated by the knowledge that the newly elected assembly would exert immense influence on policies defining national identity.

In one sense, controversies between the KMT and the opposition parties about how the December 1991 elections should be held were simply a manifestation of difficulties that emerge during transitions from authoritarian rule. Despite its efforts to liberalize the political system on Taiwan, the KMT was still controlled at the center by a handful of Mainlanders and their Taiwan-born scions, who were regarded as having ambitions regarding reunification that set them apart from the bulk of Taiwan's population. To prevail, the KMT had three distinct options. It had to persuade people that its message was preferable to that of others; it had to apply pressures on those who were susceptible to withdraw their support; or it had to overpower contenders with superior organization. In an electoral system where ideas seem not to be the sole—or even the primary—grounds on which people cast votes, it stands to reason that the KMT depended heavily on its exceptional organizational capacity to retain political power.[6]

All but 64 members of the first National Assembly were to retire at the end of 1991, and the December contest was to replace them with 225 elected deputies and an additional 100 deputies appointed by the political parties to fill at-large seats and to represent the overseas Chinese community.[7] In the course of the year, there were four major controversies concerning the regulations for the elections:

- whether people would vote for candidates only, or would be allowed to vote for a candidate and a political party;
- whether soldiers would be permitted to vote by absentee ballot from their barracks;
- how many electoral districts there would be and how they would be drawn; and
- whether the explicit promotion of Taiwan independence would be permitted in campaign literature and party propaganda.

One Ballot or Two?

There were two major proposals about how the elections should take place. Under one proposal, voters in each electoral district would simply select a candidate to represent their district at the National Assembly. The at-large assembly seats and those for overseas Chinese would be apportioned to political parties whose candidates had been elected. Prior to the election, each party fielding candidates would register a ranked list of candidates it designated to fill any at-large seats it gained. Once it was determined what percentage of the seats went to candidates from a given party, that party would receive control of the same percentage of the at-large and overseas Chinese seats to fill from its list of predesignated nominees. This was the one-ballot system favored by the KMT and the one ultimately used to determine the composition of the second National Assembly.

The two-ballot proposal, advanced by the DPP, would have asked each voter to select not only a candidate but also a political party. In that way, a voter would cast a first ballot to elect a candidate and a second ballot to register support for a political party. The at-large and overseas Chinese seats would then be distributed on the basis of the results of the second ballot. From the perspective of the DPP, the rationale for this proposal was to enable voters who were unwilling to resist the pressure to vote for the KMT candidate to cast a first ballot for that candidate but support the opposition by casting a second ballot, say, for the DPP. In this way, even though the KMT would retain a majority of the National Assembly seats, the presence of a larger opposition minority would more effectively keep the KMT in check.

Absentee Ballots for Soldiers?

Another source of contention was a plan to allow soldiers to vote by absentee ballot. The standing rules are that an individual is eligible to vote only in the place where the person has been registered as a resident for more than six months. Soldiers are generally not registered at their camps, nor are university students generally registered at the place where they attend school. With an election holiday that lasts only one day, it is not possible for most soldiers and students to get from their camp or campus to their home district. This effectively deprives both groups of the right to vote.

Premier Hau supported a proposal that soldiers and students be allowed to cast absentee ballots from polling sites near their barracks or campuses. This was depicted as an effort to extend the franchise to soldiers and students. The DPP objected to this stratagem, however, fearing that the soldiers would be too easily monitored by their superior officers and that the potential for abuse—forcing soldiers to vote for particular KMT candidates—was too high.[8] The various proposals were batted about for several months, but on June 5 the Central Election Committee announced both that it would use the one-ballot system— the system favored by the KMT—and that the proposal to allow students and soldiers to vote away from home would not be implemented—a concession to the opposition.[9]

Election Districts

The dispute over elections began when the Central Election Committee announced more and smaller districts than had previously been assigned. It was assumed that the KMT wanted to increase the number of electoral districts in regions that were known to be opposition strongholds, because smaller districts made it easier for the KMT to operate its political machine, to mobilize voters, and to exert influence by buying votes. The DPP opposed increasing the number of election districts because it would have had to field more candidates than it felt it could and it would have needed to disperse scarce resources.

When the redistricting was announced, the magistrates (county executive officers) in six counties said they would refuse to allow elections in their counties as a protest against what they viewed as the ruling party's abuse of authority.[10] The dispute continued for several weeks until July 3, 1991, when the Legislative Yuan passed the revisions to the Election and Recall Law with no objections; the DPP lawmakers had absented themselves from the legislature.[11]

On July 9, 1991, three hundred opposition activists protested the Central Election Committee's plan to divide the electoral districts. The protesters threw three thousand eggs at the building in which Wu Pohhsiung, head of the Central Election Committee, worked as minister of the interior.[12] After wrangling about the provisions in the revised election law, it was announced that the KMT had accepted a DPP counterproposal to the one-ballot system. The eighty at-large and twenty overseas Chinese seats were to be distributed according to the number of votes gained by each party, rather than according to the percentage of elected candidates associated with each party.[13] The next day, the KMT went back to its original plan to distribute at-large and overseas Chinese seats according to the percentage of candidates elected under each party's banner.[14]

Campaign Literature and Television Advertisements

The 1991 elections were the first in which it was possible to broadcast campaign advertisements on television. As a rule, election campaigns are limited to a period of about ten days. During that period, Taiwan is transformed into a carnival of electioneering. Rallies are held in public parks, poster-bedecked sound trucks blaring candidates' entreaties to voters cruise the streets, buildings are festooned with gigantic campaign banners, and lively events are staged to increase candidates' name-recognition.

In past years, access to the airwaves had been restricted to news reports that favored the KMT. In 1991, for the first time, the government permitted all parties that met a minimal requirement to broadcast campaign advertisements on television. The formula devised by the Central Election Committee was complex and favored the KMT. Considering that the three legal television stations are national, in the sense that broadcasts are received across the entire island and there is no local programming, it was determined that campaign advertisements for particular candidates would be senseless. Also, the total amount of time available for campaign advertisements was tightly regulated.

Time was designated for each qualified party to promote itself, not to promote individuals. Six hundred candidates were registered for the election. Four parties—the KMT, the DPP, the Chinese Social Democratic party (CSDP), and the Non-Party Democratic Independent Alliance (NPDIA)—all qualified for time on television because they nominated ten or more candidates. The air time available for campaigning was divided among the qualifying parties on the basis of the number of candidates each party nominated. In addition, a "deposit" was required from each party calculated on the basis of the number of its candidates. The money was only returned to parties that were unable to win seats for at least one-tenth of their nominees.[15]

In the end, a total of 270 minutes of airtime was used. Each party was required to produce a videotaped advertisement and submit it for review by the Central Election Committee on December 3, eight days before the start of the campaign. It was made clear that the committee would not approve tapes advocating Taiwan's independence.[16] Huan Yueh-chin, chief of the political platforms review committee, stated that "[i]dentification with the nation should be the base line for the screening of the video messages." On December 5, the Central Election Committee anounced that all four qualified parties' tapes were rejected, and the tapes were returned with instructions that they be edited and resubmitted.

The KMT produced eight videos ranging in length from nine seconds to thirty minutes, but was told to revise those portions that described the other parties as disorganized and without goals.[17] The

KMT emphasized its role in dragging Taiwan up from its backward, agrarian past to enjoy the fruits of an "economic miracle." The dominant theme in the videos was "reform, stability, prosperity," the three objectives the KMT claimed it alone could provide. The protective and nurturing role of the KMT was illustrated with the image of a naked, infant boy lying on the rich blue expanse of the KMT party flag. It underscored that over the past four decades, the KMT leadership helped Taiwan to weather many storms and led the island's growth from economic, social, and political infancy to maturity.[18]

Part of the narrative described the KMT as "an experienced, responsible political party with enough flexibility for reforms." It promoted the idea that the ruling party should be viewed as "a faithful old friend." These concepts aimed at undermining the DPP, which had come to be seen as irresponsible, inexperienced, and untried.[19]

A "negative advertisement" mentality crept into some of the KMT's videos. One report stated "Viewers see the TV screen filled with dramatic scenes of suffering, civil war and chaos in developing countries such as Haiti, Yugoslavia, Sri Lanka, the Philippines, and Vietnam. The videos play vividly upon these emotional images as a way to attest to the stability maintained in Taiwan under the KMT's rule."[20] The message was clear: a vote for the KMT was a vote for "reform, stability, [and] prosperity," but a vote for the DPP was a vote for independence and chaos.

This theme, to which the KMT frequently drew attention, was strenuously opposed by the DPP. Hsu Hsin-liang was quoted as saying, "Under the high-handed control of the KMT, Taiwan society has been held in bondage, politically, socially, and culturally." He urged that the island free itself from such constraints. Taiwan's achievements resulted from the hard work of the people of Taiwan, he said, not the wisdom of the KMT leadership.[21]

The four DPP tapes were produced by award-winning film directors and were rejected at first because of passages advancing independence as a goal of the party. The passages were edited out. The DPP was advised to fill the gaps with something less objectionable, but the DPP initially said it would be just as happy for the Central Election Committee to leave those segments of the tapes blank, because that would reveal the absurdity of the KMT's policy.[22] In the end, the subtitles promoting independence were replaced with a message asking for financial contributions.

Two prominent themes were played up in the campaign videos. Drawing back from an outright call for independence, the DPP videos opposed the notion of reunifying Taiwan with the rest of China. They also promoted the idea that the president should be elected by popular vote. To tarnish the KMT's claim of providing stability, one scene hinted at Taiwan's authoritarian past. It showed "chickens living in cages juxtaposed with chickens allowed to run free. 'Stability is more than living in affluence,' the narrator tells the Taiwan TV audience, 'man needs freedom and dignity besides stability and prosperity.' " Chang Chun-tung, a DPP candidate and professor at National Taiwan University, addressed the audience to warn of disaster that comes with prosperity. He asserts that "prosperity has focused mainly on material construction and brought forth environmental pollution and social injustice."[23]

To promote the idea that citizens on Taiwan should have the right to elect their president directly, the DPP video displayed pictures of Chinese rulers from the past and suggested to viewers that "there have been some 330 kings, emperors, or presidents in Chinese history and none of them were directly elected by the people." Voting for the DPP, which promotes direct presidential elections, the video said, "offers the people the opportunity to be the real master of Taiwan."[24]

One recurrent image in the DPP videos countered the tender sight of the KMT baby-on-the-flag and demonstrated that the DPP was also capable of using an "attack-video" strategy. The video showed "mass produced, identical dolls on a factory conveyor belt. Those that look slightly different are picked out in the scene, smashed, and thrown into a fire. The opposition party uses the scene to try [to] urge the Taiwan electorate to 'have independent thought [to make] an independent choice.' "[25]

In addition to these party-produced videos, candidates were also expected to submit written campaign platforms for publication in bulletins produced by the election committee in each county. The Central Election Committee made clear that platforms recommending that Taiwan be independent would not be published. It was reported that Hsu Kuei-lin, secretary-general of the Central Election Committee, instructed that "except for platforms which carry statements strongly and clearly promoting Taiwan independence, a new Taiwan state, or the abolition of the ROC Constitution, all will be tolerated."[26] When candidates submitted platforms that violated the committee's injunction, the biographical data concerning the candidate was allowed to be published, but the offending platform was expected to be omitted, leaving blank spaces where texts that advanced independence would have appeared.

Although the Central Election Committee banned candidates from advocating Taiwan independence, opposition-controlled local governments permitted it. Local governments formed committees to screen the platforms of candidates within their districts. The opposition-controlled committees of Kaohsiung County, Taipei, Ilan, Pingtung, and Changhua adopted similar policies.[27] On November 22, Chen Han, chief of the High Court Prosecutor's Office, said that those county officials who refused to censor the illegal platforms would be considered accomplices of candidates. In response, opposition leaders of local election committees said they would resign if they were forced to censor election platforms.[28] On December 12, the day after the start of the campaign, the heads of six county election committees resigned to protest government demands that platforms be censored.[29]

KMT campaign literature emphasized the success of political reforms, the importance of domestic stability, and the widespread prosperity that the KMT had "created." Some literature attacked the independence movement and the violence associated with the opposition. Some publications, playing on the sentimental attachment of Taiwanese to their Taiwanese president, featured the slogan "To support President Lee Teng-hui, please vote for the KMT."

Formally, the elections were for one purpose only: to select delegates to the second National Assembly, who would be responsible for carrying the democratization of Taiwan to its next phase by institutionalizing changes in the form of constitutional revisions. However, despite official attempts to keep the focus of the election on the constitutional revisions that would promote democratization, it was widely understood that "the election is not just a contest between the KMT and the DPP, but a contest between the ROC Constitution and the 'Republic of Taiwan' Constitution." In short, the KMT had turned it into a no-confidence vote on the political status of Taiwan and the issue of national identity.

Chu Hsin-min, a KMT candidate, said that without resolution of the national identity issue "there is no point for us to discuss constitutional amendments." In his view, those who promoted Taiwan independence had turned the NT dollar into "worthless toilet paper."[30] Indeed, the independence issue loomed large over the election campaign. One foreign observer wrote, "Ten years ago, you could only whisper about *T'ai-tu* [Taiwan independence]. . . . A year ago, if you talked about it, you could get arrested. Now they've got campaign trucks, with flags saying 'Republic of Taiwan,' blaring independence. It's amazing."[31]

Election Results

In the end, the KMT won 179 of the total 225 seats, which represented 71 percent of the 8.93 million votes cast.[32] This entitled the party to appoint sixty of the eighty available delegate-at-large seats and fifteen of the twenty seats reserved for overseas Chinese. The DPP won forty seats in the electoral contest, which entitled it to twenty of the delegate-at-large seats and five of the seats for overseas Chinese. The CSDP and the NPDIA captured the remaining four seats, too few to entitle them to any of the at-large or overseas Chinese seats.[33]

These results ended up giving the KMT a commanding lead and clear control of the National Assembly, where a constitutional amendment required three-fourths of the votes. In addition to the 179 seats won outright and the eighty seats picked up out of those reserved for winning parties, the KMT retained sixty-four members from the first National Assembly—delegates who had been selected in supplementary elections in earlier years.

The DPP had succeeded in sharpening the focus of the election on the matter of national identity by equating constitutional revision with the status quo and a new constitution with a new country. By upping the ante on the election, the DPP was not merely competing for seats at the table but asking the electorate to pass judgment on the DPP's vision of Taiwan.

All along, the DPP had stressed its pro-independence platform, but as the campaign neared its conclusion, the opposition shifted to more moderate calls of simply opposing reunification. Reports said, "The adamant secessionist calls have apparently scared away voters who are likely to reject extremist political stances."[34]

The DPP failed in its effort to attract the electorate to the idea of a new constitution and a new country. The failure to wrest a greater number of seats from the ruling party suggested to the opposition the need to reevaluate the approach it took during the campaign. In particular, the DPP needed to determine whether it failed for doing too few of the right things or too many of the wrong things.

In the aftermath of the December elections several key members of the DPP indicated that the "era of fistfights" would end. The ostensible justification for the fist fighting was the continued tenure in office of the senior legislators and assemblymen of the Legislative Yuan and National Assembly. The seniors were cajoled and bought off into retirement at the end of December, so the major irritant was removed. As DPP representative Frank Hsieh said, "it [was] time to end the fistfight era in the Parliament and enter the age of verbal debate and persuasion."[35]

From the vantage of the KMT, its victory in December 1991 offered a renewed mandate to carry on with its twin programs of democratization and national reunification. The KMT soundly beat the various opposition forces arrayed against it and retained its commanding presence in the National Assembly.

Beyond the immediate results of the election, there is also terrific symbolic significance. All the deputies elected on the mainland were replaced. While it may still be possible for the KMT to claim that the National Assembly represents all China, not merely the island province of Taiwan, in fact that claim has become utterly transparent. Nevertheless, Lee Teng-hui struck a characteristically conciliatory note, saying, "Revision [of] the constitution concerns the development of the nation and the fortune of all people. We must listen with the greatest sincerity to all opinions. . . . No ambitions of a single party of individuals are allowed" to interfere with the reform.[36]

Elections for the Legislative Yuan

The following year, in December 1992, Taiwan elected a new Legislative Yuan. The last time the entire legislature had been elected was 1947. Since that time, there had been several supplementary elections, as there had been for the National Assembly, but 1992 was the first time since 1947 that all the seats in the legislature were contested. The election was also remarkable in that it revealed very deep divisions within the KMT that pitted Mainlanders against Taiwanese.

The election campaign developed into something of a test of popular sentiment regarding Taiwan's relationship to the PRC. The DPP had stepped back from the virulence of the independence platform it had advanced the year before. Rather than emphasize the desirability of declaring independence, it maintained its focus on the disincentives for reunification. While the KMT leadership promoted the notion of one China, the DPP advocated a formula of one Taiwan and one China —in essence, two states. Within the KMT, however, there were some Taiwanese representatives associated with the Wisdom Coalition who also adopted a two-state platform. In that way, for the first time, a significant fissure within the ranks of the KMT reflecting a division between Taiwanese and Mainlanders appeared in the national spotlight.

The "China KMT," or "old K," composed of veteran officials representing the interests of the Mainlanders, promoted the idea of one China. Some representatives of the mainstream "Taiwan KMT" faction —especially members of the Wisdom Coalition—challenged the idea of one China. As part of their platform, they advocated recognition of both Taipei and Peking in the UN and the direct popular election of the president on Taiwan. Many of these candidates ultimately ran without official endorsement from the KMT.

To receive a party endorsement and be listed by the KMT as an official candidate, an individual had to be placed on the ticket by KMT Secretary-General Soong Chu-yu. This was seen by participants and observers as the "last chance for many second generation Mainlanders . . . to stake out a place for themselves in local politics."[37]

Nevertheless, the process of forming the ticket proved to be exceedingly complicated. For one thing, there were many more people seeking to be placed on the ticket than the party could select. Of the total 161 seats to be filled, only 125 seats were to be selected at the ballot box. Another thirty-six were apportioned to the parties according to a formula that was based on the total number of candidates associated with the party ticket who were elected. Ultimately, 403 candidates stood for election.[38]

The campaign was noteworthy for the great number of wealthy tycoons who plied a crude breed of money politics in an effort to take national political power on behalf of family factions rather than as genuine representatives of the party. In the end, forty-six candidates ran under the KMT banner without approval from the party.[39] This contributed to a breakdown in the theretofore meticulous party strategy for electioneering. This breakdown was exacerbated by Taiwanese candidates within the KMT who evidently tried "to exploit ethnic resentments in their own races against their ruling party colleagues. Some liberal KMT candidates quietly told supporters that 'Taiwanese should vote for Taiwanese.' "[40]

The conflict about national identity affected the campaign in another manner. Two weeks prior to the election, the KMT expelled legislator Chen Je-nan of Kaohsiung for supporting the DPP's notion of one Taiwan, one China. The expulsion of an incumbent KMT lawmaker so close to a national election "underscored the erosion of consensus on a bedrock principle of the KMT, " that there is one China.[41]

One well-known pollster, Ting Ting-yu, said that the mood on Taiwan preceding the 1992 elections was much different than the preelection mood a year before. Ting said that the DPP was not talking as openly about independence, and the populace did not seem to think it likely that the DPP would do well enough to become the majority in the legislature. Ting predicted accurately that this condition would contribute to a popular willingness to vote against the KMT as an antigovernment protest.[42]

In the end, the KMT performed much worse than it had hoped and the DPP much better than it had expected. While the KMT still retained control of the 161-seat legislature, it took only 103 seats and 53 percent of the popular vote—the lowest level ever.[43] The DPP, by contrast, won 50 seats and 31.9 percent of the popular vote, which was more than it ever had.[44] Voters tended to shun those candidates who were clearly linked to big business or had been involved in financial scandals, "and a large proportion of voters who accepted money, gifts, or banquet invitations apparently cast their votes independently."[45]

One effect of this was that the Wisdom Coalition, comprised of moderate Taiwanese who were supportive of Lee Teng-hui, was decimated. Ten of the thirty candidates affiliated with this bloc lost their bid for reelection. In the main, these candidates had also been associated with big spending, factionalism, and vote buying. By contrast, the conservative, pro-unification wing allied with Hau Pei-tsun did very well. Of the twelve seats where such candidates were vying for election, eleven were filled by individuals who belonged to the New KMT Alliance, sympathetic to Hau.[46]

Overall, Mainlanders showed up in force for this election, indicating that they understood the significance of holding on to as many seats as possible. While they represent only about 15 percent of the population, more than 20 percent of those who voted on December 19 were Mainlanders. Forty percent of those who voted for KMT candidates were Mainlanders. Still, only 22 percent of the new legislators are Mainlanders, whereas 60 percent of the former legislature was.[47] All of this means that even though there were more Taiwanese voters than Mainlanders supporting KMT candidates, in the end, a majority of the KMT's seats were filled by Taiwanese.

The DPP did far better than even its promoters had expected, winning 51 seats in the new legislature. Although the DPP had been bruised badly in years past by rumors that the radical New Tide faction and the more moderate Formosa faction would split the party, the opposition party managed to overcome its internal differences. Hsu Hsin-liang said, "[W]e see this as a united DPP winning against a split KMT."[48] The DPP had also learned a lot from its experience in 1991 when it championed the independence issue more forcefully than voters seemed willing to support.

Chiu I-jen offered several explanations for the success of the DPP. He said that the DPP learned a lot about campaigning techniques from the 1991 experience and, therefore, changed its strategy—but not its position—in 1992. Chiu also acknowledged that the power struggle in the KMT and the large number of people opposing the money politics of the KMT—even if they were not adamant supporters of the DPP platform—also contributed to the success of the opposition. Finally, he said, there were a lot of very popular vote getters running on the DPP ticket.[49]

In the wake of the 1992 election, Lee Teng-hui directed a major shake-up of the KMT leadership and of cabinet positions. The most stunning shift occurred when Lee appointed former governor of Taiwan Lien Chan to succeed Hau Pei-tsun as premier when Hau resigned after the election. Soong Chu-yu, who resigned his post as secretary-general of the KMT as a way to accept responsibility for the KMT's poor performance, was given the post of governor. So, in an ironic twist, after an election in which the Mainlanders within the KMT did better than expected and the Taiwanese loyal to Lee did poorly, Soong —a Mainlander who was born in Hunan—was made governor of Taiwan, Lien—a Taiwanese who was actually born in Shensi—became premier, and Hau—a Mainlander from Kiangsu—was edged out entirely. One commentator observed that "Hau's removal shows that the president is achieving his goal of eliminating powerful Mainlanders from key posts and reforming the structure of power" within the KMT.[50]

Voters may have made choices on the basis of issues other than national identity and the reunification/independence (*t'ung-tu*) debate, but for many voters questions of identity figured prominently in their choice at the ballot box. As Taiwan's political system matures, it may be that other matters come to the fore, as well they should. During this early phase of political liberalization and democratization, however, the citizenry and the government are engaged in the awful task of reconfiguring the system by which the polity will be governed. Thus far they have done it with relative success and in comparative stability. Yet it is easy to understand that in such an elemental process as this the question of national identity affects the choices people make about who will represent them.

Notes

1. See George H. Kerr, *Formosa: Licensed Revolution and the Home Rule Movement, 1895–1945* (Honolulu: University of Hawaii Press, 1974), especially chapter 10.
2. Interview with K'ang Ning-hsiang, Taipei, July 1, 1991.
3. Arthur J. Lerman, *Taiwan's Politics: The Provincial Assemblyman's World* (Washington, DC: University Press of America, 1978), p. 32. See also Tang Mei-chuan, *Urban Chinese Families* (Taipei: National Taiwan University Press, 1978), pp. 35–41.
4. Andrew Nathan, "The Legislative Yuan Elections in Taiwan: Consequences of the Electoral System," *Asian Survey*, vol. 33, no. 4 (April 1993), p. 425.
5. Samuel P. Huntington, *The Third Wave: Democratization in the Late Twentieth Century* (Norman: University of Oklahoma Press, 1991), p. 182.
6. Donald Share and Scott Mainwaring, "Transitions Through Transaction: Democratization in Brazil and Spain," in *Political Liberalization in Brazil: Dynamics, Dilemmas, and Future Prospects*, ed. Wayne A. Selcher (Boulder, CO: Westview Press, 1986), p. 181.
7. The sixty-four holdovers from the first National Assembly are those who had been elected in supplemental elections on Taiwan since 1949.
8. *China Post*, May 20, 1991, p. 1.
9. *China Post*, June 6, 1991, p. 1.
10. *China Post*, June 24, 1991, p. 4.
11. *China Post*, July 4, 1991, p. 1.
12. *China Post*, July 10, 1991, p. 1.
13. *China Post*, July 12, 1991, p. 1.
14. *China Post*, July 13, 1991, p. 1.
15. The original formula is detailed in the following table:

Number of Candidates	Airtime	Deposit
15–50	5 minutes	NT $200,000 (U.S. $7,400)
51–100	10 minutes	NT $400,000 (U.S. $14,800)
More than 100	15 minutes	NT $600,000 (U.S. $22,200)

Source: Free China Journal, August 30, 1991, p.2.

This proposal was later amended so that a deposit of NT $20,000 (U.S. $740) was required for each candidate who appeared on camera. See Free China Journal, September 20, 1991, p. 2.

Ultimately, there were 471 candidates registered for election in fifty-eight districts. There were 270 minutes of airtime, divided as follows:

Party	Number of Candidates	Television Airtime
KMT	215	149 minutes, 12 seconds
DPP	94	65 minutes, 15 seconds
CSDP	45	31 minutes, 15 seconds
NPDIA	35	24 minutes, 18 seconds

Source: Free China Journal, November 11, 1991, p. 1.

16. *Free China Journal*, September 20, 1991, p. 2.
17. *China Post*, December 6, 1991, p. 1; *Free China Journal*, December 17, 1991, p. 4.
18. Ibid.
19. *Free China Journal*, December 17, 1991, p. 4.
20. Ibid.
21. *China Post*, November 15, 1991, p. 4.
22. *China Post*, December 4, 1991, p. 1.
23. *Free China Journal*, December 17, 1991, p. 5.
24. Ibid.
25. Ibid.
26. *China Post*, November 27, 1991, p. 1.
27. *China Post*, November 22, 1991, p. 1.
28. *China Post*, December 2, 1991, p. 1.
29. *China Post*, December 13, 1991, p. 4.
30. *China Post*, December 19, 1991, p. 4.
31. *China Post*, December 26, 1991, p. 4. Other bones of contention pertaining to the electoral law were the KMT's desire to require that all candidates be high school graduates and its refusal to allow those sentenced to prison for treason or collaborating with other states to overthrow the government of the ROC to run

in the elections. In both cases, the DPP opposed the restrictions but was able to extract the concession that those convicted of sedition or advocating the overthrow of the government would be permitted to run if they addressed their calls exclusively to those living in Taiwan and not beyond the island. *China Post*, June 29, 1991, p. 1; July 15, 1991, p. 1.

32. There were 13,083,119 eligible voters, of whom 68 percent, or 8,938,996, cast votes. *China Post*, December 23, 1991, p. 1.

33. *China Post*, December 23, 1991, p. 1.

34. *China Post*, December 20, 1991, p. 1.

35. *China Post*, December 27, 1991, p. 4.

36. *China Post*, December 26, 1991, p. 1.

37. Julian Baum, "Building the Ballot: Enter a New Generation of Politicians," *Far Eastern Economic Review*, October 1, 1992, p. 14.

38. *Voice of Free China*, in FBIS-CHI–92–246, December 22, 1992, p. 52.

39. Julian Baum, "Tactical Alliance: Ruling Party's Local Factions Block Opposition," *Far Eastern Economic Review*, December 17, 1992, p. 17.

40. Ibid.

41. Julian Baum, "Split in the Ranks," *Far Eastern Economic Review*, December 24–31, 1992, p. 25.

42. Julian Baum, "Parting of the Ways," *Far Eastern Economic Review*, November 12, 1992, p. 20.

43. Nathan, "The Legislative Yuan Elections in Taiwan," p. 425.

44. Ibid.

45. Ibid., p. 429.

46. Julian Baum, "The Hollow Center: Poll Result Undermines President's Power," *Far Eastern Economic Review*, January 7, 1993, p. 14.

47. Nathan, "The Legislative Yuan Elections in Taiwan," p. 431.

48. Baum, "The Hollow Center," p. 14.

49. Interview with Chiu I-jen, Taipei, August 23, 1993.

50. Julian Baum, "Mainlanders Adrift: Premier's Resignation Weakens KMT's China Faction," *Far Eastern Economic Review*, February 11, 1993, p. 17.

8

The Impetus for and Impediments to Democratization

The ruling system of the KMT has thoroughly collapsed because it is based on a structure of lies. . . . Once people saw through the KMT's lies, the entire dynasty disintegrated.

—Chang Chun-hung, secretary-general, DPP

The Impetus

It seems unlikely that the KMT of the mid-1980s envisaged the Taiwan of the early 1990s (to say nothing of the KMT of the early 1990s). Despite the KMT's ideological commitment to democracy, reform would probably not have been undertaken were it not that the various forces opposed to the KMT on Taiwan ultimately became such a threat. Had the KMT been able to withstand both the threat and the cost of suppressing it, there may have been much less incentive for change. As it turned out, those within the KMT leadership who were more comfortable with an authoritarian style of rule were edged ever closer to the precipice of change by those within the party hierarchy who understood that, to survive, the party would have to change. Sensing the KMT's slackening resistance to political change, the opposition intensified its pressure on the regime and forced those in power to respond. Had the ruling figures in the KMT reacted to the challenges posed by the opposition in the same reflexively autocratic fashion as they had in the preceding decades, a different outcome would have ensued. That the KMT did not repress the opposition with the same vigor for which it had been known in the past suggests that something was changing in the KMT, too.

A new generation of KMT power holders—some born on Taiwan and others raised on the island after leaving the mainland as young children—was able to persuade party conservatives that a more flexible approach to the opposition would yield a more stable and, in the end, more desirable outcome for the party. To ensure Taiwan's continued economic prosperity, political stability was essential. The reformist figures in the KMT hierarchy might have reasoned that their party could claim credit for Taiwan's economic and political development while ceding power on the margins to an opposition they viewed as too extreme and too divided to undermine the perpetuation of KMT control. Whether those figures themselves understood what might happen if liberalization was tolerated is hard to know. It is also hard to know how many Taiwanese within the KMT saw reform as a way to advance their own interests within the party and whether those interests were affected by the sense that Taiwan should be governed by those born on Taiwan, even if that did not amount to independence.

Much like the driver of a vehicle careening down a mountain road after the brakes have failed, reformers had no hope of stopping liberalization once the process began. The cost would have been too high. The best they have managed to do is to negotiate each hairpin curve to slow the process sufficiently that they have not lost control in a cataclysmic finale. This they have done fairly well. While these individuals may not have anticipated the results of their efforts at restraint, dodging disaster by holding open the possibility of compromise has enabled them to create a system that—although still unsatisfactory to many—is more viable than the system that existed before the process began. This chapter addresses the questions: Why has reform unfolded the way it has? And what impediments lie in the path of continued democratization?

Economic Preconditions

It is not possible to know with certainty all that led to the political reforms of the late 1980s and 1990s. Typically, political analysts seek causes for the onset of political reform and often specify these causes in terms of particular economic preconditions. Reams of analyses have been published about the economic evolution that led to the "Taiwan miracle" and the rise of Taiwan as one of the "four small dragons" in East Asia. The sequence of changes on Taiwan apparently bolsters the idea that economic development in authoritarian regimes leads to political and social pluralism, which brings with it demands for the liberalization of the authoritarian regime under which the economic development was managed.

Indeed, many of the socioeconomic factors that theorists generally consider to affect the emergence of democratization, such as "high levels of urbanization, industrialization, rising per capita income, high literacy rates, and mass communication," can be observed on Taiwan.[1] These socioeconomic factors evidently have influenced the political climate on the island.

By the middle of the 1980s, Taiwan had developed many of the socioeconomic conditions typically associated with political liberalization, including a sizeable, prosperous, well-educated middle class that demanded a diminution of authoritarian practices, sought greater opportunities for participation in the political process, and pressed for institutional reform.[2] Gradually, the expectation that public institutions be reformed insinuated itself into the KMT itself. Once that happened, the party was pressured to reform by "young Turks" dissatisfied with playing a subordinate role in a political hierarchy governed by party elders.

Coincident with the pressure to reform the way the ruling party ruled the state and governed itself, an expansion of private wealth enabled individuals to sever their dependence on "KMT patronage" and exert greater autonomy over their own lives.[3] Economic development changes people's values and tends to bring in its wake political reform. Once individuals find themselves with a degree of economic autonomy—the freedom to purchase what they want, beyond what they need—they become invested with a new mentality. This shift in their economic impulses introduces a degree of autonomy that they may not have had before. Experience with economic autonomy can lead to the expectation of or desire for political autonomy and ultimately to the end of quiet acquiescence to political control from above.

It would be difficult to expect an individual who can fly to Disneyland for a family vacation, send his children to MIT for an education, invest a fortune in a small factory on the mainland, and buy any number of foreign-made consumer products, apparel, or automobiles to accept that the government dictates what he reads, what he thinks, and for whom he should vote when he goes to the polls. If it is possible for an individual to learn how to exercise autonomy in the economic realm, it is also possible, though not easy, for that individual to learn how to exercise comparable autonomy in the political realm. Just as the transformation of the economic realm will be accompanied by unintended consequences, disruptions of established social patterns, and cataclysmic shifts in long-standing values, so too will the transformation of the political realm.

Greater individual autonomy on Taiwan caused people to make demands on the state based on individual preferences. Communities of like-minded people were emboldened by the freedom to make economic choices to assert their political preferences, too. Autonomy also empowered people to act—individually or communally—in their own perceived best interest without regard for the wishes of the state. This increase in social pluralism—a precursor to political pluralism—enabled more and more "issue-oriented groups" and associations to move beyond the effective control of the KMT or state apparatus. In addition, Taiwan's increasingly independent media grew beyond the grasp of the KMT and the state and became a part of the process, not simply the source of information about it.[4]

As the state and the party were formerly indistinguishable, this circumvention affected the power of both. The party was no longer able to dominate the state apparatus with the same impunity, which meant that the state was no longer as rigid and intrusive. Whether the party no longer dominated the state because it was not as powerful a party or whether it was no longer as powerful a party because it no longer dominated the state apparatus, the fact was that the party was demonstrably less powerful than it had been for most of the preceding four decades.

Over time, it became clear that the KMT's own interests had often been misrepresented as those of the state. This was a prime concern of the opposition, and when it was voiced in the context of early liberalization it was one that the KMT had difficulty refuting. In the end, the opposition's attention to this matter hastened the disentanglement of the state and the KMT.

While measurable results in the development of Taiwan's economy were noticed before significant progress in political reform occurred, the *causal* relationship between those factors cannot be determined. Viewing the link between these processes from a conceptual perspective, theorists such as Seymour Martin Lipset find a strong *correlation* between economic and political development, but others, notably Samuel Huntington, caution that countries "do not automatically become democratic when they reach a certain level of material well-being. Institutional and political factors constitute a second influence on the process of democratization."[5] This does not invalidate the role of socioeconomic factors, but underscores that these are some—not the only —ingredients in the recipe for democratization.

Chiang Ching-kuo's Prescience

KMT and government officials typically explain that Taiwan's democratization resulted from the farsightedness of the KMT or, more precisely, of Chiang Ching-kuo. There are certainly other notable cases in which democratization was initiated from above by political leaders who emerged from the authoritarian regime they sought to reform. The joint efforts by King Juan Carlos and Prime Minister Adolfo Suarez in Spain and of General Ernesto Geisel in Brazil helped to bring democracy to states that had long been ruled as authoritarian, military regimes. Mikhail Gorbachev—a product of the system he ultimately helped to dismantle—unleashed a process of reform that rapidly moved beyond his own capacity to control it.[6] So, on its face, the explanation that Chiang Ching-kuo led the process of reform deserves consideration.

In a 1988 speech delivered in Washington, DC, Shaw Yu-ming, then the ROC government spokesman, commended Chiang Ching-kuo's "foresight" as the impetus for reform. While he admitted that Chiang "did not publicly declare what motivated the rapid moves toward liberalization that took place under his direction, some educated guesses are possible." In Shaw's view, Chiang always looked toward the future. He saw early on the need for various forms of infrastructural development of the island that ultimately fostered Taiwan's spectacular economic growth.

According to Shaw, "Toward the end of 1985, he [Chiang] must have sensed that the time was ripe to push for much bolder moves toward full democracy." Shaw suggested that the most apparent clues that the "time was ripe" were economic (even though there had been demands for political reform for many years before 1985). Shaw acknowledged that socioeconomic preconditions must exist for democratization to take place. Rather than view the presence of these conditions as the impetus for popular demands for greater pluralism and autonomy, however, he saw political reform beginning when Chiang Ching-kuo recognized that economic and social changes had been successfully effected.[7] This view has been endorsed by several sympathetic scholars who explain that on Taiwan the commitment of the ruling elite to "pursue democracy is at least as important as the existence of requisite socioeconomic conditions."[8] John Copper agreed that "democratization followed economic and social change" but observed that it was initiated by "the edicts of President Chiang Ching-kuo. In other words, it started by fiat. . . ."[9]

Consistent with the reasoning that democratization occurred on Taiwan from the top down is the view that this process was utterly compatible with, indeed dictated by, Sun Yat-sen's Three Principles of the People, the ideological touchstone of the KMT. From this perspective, there was never any question that the ROC would become democratic: the only issues were when constitutional democracy would be permitted and how long a period of transition would be necessary to make it effective.[10] This has led one observer to comment that because of the KMT's internal commitment to reform, democratization on Taiwan has not had the sort of cathartic effect on the populace that is often evident when a regime is forced to dismantle its autocratic system, as in the Soviet Union, or when it is toppled by a popular opposition movement, as in the Philippines or states in Eastern Europe.[11]

While Chiang Ching-kuo and the KMT certainly deserve enormous credit for maneuvering the state through the process of political reform, there are critical factors for which this argument does not adequately account. Those who posit that democratization began, deus ex machina, when Chiang Ching-kuo recognized that certain socioeconomic conditions were "ripe" have displaced theoretical logic with hagiographical rationalization.

Collapse of Authoritarianism: Crisis Within

A third explanation for the initiation of political reform is the recognition by the KMT leaders that there was a crisis within the party. The Chiang dynasty was nearing the end of its reign and there was no adequate system of succession that could accommodate the major forces within the party. In addition, the continued legitimacy of the party itself was no longer taken for granted. Chiang may have realized that the age of the charismatic, autocratic "strongman" was passing, and he was afraid of "what happens in a strongman regime when the man is no longer that strong."[12]

In this scenario, the need for reform came about as the party that had piloted the ROC ship of state for six decades began to accept that it had lost its way, its skipper was aging, and no successor presented himself as capable of taking over the helm. Even this realization did not emerge overnight, but in the wake of a growing loss of control stemming from the Chung-li Incident of 1977, the Kaohsiung Incident of 1979, and the Henry Liu Incident of 1984.[13] Just as Gorbachev had done in the Soviet Union, Chiang Ching-kuo was able to impose liberalization on Taiwan because his leadership was "strong and prestigious enough to roll over the inertia of the oligarchies and institutional interests" of the party and state.[14]

While this approach moves beyond the formulaic notion that liberalization occurs when the state reaches a certain level of economic development and is certainly more persuasive than the idea that Chiang simply woke up one morning and decided to become a democrat, it ignores the importance of the opposition as an influence on the regime's attitude toward reform. Advocates of this view consider the international context in the form of pressure from the United States in the 1970s to improve human rights and the downfall of Marcos in the Philippines as influential, but represent the opposition as incidental and aggravating, not elemental or motivating.

The significance of socioeconomic development and a receptivity on the part of the authoritarian regime to the potential for reform are important, but an opposition of some form is a necessary ingredient in this recipe because otherwise there would be no incentive to change the structure of government or the relations of power within society. It makes little sense that a crisis of authority within the party was the cause of a liberalization even if one believed that the opposition was not sufficiently organized to present a serious threat to the power of the KMT.[15]

While it is undoubtedly true that the opposition represents a spectrum of views that may not easily be subsumed under one organizational umbrella, a central reason why the opposition was not better organized and more effective is that the regime forbade its existence and activities. The KMT suppressed the opposition as long as it could. Those who were not intimidated into silence or inactivity were thrown into prison. Knowing this, one must wonder why the regime suppressed opposition unless it found opposition—regardless of how poorly it was coordinated—to be intolerable. The growing sophistication of the island's economy and the ever more brazen quality of dissent ultimately made the cost of suppression rise beyond a level that even the KMT was willing to pay.

It is probably true that Chiang's physical deterioration, pressures from abroad, and the growth of Taiwan's economy affected the way party leaders thought about the balance of power on Taiwan. Still, the primary reason why reform was undertaken when it was and in the manner that it was had to do with the challenge mounted by the opposition movement. Even before it was reorganized in 1986 as the DPP, the efforts of the *tang-wai* politicians in winning elections and staging protests demonstrated that the opposition was "not just a transitory phenomenon" and "posed a serious, vigorous challenge to the government by conducting interpellations of officials and examining the state budget," even though only about 4 percent of the Legislative Yuan representatives were affiliated with the opposition.[16] So, while other factors were influential, the centrality of the pressure from the opposition is also incontrovertibly a factor that one must consider.

Lu Ya-li rejects both the notion that Chiang Ching-kuo's foresight and sensitivity to the changing political imperatives were the source of reform and the view that Chiang was "forced by domestic and external pressures to undertake political reforms."[17] To credit a single man for the reforms that have been undertaken is too simplistic. Although Chiang Ching-kuo accelerated the process of liberalization, changes might have occurred anyway, even if later.

The International Political Climate

Another factor that may have influenced the course of reform on Taiwan was the international political climate of the mid-1970s and 1980s. Other former authoritarian states undertook liberalization during this "third wave" of democratization and the KMT may have responded in a manner that Huntington explained as the "demonstration effect, contagion, diffusion, emulation, snowballing, or perhaps even the domino effect. Successful democratization occurs in one country and this encourages democratization in other countries either because they seem to face similar problems, or because successful democratization elsewhere suggests that democratization might be a cure for their problems whatever those problems are, or because the country that has democratized is powerful and/or is viewed as a political and cultural model."[18] Political conditions that may have been tolerated for some period gradually became intolerable, even though the system itself has not changed.[19] Television, movies, travel, and the press enable individuals in one place to know how their own political and social systems stack up against the systems of others, and this, in turn, affects people's notions of what is tolerable. For instance, Hsu Hsin-liang commented while serving as DPP chairman that "developments in Eastern European countries and the democratic development in Russia" may have emboldened the DPP to include independence as a clause in its newly adopted constitution in October 1991.[20]

Significantly, after June 4, 1989, the KMT was gratified that its depiction of the Communist regime on the mainland was reinforced by events in Peking, but also pressured into demonstrating how differently it treated political dissidence and opposition on Taiwan. This, too, may have influenced the way the KMT dealt with the opposition on Taiwan once reform was under way.

Opposition as Primary Impetus to Reform

It is true that democratization on Taiwan has been managed by the political elite—especially those who held the reins of state power in the KMT—and conferred from above. That the transformation has been effected from the top of the political structure tells only half the story, though. Those who view democratization as initiated from "above" or because of external pressures or influences must still explain "why the regime, having shown little interest in political change prior to the emergence of the opposition, suddenly reversed its stand."[21] One must acknowledge that the leadership that is credited for guiding Taiwan to democracy was responding to popular demands voiced in opposition to the KMT and the ruling elite itself.

Cheng and Haggard correctly wrote, "The most appropriate view of the transition is one that focuses on the strategic interaction between state and opposition yet is careful to remember that neither constitutes a monolithic block."[22] This interaction began to occur when certain socioeconomic conditions prevailed, but was then "advanced by the ability of the opposition to set the agenda, to use extra-legal methods, to shift bargaining arenas, and eventually to push the ruling elite toward new rules of the game."[23] Cheng and Haggard point out that while one must consider the role of the opposition, it is also important to distinguish between the role of the opposition on Taiwan and that in a place like the Philippines where a popular uprising ousted an unpopular leader.[24]

Had Chiang Ching-kuo been a weaker leader or a man of lesser vision, the efforts of the opposition might have been met with a more brutal and uncompromising reaction. That Chiang was able to smell the wind of change and bow to its current is a mark of his leadership skill and, in a Confucian sense, noble qualities. Still, it is worth bearing in mind that he did not take up the cause of liberalization impulsively or out of a sudden sense of benevolence to the Taiwanese majority, who for decades he had actively helped to suppress.

Accepting the role of the opposition as a critical component of the liberalization process is only the first step. There is a tendency among analysts of Taiwan's politics to discuss the opposition in a categorical sense. Taiwan's is depicted as an authoritarian regime bound to have some opposition, and the role Taiwan's opposition plays in the interaction with the KMT is merely a reflection of its status as that opposition. From the comparativist perspective, the interaction between regime and opposition on Taiwan is no more remarkable than it is in any other state undergoing democratization. To understand the particular texture of politics on Taiwan, however, one should consider what has impelled people to fill the role that analysts label as the "opposition." On Taiwan, the single most compelling cause for dissent is still the divisive controversy about national identity. Not only does national identity divide the KMT from the opposition parties; it is also a central factor shaping the internal division within the KMT itself.

Opposition to Unfairness

Lin Cheng-chieh said, "This is clear: the opposition is the source of power for the democratization process."[25] This power comes from the tension between the "newly arrived immigrants" [Mainlanders] and the "immigrants who came before" [Taiwanese].[26] He explained that the tension itself reflects deep grievances, the most important of which is that there has been an asymmetry of power and an inherent unfairness in the political process. Lin said about the Mainlander elite, "They control every avenue of power, the National Assembly, the bureaucracy, the legislature; this is the rallying point of dissatisfaction."[27] In his eyes, the impetus for the opposition to press for democratization was an abiding objection to foreign domination.

This sense of unfairness was noted by Hsiao Hsin-huang. In a study of the social movements and civil protests that emerged with the onset of reform in the mid- to late 1980s, he found that although the various groups that took to the streets to protest did not necessarily identify with the opposition party, they all expressed a sense of the unfairness of the prevailing system. Hsiao examined eighteen protest movements organized around different kinds of grievances and found that "the most significant collective sentiment expressed in most of the emerging social movements has been a feeling of 'victim consciousness,' the feeling of being ignored and excluded. Most participants in the new social movements subjectively identify themselves as victims. They feel that they have not been treated fairly even though they are not necessarily isolated from society."[28] This sentiment seems to underlie much of the rhetoric one heard from the opposition, yet KMT officials and prominent Mainlanders interviewed seemed not to appreciate or acknowledge it. Their response to the suggestion that Taiwanese felt the "system" was unfair was to point out how the Taiwanese, as a whole, control more of Taiwan's economic resources than do Mainlanders. There is also a tendency among defenders of the KMT to point to prominent Taiwanese in government—especially the president—as evidence that there is no discrimination against Taiwanese.

For instance, Hau Pei-tsun said, "In the past the Taiwanese said that the Mainlanders governed Taiwan, but this is not really what happened. Mainlanders did not really enrich themselves, right? Mainlanders have let Taiwanese become the president, and now the premier, and party chairman, right?"[29] Some Mainlanders even suggested that in recent years if there was any unfairness about the system, it was that they were rapidly being excluded from society as they became a smaller and smaller portion of the population.

Lin Cheng-chieh noted that democratization and Taiwanization have developed along parallel lines. He recalled a confrontation between the maverick legislator Chu Kao-cheng and some of the established KMT legislators. Chu swore at them crudely and characterized the inequity of the political circumstances in Taiwan using a proverb about a beggar who goes to a temple to plead for food and, once fed, kicks out the monks and takes over the temple himself.[30] This illustrated the point that the KMT came from the mainland as a "bunch of losers" defeated by the Communists and then expected to be allowed to take over the island of Taiwan, barring the native population from participating in their own governance. Many Taiwanese viewed this as outrageous.

Chiang Chun-nan recalled a speech in which opposition leader K'ang Ning-hsiang ridiculed the KMT claim that the people of Taiwan should be grateful to the party for all the prosperity it has brought the island. According to Chiang, K'ang challenged the KMT, saying, "The *Kuo Min Tang* was defeated on the mainland. They had nowhere else to run. And we Taiwanese accepted them; [we gave them] asylum. We gave them rice, and we fed them, we clothed them, we paid taxes. [When] they came here, [they] had no where [else] to run. . . . [T]hey would have disappeared without Taiwan. . . . And now the KMT is so arrogant. They ask Taiwan to be grateful for them."[31] Chiang added that another opposition leader remarked that if history ever repeats itself, next time he hopes that an atom bomb will be dropped on Taiwan and the Japanese will get stuck with the KMT. Over the years, this sort of resentment about the KMT expanded. Taiwanese simply became fed up, and when their willingness to confront the KMT exceeded the KMT's willingness to repress dissidence, the need for liberalization became evident.

So, it may be true that Taiwan was not prepared for political liberalization until a certain level of economic prosperity had been reached, and Chiang Ching-kuo is most assuredly to be credited for legitimizing the need for reform by setting the government apparatus on the path toward democracy, but one should not ignore the vital role played by the Taiwanese opposition to Mainlander control. The reaction of the Taiwanese to the constraints on their national identity may be difficult to quantify, but it is a factor that not only incited the need for reform but also shaped the way reform unfolded.

Democracy, Self-Determination, and Independence: Means Versus Ends

For most of the 1980s and early 1990s, the opposition emphasized a desire for independence and democracy. Yao Chia-wen, the second chairman of the DPP, spoke of self-determination as a "stepping stone to independence." Huang Hsin-chieh, Yao's successor as DPP chairman, sympathized with the view that political conditions on Taiwan are "not yet conducive to the island's independence and, for the time being, it would be more realistic to advocate the right of the Taiwanese people to self-determination."[32]

Perhaps advocates of independence expect that continued opposition to the idea of unification will undercut the legitimacy of the KMT, lead to its disintegration or collapse, and make room for a ruling elite drawn primarily from among the Taiwanese.

As democracy is evidently an effective way for the Taiwanese to exploit their numerical superiority over the Mainlanders, this too is an effort to ensure that the future rulers of the island are Taiwanese, not Mainlanders. Simply put, both "independence" and "democracy" may be means to another end: Taiwanese sovereignty—a reflection of Taiwanese nationalism.[33]

As to the difference between independence as an objective and self-determination, in a survey of 600 students at National Taiwan University, Taiwan's premier university, 60 percent drew a distinction between the two concepts. In a 1983 survey conducted by *Lien-ho pao* (United Daily News), 68 percent of the respondents "felt that self-determination did imply eventual independence," and a 1989 survey about the two matters revealed that "thirty-seven percent of the respondents favored self-determination while a much lower percentage favored independence."[34] According to one analyst, between 1979 and 1990 "supporters of Taiwan's independence have only ranged from 1.5 percent to 16.2 percent of the population on the island."[35]

This evidence is entirely consistent with information gathered by Taiwan's Public Opinion Research Foundation. In June 1990, it found that 12.5 percent of 1,000 respondents to its survey approved of the Taiwan independence movement, whereas only 12 percent of respondents in December 1990 approved of the movement. By contrast, 67 percent in June and 61.7 percent in December disapproved. In a June 1990 survey, *Lien-ho pao* (United Daily News) also found that 42 percent of 1,128 respondents supported independence "if the Chinese Communists continue one-party dictatorship," but only 5 percent supported independence if the Chinese Communists "practice democracy and freedom."[36] It does not make clear what is meant by Chinese Communists practicing "democracy and freedom."[37]

The implication of these figures is brought into even sharper focus by a survey conducted by the Mainland Affairs Council in May 1991. It found that only 6.6 percent of its 1,230 adult respondents wanted to engage in "immediate negotiation leading to unification"; even fewer, 6.4 percent, wanted a "permanent separation leading to a new and independent country." However, a hefty 82 percent wanted to "maintain [the] *status quo* and begin unification negotiations only when the time is ripe."[38] It should come as no surprise that this is precisely compatible with the stated objectives of the KMT, which has promulgated the multistage Guidelines for National Unification. Similarly, it is consistent with the view that many—perhaps most—of those who support the opposition are generally inclined to form some sort of relationship with the mainland, but hope to do so when the time is appropriate and only when it can be done on their own terms.

These polling results are very difficult to interpret because it is hard to know how the phrasing of the question and the context of the survey affected people's responses. It is clear how the survey results are used, but it is not at all as clear whether the results are as meaningful as those who use them claim them to be. Finally, the question of self-determination itself is a thorny one.

Despite the KMT's earlier bellicose plan to "recover" the mainland, the unexpectedly successful economic development of the island has led the KMT to maintain the justification that it is interested in reunification as an ideal, but recognizes that the time is not right for that ideal to be realized. Chang Wen-chung, formerly director-general of the Boston office of the Coordination Council for North American Affairs, spoke about the KMT's current view of reunification. He said that the government is not talking about "immediate reunification" because economic and political differences between Taiwan and the mainland are too great. It is not the aim of the KMT that Taiwan be unified with the PRC in its current form and "be pulled down to their living standards; to sacrifice the civil rights, the political rights [that] the people in Taiwan are now happily enjoy[ing]."[39]

This theme was advanced by Chu Chi-ying. He explained that the rise of the middle class on Taiwan diminished the interest by the populace in the issue of independence. He said that the two most important things on people's minds were democracy and stability.[40] These became the stated goals of the government and the basis on which the KMT differentiated itself from the opposition. By contrast, the DPP developed a reputation for causing internal disorder and ignoring the irritation it evoked in the PRC by its persistent calls for independence.

The KMT policy toward the PRC is that the two sides should first "recognize each other as political entities on an equal basis," solve common problems such as smuggling, crime, and piracy, and help each other with economic development. In the second phase, the ROC and PRC should "treat each other as equal partners" and encourage "more interflow of people and goods across the straits." Then, in the third phase, "when the living standard of mainland China is approximately close to ours, when people over there enjoy political freedom, equality, they have a democratic form of government, then, only then, we can talk about political reunification. That may be ten years, twenty years, fifty years, maybe a century away. . . . The government on Taiwan is choosy."[41] From the perspective of Taiwanese in the opposition, however, this is unacceptable. They want to submit the question of reunification to a referendum of citizens on Taiwan. Chen Shui-pian explained that seeking a referendum is democratic "because we are not saying that our position of Taiwan independence is the only choice for the future of Taiwan. It is not the only choice. It is one of the choices, one of many choices."

On the issue of who should be eligible to participate in such a referendum, Chen stated that this issue is too important to leave to one party to determine. It must be resolved after the population of Taiwan has been given a chance to express its preference. "Let the 20 million people of Taiwan vote either for independence, for reunification, or for the status quo, or for some better choice. The DPP takes a position in accord with the spirit of democracy, but the KMT does not. The KMT advocates that China should be unified and proposed the National Reunification Guidelines as the only choice for the future of Taiwan. It's already a final conclusion. We consider this to be wrong. It is overbearing. It is not democratic."[42] In response to a question about how small a political unit may be and still be entitled to self-determination, Chen said that whatever population believes it has the conditions for independence should be permitted to exercise that right. There is no absolute number of people necessary to have a separate nation. He pointed out that the number of countries that exist today is far higher than it once was because large empires and countries have broken into smaller units. In fact, he added, there is no way to guarantee that what is now considered the People's Republic of China will not eventually break up into smaller states. Perhaps, he said, the days of the large state will soon pass.[43]

Not surprisingly, the KMT has seen reunification and independence as issues that go well beyond the people of Taiwan, and therefore it opposes the idea of a referendum. Ideologically, the KMT cannot submit the question to a vote because that would admit that the possibility of independence is tolerable. The core of KMT philosophy, as the creed of a nationalist party, is the reunion of the entire population in one nation. Independence is simply unacceptable. From a pragmatic perspective, even though the KMT is apparently no longer interested in rapid reunification while Communists are in power on the mainland, it cannot abandon the idea of reunification. Without it, the KMT would be an emperor with no ideological clothes. As it is, the KMT is wearing far fewer ideological robes than it once did.

One senior KMT official reasoned that the question of independence was not just a matter for the people of Taiwan to settle among themselves. He said it was important to recognize that the PRC had made this question its business, too. The reason the PRC takes such interest in the matter of Taiwan is not simply a question of sentimentality. He explained that the fifty-five minorities in the PRC constitute 8 percent of the population but occupy 60 percent of the land mass. It is not surprising, therefore, that the PRC reacts so sensitively to discussions of Taiwan independence. If the PRC allows a group of 21 million Han Chinese to declare independence from the rest of China, how can it justify refusing the demands of the 8 percent of the population that is not even Han Chinese to seek independent status?[44]

The foregoing would suggest that the opposition did indeed provide an essential impetus for the political reform that occurred after 1987. It is not clear, though, what the opposition really represents. On the one hand, if one is to believe the KMT officials, the opposition has only been interested in promoting independence. Leading figures in the DPP state their views differently. Hsu Hsin-liang, after the DPP's successful showing in the 1991 National Assembly elections, denied that independence was the exclusive aim of the DPP. "Making Taiwan independent of China is not our only choice . . . and we would consider conditions at the time [we take over] before deciding whether to adopt this as our national policy. . . . If we have to choose between the pro-independence movement and the pro-democracy movement, I think our party would choose to build a modern, democratic system on the island."[45] Of course, one could say that Hsu is simply being shrewd. He knows that if the DPP is to succeed, it has to persuade the population that it is responsible, and many people—Taiwanese included— view the advocacy of independence as too risky. Saying that the DPP prefers democracy over independence is the "right" answer, politically. It also clouds the issue. The DPP does not have to choose. It can advocate democratic reform, come to power, and then promote independence. The two are not mutually exclusive if democracy is viewed as the first objective.

Whether democracy is a means to another end is difficult to discern. Different people in the opposition hold different views. It certainly seems that, from its actions, the DPP has decided that democracy must come first. In that regard, one should consider the remarks of Lin Cho-shui, a DPP legislator. Lin said that he hopes the DPP will be an "engine" for the promotion of independence. "We will gradually make the DPP the party of Taiwan independence and with each step we will consider what the degree of acceptance of the political environment is at that time. We will always put forward a program that is a little more than people will be able to accept and after everyone has compromised a bit, then it will be just right."[46] This is a delicate strategy. The DPP has used the banner of independence fruitfully to capitalize on underlying tensions between Mainlanders and Taiwanese that reflect different notions of national identity. Ultimately it may care less about independence per se than about securing power in the political system, but to maximize its competitive advantage the DPP has cloaked itself in the mantle of independence. Of course, this has provided the KMT with a ready weapon for its own defense and, naturally, the KMT has focused on the irresponsibility of the independence movement. In a manner that reflects the national identity of Mainlanders, the KMT has continually emphasized the importance of eventual reunification with the rest of China.

Chiang Chun-nan commented that there really are not very many people in the KMT who want reunification, but they are locked into the rhetoric of their ideology and feel they have to persist with it. When the KMT first came to Taiwan, he said, the recovery of the mainland was emphasized as a military issue. With time, it became a moral obligation. Now, he said, it has become a political expedient. The KMT claims that if it gives up the hope of reunification, the PRC will attack the island. In fact, he said, the KMT more likely wants to preserve the status quo and emphasizes reunification as a way to preserve itself, even though few people actually see reunification as a value in and of itself. He added that the KMT is fond of labeling Taiwan independence as "dangerous," but if the party leaders could find a way to stop saying that it is dangerous, Chiang believes that even they would support the idea of independence.[47]

At the same time, to ensure the survival of the KMT in the short term, the party leaders gave in to demands for liberalization and democratization. This has resulted in a significant shift in power from the Mainlander minority within the KMT to the Taiwanese majority. The peaceful Taiwanization of the KMT leadership has accomplished by other means the unstated objective of the opposition: for Taiwan to be governed by Taiwanese. Still, the emergence of democracy in the period 1987–1992 does not signify that Taiwan has put its undemocratic past to rest. There are still factors that may impede the final consolidation of the political gains that have been made.

Impediments

> Reunification is always in conflict with democracy.
>
> —Chiang Chun-nan

> The national identity question is . . . the most serious problem.
>
> —Shaw Yu-ming

> The biggest difficulty we have in democracy is national identity. . . . Before the . . . problem between the mainland and us is solved, there will be pressure on our democracy.
>
> —Lin Cheng-chieh

One factor that is still difficult to explain is how democratization materialized on Taiwan despite the sharp contrast of views concerning national identity. One will recall that theories of democratization specify the importance of consensus among the political elite about national identity as a necessary precondition for the consolidation of democratic reform. Taiwan seems to lack such an elite consensus, and yet Taiwan was able to accomplish between 1987 and 1992 what few other authoritarian states have been able to: a peaceful transition to democracy. If the theories about democratization are accurate, the democratic reforms established in the early 1990s will not be long-lasting unless some agreement can be reached about the issue of national identity. That democracy has emerged is not itself a violation of the principles theorists expressed. If democracy is consolidated—if it lasts—in the absence of consensus, that would undermine the theoretical notions about the importance of agreement about national identity.

If one views consensus as an explicit agreement, there is little hope that consensus about a common identity for the people living on Taiwan will emerge soon. On the other hand, if one considers tacit acceptance of a condition as a functional equivalent of explicit consensus, one would have to say that there is already agreement about the current and desirable political status of the island, even if this agreement does not extend to people's ideals. One hears very few voices opposing the de facto political, social, and economic autonomy Taiwan has enjoyed since 1949. If advocates of independence are primarily interested in the autonomy of Taiwan, their objectives were realized in 1949. Since that time, the first since Cheng Ch'eng-kung ruled the island in the seventeenth century, the island has been governed only by powers that live on the island and not by powers that take orders from a central government based elsewhere.

This leaves open the question of whether democratic reforms of the late 1980s and early 1990s could be overturned. That is, will the failure of the political elite to arrive at an explicit consensus subvert the political gains they have worked so hard to achieve? Students of democratization must be concerned not only about whether democracy can emerge from the clutch of an authoritarian regime, but also about whether the democratic institutions newly established in the wake of the regime can survive. This underscores the importance of examining the potential impediments to democracy.

There are many factors that might limit the life of a newborn democracy. In the case of Taiwan, the most apparent question has to do with the essential contest between Mainlanders and Taiwanese about the matter of national identity. As of the late 1980s, it was not at all clear whether the Mainlander-dominated KMT would, indeed, surrender enough power for the Taiwanese to assume control of the island's political system. While liberalization proceeded at a rapid clip, it was always reined in just shy of democracy to ensure that Taiwanese did not exploit their superior numbers and to ensure that self-determination was not actually possible. By the early 1990s, however, the system had advanced to the very cusp of the phase when self-determination is a reality. Both the National Assembly and the Legislative Yuan had been selected by popular election, as had a host of local and provincial positions. The last central-level government office to be contested openly was the presidency, and that, too, was slated for a popular election. From the perspective of the early 1990s, complete self-determination seemed nearly attainable by the end of the decade. In most other respects, Taiwan had become essentially democratic. Whether that democracy could be sustained was still difficult to assess.

Compatibility of Chinese Culture and Democracy

One potential impediment to the consolidation of democracy on Taiwan is the underlying political culture of the island, which stems from Chinese political traditions. Raising this question, one is aware that the Weberian problematik that dominated Western analysis of China's modernization for many years has been somewhat discredited by the very development Weber suggested would be unlikely to occur. "In these days of East Asian economic potency it is difficult to take seriously any universal claim about the incompatibility of Chinese culture and modernization."[48] Yet, when one considers the prospects of marrying democracy and Chinese culture, one must wonder which of the two forces is likely to yield more to the other. Will a Chinese society that becomes democratic be less Chinese than one that remains undemocratic? Or will the form of democracy adopted by a Chinese community be molded to its preexisting social and cultural norms to such a degree that it is substantially different from democracy practiced elsewhere?[49]

Two features of democracy as it has been practiced elsewhere may be difficult to cultivate on Taiwan. One is the acceptance that uncertainty is a necessary and desirable feature of political life because political outcomes are determined by elections, the results of which cannot be known in advance. The other is the need to trust that one's opponents are loyal to the political system so that it is at least conceivable that different political actors can alternate in power, even if, in fact, they do not do so.

Faith in the newly acquired ideal of rule by popular consent does not necessarily extend to faith in institutionalized uncertainty, which, in the context of China's political history, may be equated with disorder. In the literature about Chinese politics, all too much is made about the fear of disorder. It is often described as though the intolerance of chaos is an attribute peculiar to the Chinese. This is misleading. Governments exist to order society by regulating the legitimate use of power and to distribute goods among those who live within the society. To some degree, every political system is intended to avoid the chaos that would come with anarchy, and societies everywhere struggle to avoid disorder. There are certainly different degrees to which societies tolerate disorder, and it may be that the Chinese are comparatively intolerant of some forms of disorder. Still, one should not conclude that politics in China reflects a desire for order whereas politics elsewhere stems from an interest in some other end.

To minimize the disorder that comes from uncertainty, Chinese have generally lived under authoritarian systems in which political outcomes were carefully controlled by the rulers. China's political history is marked by efforts of rulers to maintain control, not invite contestation. Yao Chia-wen said, "[B]asically Chinese culture is a controlling culture, not a democratic, not a free, not an equal [one]. Chiang Kai-shek said it was an ethical system [but] ethical is not equal."[50] Enforced conformity and strict maintenance of public order has been justified over the years by a perversion of Confucian values. Challenging authority, basing policy on the expressed will of the governed, institutionalizing regular methods for the citizenry to select its ruling figures and bodies, and the host of freedoms, rights, and privileges associated with democracy are not natural outcomes of the political and social values that have prevailed in Chinese communities.

The tendency on the part of the ruling authorities to control political outcomes and the acquiescence of the populace to that control are features of political life in the Chinese cultural milieu that are antithetical to democracy. The need for competition, and the incumbent uncertainty that accompanies a fair competitive system, comprise a style of political interaction that will have to be learned if democracy is to survive on Taiwan. Although it will require that people reorder their political values, it is entirely plausible that this change can be effected.

If the incentives to change overwhelm the inertia in which most people wallow, then whatever disinclination people feel about surrendering the certainty that comes with control may be swiftly brushed aside. Economic development is only one force that may help to define people's incentive to change. Frustration, fear, and anger may also lead people to view themselves differently than in the past, to recognize that they are fed up with the status quo, and to reach for goals that require a fundamental alteration in the way they interact in political and social contexts.

Just as the tendency to control political outcomes, rather than to accept the uncertainty that comes with fair competition, is a reflection of Chinese political traditions, so is the tendency to distrust political opponents. This distrust makes it difficult to institutionalize the sort of competition that is necessary for a democracy to function. In any stable system of democracy, as Przeworski suggests, one may disagree with, or even dislike, one's opponents, but one understands that the opponent's loyalty to the system itself and to the interests of the state are sufficiently intense that if the opposition wins, one will not be prevented from competing with it for power in the future. Not only does this rest on an acceptance of uncertainty; it is founded on a trust in one's opponents. This is a spirit alien to Chinese political culture.

Aside from the apparently inevitable desire of power holders to retain power, the KMT might be justified in fearing that if it loses the popular mandate to rule, and new authorities are voted into office, those new ruling authorities might treat the KMT as an opposition party with the same intolerance and brutality that the KMT has, over the years, used against its opponents. Whether these fears are well founded or not, it is easy to appreciate that they exist because Chinese have lived under a system, informed by a culture, that bolstered these fears longer than they have lived with the prospect of alleviating such anxieties by institutionalizing regular means to select and replace political leaders.

It is also easy to understand why the opposition remains as skeptical of the KMT as it is. The distrust and hostility built up over four decades of KMT rule cannot be swept aside by a few years of liberalization, even though, by any objective standard, the changes since the mid-1980s have significantly altered the balance of power and continue at a pace that, by comparison to other states engaged in democratization, seems far more accelerated.

Just as the KMT has been hostile and suspicious of the CCP, the opposition on Taiwan remains highly distrustful of the KMT. It is essential to the future of democracy on Taiwan, though, that that distrust ultimately be diminished by experience with cooperation. "Cooperation has always been a central feature of democracy. Actors must voluntarily make collective decisions binding on the polity as a whole.

They must cooperate in order to compete. They must be capable of acting collectively through parties, associations, and movements in order to select candidates, articulate preferences, petition authorities, and influence policies."[51] Although political development on Taiwan since the onset of liberalization has fostered to a limited degree the types of attitudes about which Schmitter and Karl wrote, at this writing it would be hard to characterize the political system on Taiwan as based on the sort of trust that makes cooperation possible. Still, Schmitter and Karl expressed faith in the possibility that democracy can emerge from such an incipient condition as already exists on Taiwan. They suggested that democracy does not rest on "deeply ingrained habits of tolerance, moderation, mutual respect, fair play, readiness to compromise, or trust in public authorities. Waiting for such habits to sink deep and lasting roots implies a very slow process of regime consolidation—one that takes generations—and it would probably condemn most contemporary experiences *ex hypothesi* to failure."[52] If this view is correct, then the preference for control rather than uncertainty and the inhibition about trust and cooperation are not, in and of themselves, powerful enough impediments to prevent the consolidation of democracy. These tendencies may be difficult to alter, but it is possible for people to learn a new mode of political interaction. Initially, these elements may seem like obstacles to the consolidation of democracy, but with patience, creative leadership, and determination, these difficulties may be overcome. One analyst observed, "[T]he real reason why Taiwanese politics have remained unsettled has been that the KMT people brought the worst aspects of traditional Chinese politics to Taiwan, an island without strong ideological tendencies. The KMT people are accustomed to speak differently than they think and to act differently than they speak."[53]

How Taiwan Votes

Quite apart from those impediments that reflect Taiwan's Chinese cultural underpinnings are those that reflect Taiwan's own peculiar history. One of these issues pertains to the basis on which people vote. The question that seems most pressing is whether people vote on the basis of their own political views or whether other factors affect their choice. These matters are widely discussed among the political and intellectual elite. Many of those consulted for this study suggested that voters are not concerned with a candidate's position on a set of issues or even with a candidate's party affiliation. Instead, it is assumed that people vote on the basis of connections they may have either with the candidate or with the local party operative who represents the candidate.

If one is curious about the degree to which voters on Taiwan are interested in democracy, or how they feel about Taiwan's national identity, it is important to determine whether one can view election results as an accurate gauge of popular political opinion. It is unclear whether a landslide victory for one party should be viewed as an endorsement of its policies, or whether it is simply the case that the electorate is insufficiently attuned to the power of the ballot and will respond to pressures or suggestions by local party operatives to vote in a certain way. In their official statements, both the ruling party and the opposition refer to the elections as endorsements of particular political positions, but it is not at all clear that this is an accurate reading of the public mood.

Kau Hui-yu, who was elected to the National Assembly in December 1991, said it will be very difficult to wean people of the idea that they vote for someone they know, rather than for some abstract issue—such as constitutional reform or even independence. She stated her belief that people still vote according to interpersonal relations—for the candidate who comes from the same town or from the same province on the mainland, or who is associated with the same faction. People persist in viewing their elected official as the person who will be empowered to help them with personal problems: preventing a road from being built through their farmland, installing lights on the city street in front of their shop, having a park constructed, and so forth.[54]

A persistent feature of elections on Taiwan that clouds one's view of the reason why people vote as they do is the practice of vote buying. In studies of voting behavior conducted in rural districts during the late 1960s and 1970s, before the onset of liberalization, it was found that "[v]irtually every vote was bought and paid for by cash on the barrel-head. The price ranged from a token NT $10 (which was the value of a package of cigarettes) in unopposed elections for district heads, to NT $100 (U.S. $2.50) in the always hotly contested elections for county headships. The sum depended on the degree of competition and the potential spoils of office, which in some cases were enough to make sizable investments in an election well worthwhile."[55] When one reads about vote buying, it is tempting to assume that people are being bribed, in the sense that they would not have voted for the particular candidate were it not for the money involved in the transaction. To some degree, this may be true. However, to view vote buying as merely bribery may be to misunderstand the essence of the exchange. One analyst determined that the principal function of vote buying was to "make the voter aware who is running" and to convince the voter to vote, not to bribe the voter to select the highest-paying candidate.[56] Indeed, within a given electoral district, the cost of buying a vote "tends to become settled in such a manner that competing candidates offer the same amount of money for the vast majority of votes they buy. Thus, most voters have no economic incentive to vote for any particular candidate as all candidates will pay the same amount for their vote."[57] One official said that in the 1970s, before urbanization and modernization were well under way, one could buy a vote with a cigarette. With time, the greater sophistication of the voter, and, of course, economic development, the cost of buying a vote has increased. It is probably the case that vote buying is now more prevalent in rural areas than in urban centers, but it is still known to be a common practice.[58]

A senior member of the KMT reasoned that this practice was not necessarily an impediment to democracy. In his view, it is possible to view the exchange as a symbol of equality. The voter demands some recognition of his status—even if the amount is not great—as a way to ensure that the candidate is beholden to him. Often the transaction is sanitized by saying that the money exchanged is to offset the carfare incurred when the voter goes to the polls.

Officially, vote buying is illegal, and although it undoubtedly continues, it would be difficult to determine the degree to which such activity persists and to what degree it shapes the outcome of elections. If the primary function of vote buying is not bribery, in the sense of making a voter an offer he cannot refuse, then the question remains regarding the basis on which votes are bought.

Listening to the political elite discuss the way politics operate on Taiwan, one gets the sense that the most influential factor affecting electoral outcomes is the personal connection—perceived or actual— between candidates and voters. The concept of *kuan-hsi*, often translated as "connections" or "relationships," is a complex and pervasive dimension of Chinese social interaction involving the cultivation of personal loyalties to others. The term is frequently misused to cover a multitude of behavioral patterns and in much of the literature about China is discussed in mystical or exotic terms. Although this concept is worth exploring in fuller measure, for the purposes of this discussion suffice it to state that *kuan-hsi* implies a bond of loyalty to another individual who shares some common social category (family, village, province of origin, school, place of work, military class, and so forth). In addition, and of particular importance in politics, *kuan-hsi* may be extended to others who are not of that social circle when introduced or recommended by one who is.

Interactions on the basis of *kuan-hsi* and the notions of obligation and entitlement they entail are pervasive throughout all levels of Chinese society, both on the mainland and on Taiwan. To the foreign observer, they may appear more explicit and evident than they do to Chinese, who routinely deny that they "keep score" of what is owed them and what they owe. Still, one need not spend too long living in a Chinese community before it becomes evident that invoking the loyalties that come from *kuan-hsi* is not an occasional aberration to get around "the system." It is the daily pattern of interaction that constitutes the system.

Kuan-hsi is a potent force in politics, too. This system is rooted in China's past to a style of political allegiance that predates the rationalization of politics, which has produced the representative style of democracy associated with contemporary electoral politics. One can observe how social networks operate in spheres of the society other than the political realm and it is obviously not difficult to find evidence in the world of electoral politics. For example, when one examines the bases of support for the opposition, one finds that "most opposition politicians won their elections primarily because of their individual long-term efforts in establishing personal reputations and social networks. In fact, neither opposition organizations nor alliances played crucial roles for most successful opposition politicians in the past."[59]

Chiu I-jen said that the role of patron–client relations that is the basis of factional politics affects both the KMT and the DPP. He said that the KMT depends on superior organizational skills to prop up local factions to ensure that the KMT does well in elections. The party grants substantial benefits to the leaders of the factions in each locality, which are then divided up among members of the faction. This keeps the faction leader strong in his locality, receiving support in exchange for benefits, and makes the KMT stronger by assuring that the faction leader will sway his subordinates to vote for the KMT candidates. Rival factions, each supported by the KMT, are set up so that one or another faction may lose, but the KMT always wins. People have not developed a strong sense that they should vote according to the policies advocated by their factional bosses. Instead, they vote to assure their continued access to the channels of power and receipt of benefits in return.

Chiu expressed doubt that democratization would be successful unless this sort of clientism is undermined. In 1991, he said that the changes that had occurred in the past several years appear to be democratic, but "what has happened so far is a change within the political system, not a change of the system."[60] These changes are really not moving Taiwan toward democracy, but toward "Taiwanization." It is his view that Lee Teng-hui realized that he would not be able to survive indefinitely on support derived from within a party that is largely hostile toward him, because he is both a Taiwanese and a reformer. So, he had to recruit new sources of power from outside the party.

Chiu said that Lee looked to local factions and big enterprises, both of which are dominated by Taiwanese who might see fit to support Lee because he is also Taiwanese. Needless to say, these new sources of power recruited into the party were a threat to the old guard. In 1991, Chiu predicted that this situation would lead to a power struggle within the KMT in three to five years. It was his opinion that Lee would win the struggle and solidify his power base among Taiwanese loyal to the KMT.

Chiu forecast that "[a]fter the power struggle, things will settle down and the KMT will still dominate Taiwanese politics and democratization will stop."[61] He stated that this pattern in Taiwan's politics can be detected in both Chiang Kai-shek's and Chiang Ching-kuo's political behavior. Chiu concluded that "[e]ven if Lee Teng-hui wins the power struggle, it will only [result in] 'Taiwanization,' not democratization. If the power struggle ends and clientism still exists, there is no hope for democratization."[62]

In fact, Chiu predicted the power struggle accurately. In the early 1990s, KMT internal politics was characterized by a split between the "mainstream" faction, largely comprised of Taiwanese loyal to Lee Teng-hui, and the "nonmainstream" faction of Mainlanders. Just before the Fourteenth Party Congress in August 1993, several prominent members of the nonmainstream faction defected and formed the Chinese New party. In the course of the KMT Party Congress, Lee Teng-hui was able to establish his primacy in a party that had, only a few years before, been deeply divided about whether he should be appointed president. This was the power struggle that Chiu anticipated.

On the day after the KMT Party Congress concluded, Chiu I-jen said that on Taiwan, one gets the illusion of democracy, but that liberalization is not the same as democratization. He said that patron–client ties still dominate the electoral process and that mobilization of voters is done not through persuasion based on political preferences but through *kuan-hsi* and vote buying. It is necessary, he said, to establish democratic procedures to have a democracy, but that is not sufficient.

Chiu said that Taiwan still needs to be governed by the rule of law. Laws that are intended to protect the sanctity of democratic procedures must be enacted and enforced. The bureaucracy must also be trained to maintain its neutrality in order that the rule of law be upheld. Regarding the factionalism, Chiu said that local factions, once dominant at the local level only, have now begun to affect politics at the central level. In his view, this threatens the democratization of Taiwan.[63]

To the extent that clientism does not encourage people to think for themselves about political decisions that affect them, this practice makes it difficult to assess how people genuinely feel about the value of democracy and self-determination. One clue about people's sense of national identity may come from the way in which voters choose between Taiwanese and Mainlander candidates. If people vote for candidates with whom they share certain imagined or actual bonds, it would be worth knowing more about how people view the matter of provincial origin. There is some evidence that provincial origin "is clearly the most important factor that could explain . . . partisan preferences."[64] Still, it is hard to determine whether Taiwanese voters are more likely to vote for candidates from Taiwan, regardless of party affiliation, than for candidates who are Mainlanders.

One gets some sense of the dynamics of provincial chauvinism from a study that examines the results of three elections for mayoral posts in Chia-yi County. The results of these contests suggest that "[t]he provincial origin variable had the strongest impact" on the choice voters made and was more influential than age, gender, education, and class. In nine surveys conducted between 1986 and 1987, 71 percent of those who supported the KMT were Taiwanese and 28.9 percent were Mainlanders. However, 94 percent of those who favored the opposition were Taiwanese, but only 5.2 of those who were pro-opposition were Mainlanders. Of those who consider themselves to be neutral, 92.7 percent were Taiwanese and 7.3 percent were Mainlanders.

Other factors may be correlated with party identification. Overall, those who identify with the KMT are older, better educated, and middle class. Those who identify with the opposition tend to be younger, less educated, and more likely to be farmers, laborers, or housewives.[65]

Despite the steady success of the opposition, it is clear that most Taiwanese still support KMT candidates. Chiu said there are several plausible explanations for this. First, he said, it is probably too dangerous to expect Taiwan independence at this stage. While the DPP is identified as supporting independence, the KMT is seen as preserving the status quo. Second, most people probably feel that regardless of which party they support, it is unlikely to affect their daily lives very much, so why not continue to support the party most able to provide social, political, and economic benefits? Third, Chiu said, the KMT has been very successful in its efforts to socialize the population. There are many people who view themselves as Taiwanese, but primarily as Chinese. For some, this translates into support for unification and, therefore, support of the KMT. Finally, there are some Taiwanese who support the KMT because they simply do not like the DPP.[66] One thing that seems reasonably clear is that even those Taiwanese who support KMT rather than the DPP candidates tend to prefer Taiwanese candidates in the KMT to Mainlanders. One assumes that Mainlanders are more likely to support Mainlander candidates than Taiwanese even when both are associated with the KMT.

P'eng Ming-min shared the view that many Taiwanese feel that they have a common interest with the KMT, so they support the party's candidates. Of course, he added, there are also those who support the KMT because the DPP is still relatively unknown. Still, he said, many who vote for KMT candidates complain about the internal corruption of the party and the government. However, they continue to support the KMT because they derive benefits personally. P'eng pointed out that voting is not generally done according to political ideals, or on the basis of a candidate's platform, but in response to *kuan-hsi*.

On that note, P'eng said that the KMT still controls most professional organizations in the country, so failure to support the KMT can affect one's professional standing. Conversely, there are many middle-class Taiwanese who are afraid to support the DPP. Individuals fear official retribution in the form of a tax audit or the imposition of red tape on a business deal. People are very much afraid, especially businesspeople and the civil servants, for whom supporting the DPP would be professional suicide.[67]

Conclusion

While factionalism, clientalism, vote buying, and ballots cast on the basis of *kuan-hsi* certainly affect the way democracy functions and limit the usefulness of electoral results as a gauge of public opinion, they do help to institutionalize the practice of voting. Learning about these practices reinforces the notion that the populace of Taiwan is generally apathetic about the sort of questions pertaining to national identity that the elite in the opposition cling to as the reason for its existence. It also negates the arguments of the KMT elite that people reject the notion of independence and support the ruling party because it is committed to ultimate reunification with the mainland. In and of themselves, however, these factors do not constitute a reason to doubt that democracy can be consolidated and can function with vigor on Taiwan. In fact, they are reminiscent of the sort of political-machine politics that were well known in Boston and Chicago during more colorful periods of those cities' political past. A system can be democratic —where democracy is understood in terms of Huntington's procedural definition—even if it is sullied by practices that are inconsistent with the highest ideals that are associated with democracy. Time and practice are needed for a well-functioning democracy to take root. Once it has taken root, it requires constant tending.

This may be especially true in a state that has no prior experience with democracy. One senior official was rather pessimistic about the prospect for democracy on Taiwan. He commented that in Chinese society there is often a great deal of latitude between the mask one wears and what lies behind it. "Every man can speak as though he is Confucius, but really be a thief." This dualism is deeply rooted in the Chinese psyche. Under these circumstances, this senior official felt it would be exceedingly difficult to establish rule of law, order, and democracy on Taiwan. For example, he said that it is unthinkable that a jury system could be implemented. If it were, everyone would endeavor to buy or sell the jury.[68]

As with other states that seem to resist reform because of political cultural factors that are opposed to the underlying principles of widespread participation and political competition, on Taiwan the transition to democracy may be difficult, but not impossible. One must not assume that those states with political cultures that appear to resist democracy are not capable of change. Change is inevitable. At issue is what form these changes will take.

States that are now democratic did not always embrace democracy. It is true that some political cultures may be more hospitable to democracy than that of the Chinese. Still, the progress that Taiwan has made since the mid-1980s suggests that transformation is possible within the Chinese political context. Whether Taiwan succeeds or not in consolidating the democratic gains it has made, one must acknowledge that it has already progressed much farther down the road toward democracy than was expected by those who hold up the authoritarianism of China's past as the only chart of its future.

Democratization on Taiwan did not occur because the KMT simply decided that the moment had arrived to recognize the party's original aim of establishing a democratic republic. It is a process that was spurred by the Taiwanese opposition. Those who disparage the role of the opposition in the process of transition are wrong. Were it not for the increasing sense of vulnerability the KMT leadership felt vis-à-vis the Taiwanese majority, there would have been little impetus for change. Recognizing the potential power of the Taiwanese, the KMT has used its considerable experience in office to persuade voters that it is not a party of Mainlanders and that only under its continued leadership will the state continue to prosper, retain stability, and safeguard national security.

To date, the KMT has done this reasonably well. The party has also used its superior organization, cohesiveness, experience, focus, wealth, and sophistication to ensure that the transformation of Taiwan's political system took place peacefully. The KMT has managed to dominate the transition—opening up where and when it deemed fit—and has kept the pace and direction of reform relatively well controlled. This success is partly a reflection of the comparative strength within both the KMT and the DPP of moderate forces. If extremists on either pole had been able to assert themselves within their party, the whole delicate balance between those pushing for change and those resisting change would have tumbled swiftly. It is in the best interest of those concerned with advancing and sustaining democracy that this not happen.

Notes

1. Tun-jen Cheng and Stephan Haggard, "Regime Transformation in Taiwan," in *Political Change in Taiwan*, ed. Tun-jen Cheng and Stephan Haggard (Boulder, CO: Lynne Rienner, 1992), p. 2. See also Cal Clark, *Taiwan's Development: Implications for Contending Political Economy Paradigms* (New York: Greenwood Press, 1989).

2. Tien Hung-mao, *The Great Transition: Political and Social Change in the Republic of China* (Stanford: Hoover Institution Press, 1988), p. 251.

3. Ibid.

4. Ibid.

5. Samuel P. Huntington, "Foreword," in *Political Change in Taiwan*, ed. Cheng and Haggard, p. x.

6. Donald Share and Scott Mainwaring, "Transitions Through Transaction: Democratization in Brazil and Spain," in *Political Liberalization in Brazil: Dynamics, Dilemmas, and Future Prospects*, ed. Wayne A. Selcher (Boulder, CO: Westview Press, 1986); and Adolfo Suarez, "The Transition to Democracy in Spain," remarks to Harvard–MIT Joint Seminar on Political Development, May 25, 1983. I am grateful to Professor Samuel Huntington for these illustrations.

7. Shaw Yu-ming, *Beyond the Economic Miracle: Reflections on the Republic of China on Taiwan, Mainland China, and Sino-American Relations* (Taipei: Kwang Hwa, 1989), pp. 30–32.

8. Tien Hung-mao, "Social Change and Political Development in Taiwan," in *Taiwan in a Time of Transition*, ed. Harvey Feldman, Michael Y.M. Kau, and Ilpyong J. Kim (New York: Paragon House, 1988), p. 9.

9. John F. Copper, *A Quiet Revolution: Political Development in the Republic of China* (Washington, DC: Ethics and Public Policy Center, 1988). See also Linda Chao and Ramon H. Myers, "The First Chinese Democracy: Political Development of the Republic of China on Taiwan, 1986–1994," *Asian Survey*, vol. 34, no.3 (March 1994), p. 229.

10. Tien, *The Great Transition*, p. 252.

11. Peter W. Moody, *Political Change on Taiwan: A Study of Ruling Party Adaptability* (New York: Praeger, 1992), p. 180.

12. Ibid., p. 90.

13. Ibid., p. 187.

14. Ibid.

15. Ibid.

16. Lu Ya-li, "Political Modernization in the ROC," in *Two Societies in Opposition: The Republic of China and the People's Republic of China After Forty Years*, ed. Ramon H. Myers (Stanford: Hoover Institution Press, 1991), p. 115.

17. Ibid., p. 123.

18. Samuel P. Huntington, *The Third Wave: Democratization in the Late Twentieth Century* (Norman: University of Oklahoma Press, 1991), p. 100.

19. Seymour Martin Lipset, *Political Man* (Baltimore: Johns Hopkins University Press, 1981), p. 475.

20. Neal E. Robbins, "Enter the Little Dragon: Is Taiwan's Independence Movement Playing with China's Fire," *Washington Post*, December 15, 1991.

21. Cheng and Haggard, "Regime Transformation in Taiwan," p. 16.

22. Ibid., p. 12.

23. Ibid., p. 3.

24. Ibid., p. 16.

25. Interview with Lin Cheng-chieh, Taipei, July 8, 1991.

26. Ibid.

27. Ibid.

28. See Hsiao Hsin-huang, "The Rise of Social Movements and Civil Protests," in *Political Change in Taiwan*, ed. Cheng and Haggard, p. 70.

29. Interview with Hau Pei-tsun, Taipei, August 27, 1993.

30. The proverb is "Ch'i-kai kan miao-kung." Interview with Lin Cheng-chieh, Taipei, July 8, 1991.

31. Interview with Chiang Chun-nan, Taipei, May 20, 1991.

32. Leo Y. Liu, "Self-Determination, Independence, and the Process of Democratization in Taiwan," *Asian Profile*, vol. 19, no. 3 (June 1991), p. 198.

33. Ibid., p. 198.

34. Ibid., p. 198, especially n. 3 and n. 4.

35. Ibid., p. 199, n. 7.

36. Mainland Affairs Council, *Public Opinion and the Mainland Policy: Selected Opinion Polls Conducted in Taiwan, 1988–1991* (Taipei: Mainland Affairs Council, June 1991), pp. 5–6.

37. There has been a dramatic increase in the popularity of public opinion polls; the results should probably be viewed with some skepticism, however. For one thing, Taiwan's is not a culture that has long been used to the freedom to express political ideas without retribution. An article in *Hsin Hsin-wen* (The Journalist) noted that during its attempts to conduct a poll it encountered what it termed the "refusal response" from people uncomfortable with the nature of the questions. The article stated "If the pollster gave them a brief explanation of what was happening, they would then counter with 'how do I know you are not calling from the political headquarters or the Bureau of Investigation?' or 'how do I know that this call is not begin taped?' Despite all assurances, they refused to believe that their phone number had been selected in a random sampling from the phone book." See Luo Yuan-fu, "Our Sick Island Finally Regains Some of its Health—*The Journalist*'s poll on the 'Major Political Problems Facing Taiwan in 1991,'" *Hsin Hsin-wen* (The Journalist), no. 237, September 29, 1992, in JPRS-CAR–92–007, February 18, 1992, p. 52.

Second, statistics gathered and presented by other authorities have too often seemed tailored to create a particular impression. An article in *Tzu-li Wan-pao* (Independence Evening Post) stated that because polling had become a commercial venture, "so long as the client is happy, it is guaranteed that even a sparrow can be turned into a phoenix." The author surveyed the surveys and found that when senior officials took polls every six months to determine their "approval rating," invariably it was listed as between 80 and 90 percent. When a senior official blundered or was criticized, his rating tended to hover around 60 percent. When an official actually did something that violated the law and was in danger of being toppled, his approval ratings tended to come out at 60–65 percent. Huang

Lien, "Public Opinion Polls' Perfect Foresight," *Tzu-li Wan-pao* (Independence Evening Post), October 6, 1991, in JPRS-CAR–91–073, December 23, 1991, p. 88. It is difficult to know how to regard such reports and what to make of the voluminous public opinion polls that are released by major newspapers and polling organizations. One cannot simply ignore them all, and yet one must be troubled about their methodology and significance.

38. Mainland Affairs Council, *Public Opinion and the Mainland Policy*, p. 7.

39. Comments of Chang Wen-chung, recorded at "Taiwan Trends," a debate about Taiwan politics sponsored by the Institute of Politics at Harvard University, the John F. Kennedy School of Government, ARCO Public Forum, December 5, 1991.

40. Interview with Chu Chi-ying, Taipei, July 4, 1991.

41. Chang Wen-chung, "Taiwan Trends," December 5, 1991.

42. Interview with Chen Shui-pian, Taipei, August 25, 1993.

43. Ibid.

44. The individual who offered this comment asked that he not be identified by name.

45. Agence France Presse, "Chairman Hsu Hsin-liang Said that Independence of Taiwan May Not Necessarily Become the Policy if the DPP Takes Over," in FBIS-CHI–92–039, February 27, 1992, p. 71.

46. "Calming Fears of the Masses Is No Easy Task: Special Interview with DPP Taiwan Independence Plank Sponsor, Lin Cho-shui, to Discuss the Taiwan Independence Clause," *Hsin Hsin-wen* (The Journalist), no. 241, October 1991, in JPRS-CAR–92–004, February 7, 1992.

47. Interview with Chiang Chun-nan, Taipei, May 20, 1991.

48. Peter W. Moody, *Political Change on Taiwan: A Study of Ruling Party Adaptability* (New York: Praeger, 1992), p. 181.

49. Tu Wei-ming, "A Confucian Perspective on Global Consciousness and Local Awareness," *IHJ Bulletin*, vol. 11, no. 1 (Winter 1991), p. 2.

50. Interview with Yao Chia-wen, Taipei, June 7, 1991.

51. Philippe C. Schmitter and Terry Lynn Karl, "What Democracy Is . . . and Is Not," *Journal of Democracy*, vol. 2, no. 3 (Summer 1991), p. 79.

52. Ibid., p. 83.

53. Wu Feng-shan, "Thoughts on the Normalization of Politics in Taiwan," *Tzu-li Wan-pao* (Independence Evening Post), September 30, 1991, in JPRS-CAR–91–067, November 26, 1991, pp. 48–50.

54. Interview with Kao Hui-yu, Taipei, May 24, 1991.

55. Lawrence W. Crissman, "The Structure of Local and Regional Systems," in *The Anthropology of Taiwanese Society*, ed. Emily Martin Ahern and Hill Gates (Stanford: Stanford University Press, 1981), p. 110.

56. J. Bruce Jacobs, *Local Politics in a Rural Chinese Cultural Setting: A Field Study of Mazu Township, Taiwan* (Canberra: Contemporary China Centre, Research School of Pacific Studies, Australian National University, 1980), pp. 147–48.

57. Ibid., p. 148.

58. See Shelley Rigger, "Machine Politics in the New Taiwan: Institutional Reform and Electoral Strategy in the Republic of China on Taiwan," Ph.D. dissertation, Harvard University Government Department, 1994.

59. Ting T'ing-yu, "Who Votes for the Opposition in Taiwan: A Case Study

of Chia-yi City," in *Taiwan: A Newly Industrialized State*, ed. Hsiao Hsin-huang, Wei-yuan Cheng, and Hou-sheng Chan (Taipei: Department of Sociology, National Taiwan University, 1989), p. 287.

60. Interview with Chiu I-jen, Taipei, March 21, 1991.

61. Ibid.

62. Ibid.

63. Interview with Chiu I-jen, Taipei, August 23, 1993.

64. Chang Mau-kuei, "The Formation of Partisan Preferences in Taiwan's Democratization," in *Taiwan: A Newly Industrialized State*, ed. Hsiao, Cheng, and Chan, p. 329.

65. Ibid., pp. 301, 307, 329, 338.

66. Interview with Chiu I-jen, Taipei, August 23, 1993.

67. Interview with P'eng Ming-min, Taipei, August 23, 1993.

68. The source of these comments asked that he not be named.

Conclusion

A 1991 survey conducted by Academia Sinica reported that most people on Taiwan feel that the conflict between people of different provincial origins is no longer much of a problem. Those who reported feeling any discrimination or harassment felt that it occurred in the workplace. When asked to comment about the severity of the problem as it affected the political realm at the central level, 5 percent said it was a very serious problem, 19.2 percent said it was serious, 22.2 percent said it was not too serious, 22.7 percent said it was not even a problem, and 30.3 percent either had no opinion or claimed not to know.

Asked about the extent of the problem as it affected politics at the local level, 3.8 percent said it was very serious, 14 percent said it was serious, 25.9 percent said it was not too serious, 32.4 percent said it was not even a problem, and 23.5 percent said that they had no opinion or did not know. If these results are valid, it suggests that in the course of daily affairs, most people are not much affected by the Taiwanese/Mainlander difference.[1] The sense of tension born of difference may be greatest among those who were adult at the time the KMT arrived on Taiwan. For most people, though, even if they acknowledge the difference between Taiwanese and Mainlanders, the difference does not affect them much.

Still, the opposition on Taiwan and its conflict with the KMT has not been simply a matter of reasonable people differing about political choices. The division between the KMT and the opposition was not a division reflecting a conservative/liberal spectrum. The most conflictual party relations, those between the KMT and the DPP, did not stem from differences of class origins or political temperament. Theirs is not essentially a conflict about guns or butter. It is a conflict about power.

Those in the opposition have a considerable desire to be in power, rather than to be on the outside of the ruling circle, and those in the KMT have a desire to stay in power. The conflict between them, however, has not been simply a competition between those who have power and those who want power but do not have it. For most of the period leading to democratization, Mainlanders had power and Taiwanese did not. Gradually, the equation began to shift. Mainlanders had most, but Taiwanese had some. With time, as democratization spread, that balance was reversed.

It is essential that one bear in mind that although "the KMT . . . is seventy percent Taiwanese . . . the opposition is almost 100 percent Taiwanese."[2] KMT officials are fond of citing the high proportion of party membership that is Taiwanese. It is odd, though, that the KMT feels it is noteworthy that 70 percent of its party membership is Taiwanese; after all, about 85 percent of the island's population identifies itself as Taiwanese. Conversely, that the opposition has been so thoroughly Taiwanese demands further explanation. The DPP has appealed to sentiments of Taiwanese national identity to distinguish itself from the KMT and has portrayed itself as a party of Taiwan, not China.

One cannot overlook the simple verity that during the period up to the Legislative Yuan election of 1992, the most significant opposition to the KMT existed as an expression of Taiwanese identity. That does not mean that all Taiwanese support the DPP or even the idea of an independent Taiwan. It does mean that the most basic point of conflict between the KMT and the opposition stems from the matter of identity.

Even the Chinese New party, founded in 1993, which strongly identifies with Sun Yat-sen and the ideology of the KMT, has differentiated itself from the KMT in part on the basis of identity. While the stated rationale of its founders for splitting with the KMT was an interest in dissociating themselves from the corruption of the KMT, the Chinese New party also provides a haven for former KMT Mainlanders who may feel that their old party, heavily populated by Taiwanese, no longer represents their interests as vigorously as they would like.

So, while matters of identity may not play a significant role in the daily lives of most people on Taiwan, they have occupied a position of some prominence in the political discourse of Taiwan. When asked to specify how this gap has had a negative influence on democratization, Hsu Hsin-liang said that because of the attitude of the Mainlander power holders, advocating an independent Taiwan was for many years a criminal offense. The political persecution that has followed from that policy has, in his view, slowed the progress of democratization. This had the effect of sharpening the conflict between the ruling elite and the opposition.[3]

Chen Shui-pian put it more bluntly:

> Basically, the road we took has been difficult in the past. Over the past forty years, to pursue party politics and democracy, our predecessors went through the 2–28 Incident, the period of white terror, the Kaohsiung Incident, and many bloody and horrifying assassinations. Even I have experienced this: my wife has to use a wheelchair for the rest of her life because of a "political car accident." I have also been jailed. None of this matters. But, it has been a tough road. How many people sacrificed their lives? How many people were deprived of happiness? How many people were deprived of liberty? To give up all that for a minimal level of party politics today which is not really genuine party politics. We have given our blood and sweat for the lifting of martial law, for the easing of restrictions on the formation of political parties, for the liberalization of media restrictions, and the election of the legislature. It has not been easy to get what we have gotten, but we still have not achieved the ideals which we expected.[4]

Chen claimed that the KMT controls the system loosely enough to give the impression of a democracy, but tightly enough to ensure that it remains in power. He cited the armed forces and the media as two organs the KMT continues to manipulate in its own interest.

Hsu Hsin-liang also spoke quite bitterly about what he perceives as the KMT's effort to continue monopolizing power. He particularly resents the fact that the KMT persecuted those who advocated independence when, in reality, the KMT has done everything it can to maintain Taiwan as an independent political entity.[5] In the end, Hsu asserted that the way to resolve the identity problem is to allow democratization to proceed. He objected to the proposition that the identity problem impedes democratization. According to him, "[d]emocratization could help solve the identity problem."[6]

Despite the legitimate concerns of the opposition about the ground still to be covered before Taiwan's political system operates according to democratic ideals, since the onset of political liberalization in the mid-1980s, Taiwan's leadership has done a good deal to change. They have moved from moral authority as the basis of legitimacy to what Huntington termed "performance legitimacy"—legitimacy based on the delivery of political goods. The moral authority that the KMT had when it arrived on the island was its claim to represent all of China. It is currently relying on its capacity to preserve stability on Taiwan and promote prosperity for continued legitimacy.

Taiwan's political culture has also changed through a gradual process of experimentation and learning. The period 1987–1992 saw the growth and flourishing of a civil society that has generated the expectations that individuals are entitled to "make claims on the state." Taiwan's society can now "be characterized as a 'demanding civil society' with a new kind of 'participatory political culture' as its socio-psychological base."[7]

This change has brought about a new form of relations between the state and society. Political activists have learned to "act like respectable challengers. They demand change but not revolution" because most of them "understand that they will have more to lose if the existing political and economic system is weakened drastically."[8] If this is true, the comparative stability with which Taiwan has weathered the storms of political transformation may be attributed to the degree of investment individuals have in the system as it exists.

Perhaps the incremental and restrained way both the state and the society have approached the process of liberalization is testimony to people's preference for continued economic growth and political stability above all else. There seems to be a tacit understanding that the state will continue to loosen its reins—up to a limit—and the people will continue to press their demands—but up to a limit. Even though the boat is being rocked, it will not be rocked too violently. The willingness to compromise, on the part of both the governors and the governed, in order to protect a degree of stability may itself indicate that a sense of communal interest does exist despite differences in professed visions of national identity. There already may be a recognition that no changes are worth ruining what the people and their government have spent the past forty years building.

Since the 1991 elections of the National Assembly and the 1992 elections of the Legislative Yuan, the fever for independence seems to have subsided, though it has not disappeared. Perhaps the lower pitch of the opposition's demands has to do with the growing sense that President Lee Teng-hui is in greater control of the KMT. On Taiwan, one commonly expressed perception is that the KMT of Lee Teng-hui is not interested in reunification except as a verbal shield against attack from the PRC.

It is also apparent that the KMT has been transformed. Whereas it was once seen as a party of Mainlanders defending its right to govern all China, it has become a party composed of Taiwanese as well as Mainlanders defending its interest in retaining power on Taiwan. Whereas it was once ideologically fervent, it now practices and preaches pragmatism. Reunification is still held up as a goal, but held up at such a height that one can only surmise that it is no longer an urgent goal. Indeed, it is hard to imagine what the KMT would do if the goal were suddenly reached.

Chiu I-jen accurately anticipated that the KMT would promote democratization while Lee Teng-hui sought to dominate the party. Then, Chiu predicted, once Lee had prevailed in the internal power struggle, democratization would end. President Lee has certainly prevailed, yet it remains to be seen whether Chiu is correct about the future pace of democratic reform. Even if Taiwan progresses no further toward achieving the ideals of democracy than it did at the time of the Legislative Yuan elections in December 1992, strictly speaking it has already become democratic, even if imperfectly so.

It is not clear that people in general seek much more. The populace has certainly been much less agitated since the elections of 1991 and 1992. For many, the pace and direction of change has resulted in a perceived diminution of the quality of their lives. That is, change has gone too far and too fast. Economic prosperity coupled with a relaxation of strict political and social controls has caused a great surge in the opportunity for self-realization but has brought a concomitant plague of social ills and environmental hazards. Crime, pollution, traffic, social disorder, inflation, and dissolution of common moral values have accompanied the growth of the economy and an increasingly cosmopolitan lifestyle. While people have more of the things they used to complain they lacked (freedom, opportunity, expendable income), they also lack many of the things they never noticed they enjoyed (stability, wholesome community values, cleaner environment, and so forth).

In response to these rising concerns, the KMT has addressed issues of stability and prosperity in its campaigns. By doing so, the KMT has shown that it is more concerned about addressing the needs of the population on Taiwan than about governing a greater territory. The slogans used by the KMT in its 1991 and 1992 campaigns were aimed at attracting Taiwan's voters by targeting objectives to which they would respond favorably. The KMT offered stability to counter the opposition's propensity for public disorder. The KMT staked a claim to its role in the growth of Taiwan's "economic miracle" and suggested that under its rule Taiwan would continue to be prosperous.

By emphasizing qualities that the KMT could offer Taiwan rather than addressing the needs of the greater Chinese state, perhaps the KMT unintentionally has been drawn into accepting that Taiwan, not some greater China, is the state. By addressing the citizens of the island, rather than all Chinese, the KMT has unwittingly shifted its focus to the populace of Taiwan as the only citizens of the republic. In terms of its actions and behavior, the KMT has long since abandoned the role it claims to desire as the sole legitimate government of China and has accepted the reality that Taiwan itself is the nation.

This change in the KMT is an unintended consequence of democratization, which necessitated that the party's candidates appeal directly to voters. The DPP has also changed through electoral competition. It been edged gradually to more moderate positions. For the DPP, democracy was initially a way of using the power of the ballot box to force the issue of independence. With time, though, the opposition leaders came to see a broader interest. Yao Chia-wen said, "[W]e are not simply trying to replace the KMT [to] become [the] ruling party. What we are doing is to reform the political system here. To give people freedom, human rights, and a fair opportunity, and so on. To take away what is not good in this society—that is our ideal ... not simply ... just [to] try to take and replace."[9] During the height of the period of reform, however, the most public, vocal, disruptive, and assertive efforts of the DPP as a party seemed to be aimed at two related issues: the legitimacy of the KMT and the desirability of Taiwan's independence. These are the issues over which the DPP has risked the most and has created the greatest uproar. To say that the DPP was interested simply in reform is to ignore the relentless efforts by the opposition to ridicule and shame the KMT into making the presidency, the Legislative Yuan, and the National Assembly representative of Taiwan's voters and to raise at every turn the right of Taiwanese to exercise self-determination. One must conclude that for the opposition, reform was equated with establishing a system in which residents of Taiwan could exercise self-determination. As Taiwan's system became more democratic, the DPP was able to approach this end in a less combative fashion. However, the underlying aim may still exist.

At the heart of the tension between the KMT and the opposition has been the issue of Taiwan's political status and, necessarily, the definition of what it means to be Chinese living on Taiwan. At the rhetorical level, this issue is often cast simply as a choice between reunification and independence, but the conflicting sentiments have to do with much more than visions of Taiwan's future. Despite the focus on the *t'ung-tu* problem,[10] the more fundamental problem has been the sharing of power on Taiwan. Those who were barred by the KMT from access to political power have demanded that they be given a hand in the determination of their own lives. The opposition struggled to pry the system open enough that the residents of Taiwan alone have the right to select their governors, not people who voted on the mainland four decades ago or people who now live elsewhere. The KMT, on the other hand, was reluctant to give up the power it hoarded for itself because of fears of retribution and concerns that there were no opponents capable of assuming control of public policy in a rational manner. It also feared that if the advocates of independence gained the upper hand in the opposition and the opposition came to power, the wrath of the PRC easily could be invoked.

During the late 1980s and early 1990s the views of both sides were expressed in shrill and exaggerated terms, but nobody seemed to be listening. The compromises that were reached between the regime and the opposition were made, not on the basis of an acceptance of the validity of the other's views, but on calculations of power.

The more the KMT loosened control over the political system, the louder the complaint from the opposition about KMT rule. Hearing this demanding clamor, the conservative elements of the KMT frequently dug in their heels to resist further liberalization. When this segment of the KMT exerted its influence over government policy, it elicited even greater denunciations from the radical element of the opposition, which mocked the effort of the KMT to oversee reforms. This led the most vociferous opponents to castigate the entire KMT. The extremist voices in the opposition reinforced the views of the extremists in the KMT and left the reform-minded KMT elements sandwiched in between. Understanding the need to work with these reformers in the

KMT, the more moderate members of the opposition were driven to compromise in an effort to extract some changes, by offering the moderate members of the KMT less volatile partners with whom to deal.

The division between the KMT and the opposition reflects different views of national identity. The divisions within each of the two camps reflect different political temperaments and, within the KMT, the difference between Taiwanese and Mainlanders. The extremists on both ends are chauvinistic regarding their nation, impatient to proceed with their program, and intolerant of those who do not share their views. The moderates tend to be less emotional, take a longer-range view, and understand that compromise is a necessary dimension of stability under a democratic system.

During this early phase of political reorientation it seems that few were concerned about democracy for its own sake, but regarded democracy as a way to amass, or maintain, political power. It is a means, not an end. Similarly, the question of national identity was also exploited by both the KMT and the opposition as a way to attract popular support among given constituencies.

The absence of consensus among Taiwan's political elite about the explosive issue of national identity did not impede the process of democratization—quite the contrary. The opposition was able to harness the force of Taiwanese consciousness to forge a sense of nationalism that ignited the process of reform. Wary of unrest in a state where Mainlanders were a minority, Chiang Ching-kuo recognized the value of liberalization as a way to ensure that the KMT would not be toppled. The contest between the nationalism of the Mainlanders and that of the Taiwanese shaped the course of liberalization and led to the establishment of democratic practices.

From the perspective of theories about the sequence in which democratization occurs, the absence of consensus about national identity should have undermined the process. Theorists of democratization evidently did not envisage a situation such as that on Taiwan. While there is no consensus about national identity among the elite on Taiwan, there is a widespread consensus that the uncertain status quo is preferable to certain chaos. Taiwanese recognize that a declaration of independence might precipitate a hostile response from the PRC. Mainlanders holding power in the KMT understand that premature reunification may incite domestic unrest—or worse. Neither of these options is as desirable as the status quo.

Mainlanders in the KMT seem to accept this tacitly. They have essentially consented to defer reunification, are supportive of the prosperity and stability of Taiwan, and content themselves in the knowledge that reunification as a goal is still possible. Taiwanese, whether in the KMT or in the opposition, accept that the island is an autonomous political entity. While they may wish that it had greater international status than it does, the value of promoting an immediate declaration of independence has diminished as their role in running the island has expanded.

In this regard, both Taiwanese and Mainlanders have tacitly accepted the present autonomy of Taiwan, although each may have different visions for the island's future. That the Mainlanders are such a minority in the population suggests that in a fully democratic system their parochial interests may no longer prevail as they did in the past, when a Mainlander-dominated KMT controlled the apparatus of the state. Once the last vestiges of authoritarianism have been stripped away and democratic institutions and practices prevail, whether the government of Taiwan promotes reunification or independence will depend—as is fitting in a democracy—on the force of persuasion, not on the persuasiveness of force.

Notes

1. Hsiao Hsin-huang, "Sheng-chi jen-ting yu sheng-chi wen-t'i" (Provincial Identification and the Problem of Provincial Origin)," in *T'ai-wan ti-chu she-hui i-hsiang tiao ch'a* (Survey of Social Attitudes in the Taiwan Area) (Nankang: Academia Sinica, January 1991), pp. 46–47.

2. Peter W. Moody, *Political Change on Taiwan: A Study of Ruling Party Adaptability* (New York: Praeger, 1992), p. 60.

3. Interview with Hsu Hsin-liang, Taipei, June 3, 1991.

4. Interview with Chen Shui-pian, Taipei, August 25, 1993. Chen's wife was injured in a car accident during one of Chen's campaigns for office. There are different accounts of what happened, but Chen has asserted that the accident was arranged as a form of political harassment.

5. Interview with Hsu Hsin-liang, Taipei, June 3, 1991.

6. Ibid.

7. Hsiao Hsin-huang, "Emerging Social Movements and the Rise of a Demanding Civil Society in Taiwan," *The Australian Journal of Chinese Affairs* no. 24 (July 1990), p. 178.

8. Ibid., p. 179.

9. Interview with Yao Chia-wen, Taipei, June 7, 1991.

10. In Chinese, the term *t'ung-i* (unification) is used to refer to the condition under which Taiwan and the mainland will be unified as one political entity. In English, this is frequently translated as *re*unification, which has a slightly different implication about the relations between the two sides of the Taiwan Strait.

In Chinese, the movement to declare Taiwan an independent state is referred to as *T'ai-tu*, a contraction of *T'ai-wan tu-li*, which means Taiwan independence. The conflict between those who advocate reunification and those who advocate independence is frequently referred to as the *t'ung-tu wen-t'i* (the reunification/independence problem).

Appendix One

Individuals Interviewed

The following is a list of individuals with whom I conducted formal interviews. It does not include all those individuals who provided information and insight about the situation on Taiwan in a less formal fashion. The biographical note following each name provides only an indication of the person's role on Taiwan and is by no means a comprehensive account of the individual's background and experiences. Names in parentheses are those by which the person is commonly known in the English press.

Chang An-p'ing (Nelson), president, Chia-Hsin Cement Corporation; chairman, China Management Systems Corporation; second-generation Mainlander.

Chang Chun-hung, legislator, Legislative Yuan (DPP); formerly: secretary-general, DPP; executive editor-in-chief, *Ta-hsueh* (The Intellectual), an influential opposition journal in the 1970s; editor-in-chief, *T'ai-wan Cheng-lun* (Taiwan Political Review); member, Taiwan Provincial Assembly; imprisoned for eight years for his role in the Kaohsiung Incident; Taiwanese.

Chang Yan-hsien, Sun Yat-Sen Institute for Social Sciences and Philosophy, Academia Sinica; Taiwanese.

Chang Yu-sheng, president, Pacific Cultural Foundation; Mainlander.

Chen Charng-ven (C.V. Chen), senior partner, Lee and Li, Attorneys-at-Law; vice-chairman and secretary-general, Straits Exchange Foundation, established to communicate, negotiate, and handle relations with the PRC; consultant, Executive Yuan; legal consultant, Central Bank of China; legal consultant, Ministry of Foreign Affairs; general counsel, Ministry of Defense; member, Committee on Review and Drafting of Socioeconomic Laws, Commission for Economic Planning and Development; secretary-general, Red Cross Society of the Republic of China, another organization used for "unofficial" contact with the PRC; Mainlander.

Chen Shui-pian, legislator, Legislative Yuan (DPP); Taiwanese.

Chen Yi-jen, entrepreneur, philanthropist; Hakka-Taiwanese.

Chiang Chun-nan (Antonio), publisher, *Hsin Hsin-wen* (The Journalist); writer, *Tzu-li Wan-pao* (Independence Evening Post); formerly: reporter and editor, overseas edition, *Chung-kuo Shih-pao* (China Times); editor-in-chief, *Pa-shih Nien-tai* (Eighties Magazine); publisher, *Asian Magazine*; director, *Shou-tu Tzao-pao* (Capitol Morning Post); Taiwanese.

Chien Hsin-chu (Edward), professor, Hong Kong University of Science and Technology; formerly: professor, Department of History, National Taiwan University.

Chin Hsiao-yi, director, National Palace Museum; director-general, Party History Committee, Central Committee, KMT; member, Central Committee, KMT; professor, Three Principles Institute, National Taiwan University; professor, Chinese Cultural University; chairman, Chinese Historical Association; formerly: secretary to President Chiang Kai-Shek, 1950–1974; deputy secretary-general, Central Committee, KMT, 1961–1975; Mainlander.

Chiu I-jen, deputy secretary-general, DPP; publisher and editor-in-chief, *Hsin Chao-liu* (The New Tide), journal of the pro-independence faction of the DPP; member, DPP Central Executive Committee; Taiwanese.

Chu Chi-ying (James), director, Department of Cultural Affairs, Central Committee, KMT; KMT spokesman; Mainlander.

Chu Kao-cheng (Ju Gau-jeng), legislator, Legislative Yuan (CSDP); chairman, CSDP; formerly: member, Central Executive Committee and Central Standing Committee, DPP; gained notoriety by instigating use of violence in Legislative Yuan; Taiwanese.

Hau Pei-tsun, vice-chairman, Central Standing Committee, KMT; formerly: premier; minister of national defense; chief of the general staff, Ministry of National Defense; Mainlander.

Ho Chen-Hsiung (Earle), chairman, Taiwan Steel and Iron Industries; president, Tung Ho Steel Enterprise Corporation; Taiwanese.

Hsiao Hsin-huang (Michael), Institute of Ethnology, Academia Sinica; professor, National Taiwan University; chairman, ROC Consumers' Foundation; director, New Era Foundation; organizer, Purity Society, an alliance of liberal intellectuals who comment on social and political affairs; Hakka-Taiwanese.

Hsu Chi-ming (Steve), deputy chairman, Research and Planning Board, Ministry of Foreign Affairs; formerly: overseas correspondent; Mainlander.

Hsu Hsin-liang, former chairman of the DPP; member, Taiwan Provincial Assembly, elected on a KMT ticket; KMT membership revoked; ran for and won Taoyuan County magistrate without KMT endorsement; participated in an unauthorized political demonstration in 1977 and was suspended from his elected position for two years; associated with *Mei-li Tao* (Formosa) magazine; political exile in the United States; attempted several times to reenter Taiwan without authorization; the focus of several major political demonstrations and one riot; ultimately returned to Taiwan and was arrested and jailed for illegal reentry, January 1990; pardoned and released, March 1990; Taiwanese.

Hsu Lu, correspondent, *Tzu-li Wan-pao* (Independence Evening Post); formerly: correspondent for *Shou-tu Tzao-pao* (Capital Morning Post); gained notoriety in 1988 when she and a colleague were the first journalists from the ROC to travel to the PRC in violation of ROC restrictions on contact with the mainland; second-generation Mainlander.

Hsu Shao-p'o (Paul), senior partner, Lee and Li, Attorneys-at-Law; professor, National Taiwan University; Mainlander.

Hsueh Kwang-zu, educator; Mainlander.

Hu Fo, professor, Department of Political Science, National Taiwan University; Organizing Committee, National Affairs Conference (NAC), 1990; gained public recognition when he quit the NAC, charging that its work was not sufficiently serious and that he would not compromise his scholarly standing by participating; Mainlander.

Huang Chu-wen, legislator, convenor, Legislative Yuan (KMT); head of Wisdom Club, largest faction of Taiwan-elected legislators in KMT; Taiwanese.

Jen Chi-ping, professor, Department of Political Science, Tunghai University.

K'ang Ning-hsiang, adviser to DPP; member, National Reunification Commission; formerly: member Taipei City Council; legislator, Legislative Yuan; founder, DPP; publisher, *Shou-tu Tzao-pao* (Capital Morning Post); member, organizing committee, and participant, National Affairs Conference; Taiwanese.

Kao Hui-yu (Alice), deputy, National Assembly (KMT); correspondent-at-large and former city editor, *Lien-ho Pao* (United Daily News), Taiwan's second largest newspaper; member, Central Committee of the KMT; second-generation Mainlander.

Kuo Ying-ting (Po Yang), author, *Chou-lou ti Chung-kuo jen* (The Ugly Chinese) and other social commentary; formerly: jailed for political dissent; Mainlander.

Li Hsin Chu (Nigel), attorney, Lee and Li, Attorneys-at-Law; professor, National Taiwan University; member, Central Committee, KMT; participant, National Affairs Conference, 1990; second-generation Mainlander.

Li I-yuan, member, Academia Sinica; dean, College of Humanities and Social Sciences, National Tsing-hua University; president, Chiang Ching-kuo Foundation for International Scholarly Exchange; formerly: professor, National Taiwan University; director, Institute of Ethnography, Academia Sinica; Mainlander.

Li Kuo-ting (K. T. Li), senior adviser to the president; member, National Science Council; member, Central Standing Committee, KMT; formerly: professor, National Wuhan University; member, Industrial Development Corporation, Economic Stabilization Board; secretary-general, Council for U.S. Aid; vice-chairman, Council for International Economic Cooperation and Development; minister of economic affairs; minister of finance; minister of state; Mainlander.

Lin Cheng-chieh, legislator, Legislative Yuan (originally DPP); formerly: Central Standing Committee, DPP; writer, commentator about politics; member, Taipei City Council; jailed for over one year as organizer of street demonstrations; gained widespread attention in spring 1991 when he resigned from the DPP, charging that it did not tolerate his support of reunification; Mainlander.

Liu Chin-tien, director, People's Service Division, Kaohsiung County, Kang-shan Township, KMT Headquarters; Taiwanese.

Lu Hsiu-lien (Annette), legislator, Legislative Yuan (DPP); feminist; political activist; lawyer; author; founding director, Coalition for Democracy; founding director, National Organization for Women (ROC); deputy director, *Mei-li Tao* (Formosa) magazine; arrested and jailed for five and a half years on charges of sedition stemming from the Kaohsiung Incident; Taiwanese.

Lu Ya-li, professor, Department of Political Science, National Taiwan University; Mainlander.

Ma Han-pao, grand justice, Judicial Yuan; professor of law, National Taiwan University; formerly: commissioner, Examination Yuan; Mainlander.

Ma Ying-cheou, minister of justice; formerly: deputy director, Mainland Affairs Council; chairman, Research, Development and

Evaluation Committee, Executive Yuan; professor of law, National Cheng-chi University; deputy director, First Bureau, Office of the President; deputy secretary-general, Central Committee, KMT; senior secretary, Office of the President; second-generation Mainlander.

Ming Chu-cheng, professor, Department of Political Science, National Taiwan University.

P'eng Ming-min, formerly: chairman of Department of Political Science, National Taiwan University; arrested and sentenced in 1964 for sedition; escaped from house arrest and later spent more than twenty years in political exile in the United States; Taiwanese.

Shaw Yu-ming, formerly: director-general, Government Information Office; government spokesman; member, Central Committee, KMT; professor, Graduate School of International Law and Diplomacy, National Cheng-chi University; Mainlander.

Shieh Sen-chung (Samuel), governor, Central Bank of China; formerly: professor, National Taiwan University; special chief and secretary-general, Joint Commission on Rural Reconstruction; director of projects, Asian Development Bank; vice-chairman, Council for Economic Planning and Development; chairman, Bank of Communications; Mainlander.

Soong Chu-yu (James), governor of Taiwan; formerly: secretary-general, Central Committee, KMT; research fellow, Institute for International Relations, National Cheng-chi University; managing director, China Television; managing director, Taiwan Television Company; member, Central Committee, KMT; member, Central Standing Committee of KMT, Executive Yuan; associate professor, National Taiwan University; director-general, Government Information Office; director-general, Department of Cultural Affairs, Central Committee, KMT; Mainlander.

Ting Shou-chung, legislator, Legislative Yuan (KMT); professor, Institute of Political Science, National Taiwan University; chief executive officer, Democracy Foundation; columnist, *Chung-yang Jih-pao*

(Central Daily News); deputy director, Asia and World Institute; second-generation Mainlander.

Tsai Jen-chien, director of propaganda, DPP; Taiwanese.

Tsiang Yien-si, secretary-general, Office of the President; senior adviser to the President; chairman, Committee on Science and Development, National Science Council; adviser, Council on Agriculture; member, Atomic Energy Council; member, National Science Development Committee; Counselor, Academia Sinica; member, Central Committee, KMT; formerly: executive officer and secretary-general, Joint Commission on Rural Reconstruction (established to administer U.S. economic aid); commissioner, Joint Commission on Rural Reconstruction; secretary-general, Executive Yuan; minister of education; minister of foreign affairs; secretary-general, Central Committee, KMT; national policy adviser to the president; Mainlander.

Wang Hsing-ching, editor-in-chief, *Hsin Hsin-wen* (The Journalist); second-generation Mainlander.

Wang Yi-hsiung, attorney; formerly: associate professor, Fu Jen University; candidate for Legislative Yuan; Taiwanese.

Wu Tsu-ping, honorary consul-general to Malta, Swaziland; formerly: vice-chairman, Commission on Light Industries; general manager, Taiwan Paper Corporation; chairman, Taiwan Scott Paper Corporation; chairman, Chinese Shoppers Association; chairman, Taiwan Paper Association; Mainlander.

Yang Hsien-hung, environmental activist; author; formerly: deputy editor, *Shou-tu Tzao-pao* (Capital Morning Post); Taiwanese.

Yang Kuo-hsu, Institute of Ethnography, Academia Sinica; professor, Department of Psychology, National Taiwan University.

Yao Chia-wen, Member, Central Standing Committee, DPP; formerly: chairman, DPP; professor of law, Fu Jen University, Chinese Cultural University; arrested and jailed for eight years in the wake of the Kaohsiung Incident; Taiwanese.

Yu Tsung-hsien, president, Chung Hwa Institute for Economic Research; member Academia Sinica; professor, National Taiwan University; adviser, Council for Economic Planning and Development; Mainlander.

Yu-Chen Yueh-ying, magistrate (chief county executive), Kaohsiung County; member, Taiwan Provincial Assembly; legislator, Legislative Yuan (DPP); daughter-in-law of Yu Teng-fa; Taiwanese.

Appendix Two

Letter from Tsiang Yien-si

OFFICE OF THE PRESIDENT OF THE REPUBLIC OF CHINA

July 8, 1991

Mr. Alan M. Wachman
K. T. Li Dissertation Research Fellow
Center for International Affairs
Harvard University

Dear Mr. Wachman:

Reference is made to your letter dated June 12, 1991 to Dr. K. T. Li concerning your dissertation research.

After looking over the central issue which you want to understand as listed in your letter, I am writing in the following my views about these issues:

(1) CULTURAL IDENTITY

    a. Is there any difference between Chinese culture and Taiwanese culture?

I don't really know what you mean by "Taiwanese culture," or for that matter, what is your definition of "culture." China is a vast country. In many ways, how people do things in one area may be very different from that in another area. This is quite natural and common in many countries, and these differences, strictly speaking, should hardly be considered "cultural." For instance, some Buddhists, some Catholics . . . etc. But they are all Chinese.

I think there is no doubt that Taiwan is now very much a major center of Chinese culture, and one would find it very difficult to justifiably define the existence of a "Taiwanese culture" separated from China. Recently many people from Taiwan went to Mainland China for various reasons, most of them were struck by the remarkable resemblance between their cultural life in Taiwan and that in many areas of Mainland China, especially around the Southern coastal regions like Fukien Province. Indeed while we Chinese are being separated by the geographical division of the Taiwan Strait, we are still very much united by a common bond—the Chinese Culture.

> b. What efforts were made by the government to create a
> unified sense of Chinese culture on Taiwan?

No effort as I know of was ever made to "unify" Chinese and "Taiwanese" cultures, if this is what your question implies. However, on the other hand, we would not deny that we Chinese are always very proud of our culture and treasure our tradition and heritage. More than two decades ago, the Chinese Communists launched a "Cultural Revolution" for purposes of political power struggle, but the "Revolution" threatened the preservation and the very existence of our culture. The ROC Government on Taiwan then therefore made urgent efforts to promote what is known as the "Chinese Cultural Renaissance Movement" to counter any possible devastation of the "Revolution." Recently our President Lee Teng-hui was personally involved in the reorganization of the movement and serves himself as the President of the National Council for Chinese Cultural Renaissance. The purpose of our renaissance movement has always been to affirm and restore those traditional values in the Chinese culture which would help to enrich our spiritual life in a rapidly developing society that can become also increasingly materialistic. We believe our cultural renaissance movement will refine our socio-political life and brings more sense and stability to our society.

(2) POLITICAL IDENTITY

> a. Do Chinese feel a strong sense of identification with "the state" or do people have a stronger sense of loyalty to some smaller political units?

Patriotism is always regarded as a very high virtue in Chinese history and culture, and therefore to love and to die for a state is often encouraged and praised. Loyalty to smaller political units against the state (for instance, factional struggles) is generally not accepted and treated with contempt.

> b. How people view China—is it a state? a culture? a nation?

Different people may have different views on this question. But I personally believe more people would accept the view that China is a trinity of culture, nation, and state. We hope to build China, including both the Mainland and Taiwan, a modernized nation-state with a rich and valuable culture. Our experience in Taiwan for the past four decades, the well-known "Taiwan experience," will help us to achieve the goal of modernizing that "nation-state." Our present endeavor with regard to cultural renaissance will help us to restore and revive the value of Chinese culture. So you can see why I believe that people would increasingly reflect the view that China is a trinity of the state, the nation, and the culture.

> c. Since 1949, how did the government view of Taiwan as a political unit change?

The government's view of Taiwan as a political unit has remained largely unchanged and consistent. For more than forty years, we consider ourselves—the Republic of China—the legitimate representative for the Chinese nation, including both the Mainland and Taiwan. In other words, we have never given up our sovereignty over Mainland China.

You may not understand why we maintain our claim of sovereignty over the mainland. But why should we give up that claim? What good would it bring us? In fact the claim is a reflection of our sense of responsibility, as long as we maintain our sovereignty, we would never forsake our duty in bringing freedom, democracy and prosperity to our compatriots on the mainland.

In 1988, President Lee made it clear in an important speech that we do not deny the fact that we do not control the mainland, but this does not affect our claim of sovereignty. In 1991, when we adopted our "Guidelines for National Unification," it was also indicated that we would be willing to deal with the Mainland authorities as a political entity on a reciprocal basis. These two events do not necessarily change our view of Taiwan as a political unit, but they are not completely unrelated to your question, so I mention them for your reference.

(3) DEMOCRATIZATION

a. Do the conflicts about cultural and political identity
   influence the process of making Taiwan more democratic?

The conflicts we are seeing here in the process of democratization take various forms. They may appear to have different appeal and substance, e.g. economic, social and cultural. But in essence, they are often politically-motivated. As our political process becomes more pluralistic and democratic, these conflicts receive encouragement and reinforcement and sometimes dominate our political stage. This gives an impression that our politics is more conflictive than harmonious. When these conflicts become at times violent and law-breaking, people begin to fear that they are detrimental to our task of political reform and would ruin our hope for a more democratic political system. Just imagine, when people see parliamentarians throwing chairs around, tearing down microphones and even fighting each other, they may say "If this is democracy, maybe we could do better without it!"

However, I tend to think that some of these conflictive political behaviors are only temporary phenomena, as I believe most of the people involved in such behaviors would really want to see a more democratic system in the future. Ultimately they would not want to do anything intentionally to harm our hope for democracy. In the long run, you will see these conflicts in Taiwan today as an important part of our lessons for democratization.

b. How did the government expect to proceed with democratization?

You will find quite a lot of materials concerning this question published in newspapers and many journals. Basically speaking, first the emergency decree of the Martial Law must be lifted. This was done in 1986. After then, previous bans on publication of new newspapers and formation of new political parties were also cancelled. In 1990, a National Affairs Conference was convened to offer an open forum for people of all political persuasions to exchange views on issues relating to Constitutional revision and mainland policy. Actual work on Constitutional revision began in early 1991 with the meeting of the Extraordinary Session of the National Assembly. Before the beginning of May, this year, the Temporary Provisions were abrogated and the Period of National Mobilization for Suppression of Communist Rebellion terminated, providing a legal basis for further Constitutional revision and the comprehensive reelection for all members of the three different houses of our Parliament.

This is just a rough description of our step-by-step program of political reform, I am afraid we will not have enough time to go into details.

c. What features of democracy are likely to be most compatible with the political traditions of Chinese on Taiwan?

The political traditions of Chinese on Taiwan have been heavily influenced by contemporary democratic principles and political thinking. However, the influence did not only come from external sources. Ever since our Central Government came to Taiwan, we have never stopped stressing the importance of democracy in all classrooms and steady efforts have been made to build a system of democracy here. In fact, I don't think there is any element of the concept of democracy incompatible with our political culture here. Nevertheless I can offer the following three points for your reference:

First, in any democracy, the principle of "for the people, by the people, of the people" is respected. The interest of the people, in other words, must be the paramount concern. This is exactly what we have done in Taiwan. We have followed the "Three Principles of the People" of Dr. Sun Yat-sen, our national Founding Father, and have built, I believe, a society of freedom, democracy and equitable distribution of wealth. But we are not content with ourselves and we want to do more for the people. We presume that our people also want us to do more and are "pushing" us toward that aim. We don't mind being pushed by our people to do more for them—in a democratic system, we view such "push" as trust and support.

Secondly, regular elections are an important feature of modern democracy and we are pleased to say that in Taiwan, we have successfully built a feasible system of regular elections at many different levels.

Thirdly, the existence of a viable political opposition. Despite the fact that the Kuomintang always enjoys tremendous popular support, there has always been a viable political opposition in Taiwan. The largest opposition party is now the Democratic Progressive Party and it plays quite a significant role in our political arena. In fact, there are presently more than fifty political parties in our country.

(4) SOURCE OF PROBLEMS WITH DEMOCRATIZATION

a. To what extent are the difficulties with democratization on Taiwan a reflection of deeper, fundamental characteristics of Chinese culture or history?

China has a long imperial tradition. Many would therefore consider that democracy is an alien concept. This is not entirely correct. Although China had always been ruled by an emperor before the Republican era came into being, the value of democracy is not completely ignored. In many historical classical writings one could find references to the importance of the people in the political system. It has been stressed repeatedly that a monarch should pay attention to the welfare and opinion of the people because the people are important to the state. Those monarchs who fail to heed the need and wishes of the people will lose the "mandate of heaven" and thereby lose their legitimacy to rule. On the other hand, however, one is inclined to conclude that such a concept of democracy comes closer to the principle of "for the people," and not necessarily reflects the ideas of "by the people" and "of the people."

Many studies have been conducted on the relationships between Chinese culture and democracy, yet no conclusive findings have been produced to suggest that our cultural tradition may hamper any effort of democratization. I, for one, certainly don't think so, especially if you are talking about the democratization process in Taiwan. Given a stable and secure environment (i.e. if the Chinese Communists don't bother us), I don't think we have any serious obstacle on the road of political reform. Moreover, if we could properly restore some of the basic value of our culture, our pace of democratization will become smoother and faster.

Although the above-stated views are personal, I believe that they would be shared by many of my countrymen. Hope they will be helpful to your dissertation research.

Sincerely yours,

Yien-Si Tsiang

cc: Dr. K.T. Li

Selected Bibliography

Ahern, Emily Martin, and Hill Gates, eds. *The Anthropology of Taiwanese Society*. Stanford: Stanford University Press, 1981.

Anderson, Benedict. *Imagined Communities: Reflections on the Origin and Spread of Nationalism*. London: Verso, 1983.

Arat, Zehra F. "Democracy and Economic Development: Modernization Theory Revisited." *Comparative Politics* 21 (October 1988): 21–37.

Breuilly, John. *Nationalism and the State*. Manchester: Manchester University Press, 1982.

Chang Mau-kuei. "The Formation of Partisan Preferences in Taiwan's Democratization." In *Taiwan: A Newly Industrialized State*, edited by Hsiao Hsin-huang, Cheng Wei-yuan, and Chan Hou-sheng. Taipei: National Taiwan University, 1989.

"The Charter of the *Kuo Min Tang* of China," Article 2. In *Getting to Know the KMT: The Nationalist Party of China*, vol. 2, edited by the Department of Cultural Affairs of the Central Committee of the *Kuo Min Tang*. Taipei: China Cultural Services, 1989.

Chao, Linda, and Ramon H. Myers. "The First Chinese Democracy: Political Development of the Republic of China on Taiwan: 1986–1994." *Asian Survey* 34, no. 3 (March 1994): 213–30.

Ch'en, Li-li. "When Jackals Rule: A Defiant Year Under Chiang Kai-shek." *Mother Jones* 3 (July 1983): 12–19.

Ch'en Yung-hsing. *Cheng-chiu T'ai-wan-jen ti hsin-ling* (Saving the Heart of Taiwan). Taipei: Vanguard Press, 1988.

Cheng, Tun-jen, and Stephan Haggard. "Regime Transformation in Taiwan: Theoretical and Comparative Perspectives." In *Political Change in Taiwan*, edited by Cheng and Haggard.

——— eds. *Political Change in Taiwan*. Boulder, CO: Lynne Rienner, 1992.

Chiang Ching-kuo. "President Chiang's Address to the National Assembly at the 1984 Constitution Day Ceremony." In *Republic of China: A Reference Book, 1986,* edited by Dixson D.S. Sung and Lawrence C. Ho. New York and Taipei: Highlight International, 1986.

Chiu, Hungdah. *China and the Taiwan Issue*. New York: Praeger, 1979.

Chou Yangsun, and Andrew Nathan. "Democratizing Transition in Taiwan." *Asian Survey* 27, no. 3 (March 1987): 277–99.

Clark, Cal. *Taiwan's Development: Implications for Contending Political Economy Paradigms*. New York: Greenwood Press, 1989.

Clough, Ralph. *Island China*. Cambridge: Harvard University Press, 1978.

Cohen, Marc J. *Taiwan at the Crossroads: Human Rights, Political Development and Social Change on the Beautiful Island*. Washington, DC: Asia Resource Center, 1988.

Copper, John F. *A Quiet Revolution: Political Development in the Republic of China*. Washington, DC: Ethics and Public Policy Center, 1988.

————. *Taiwan: Nation-State or Province?* Boulder, CO: Westview Press, 1990.

Crissman, Lawrence W. "The Structure of Local and Regional Systems. In *The Anthropology of Taiwanese Society*, edited by Ahern and Gates.

Dahl, Robert. *Polyarchy: Participation and Opposition*. New Haven: Yale University Press, 1971.

Davidson, James W. *The Island of Formosa: Past and Present*. London: Macmillan, 1903. Reprint. Oxford: Oxford University Press, 1988.

Diamond, Larry, Seymour Martin Lipset, and Juan Linz. "Building and Sustaining Democratic Government in Developing Countries: Some Tentative Findings." *World Affairs* 150, no.1 (Summer 1987): 5–19.

Di Palma, Giuseppe. *To Craft Democracies: An Essay on Democratic Transitions*. Berkeley: University of California Press, 1990.

Eckstein, Harry. *Division and Cohesion in Democracy: A Study of Norway*. Princeton: Princeton University Press, 1966.

Feldman, Harvey, Michael Y.M. Kau, and Ilpyong J. Kim, eds. *Taiwan in a Time of Transition*. New York: Paragon House, 1988.

Gates, Hill. "Ethnicity and Social Change." In *The Anthropology of Taiwanese Society*, edited by Ahern and Gates.

Gellner, Ernest. *Nations and Nationalism*. Ithaca: Cornell University Press, 1983.

Gladney, Dru. *Muslim Chinese: Ethnic Nationalism in the People's Republic*. Cambridge: Council on East Asian Studies, Harvard University Press, 1990.

Goddard, W.G. *Formosa: A Study in Chinese History*. London: Macmillan, 1966.

Gold, Thomas B. *State and Society in the Taiwan Miracle*. Armonk, NY: M.E. Sharpe, 1986.

Hague, Rod, and Martin Harrop. *Comparative Government and Politics: An Introduction*, 2d ed. Atlantic Highlands, NJ: Humanities Press International, 1987.

Hsiao Hsin-huang. "Emerging Social Movements and the Rise of a Demanding Civil Society in Taiwan." *The Australian Journal of Chinese Affairs* 24 (July 1990): 163–79.

————. "Sheng-chi jen-ting yu sheng-chi wen-t'i" (Provincial Identification and the Problem of Provincial Origin). In *T'ai-wan ti-chu she-hui i-hsiang tiao-ch'a* (Survey of Social Attitudes in the Taiwan Area), edited by Chung-yang yen-chiu yuan. Nankang: Academia Sinica, January 1991.

Hsiao Hsin-huang, Wei-yuan Cheng, and Hou-sheng Chan, eds. *Taiwan: A Newly Industrialized State*. Taipei: Department of Sociology, National Taiwan University, 1989.

Hsieh Chang-t'ing. "T'ai-wan ming-yun Kung-t'ung-t'i ti chung-chi kuan-hua" (The Ultimate Concerns of Taiwan's "Body of Common Destiny"). *Hsin Wen-hua* (New Culture) (February 1989): 4–7.

Hu Chang. "Impressions of Mainland China Carried Back by Taiwan Visitors." In *Two Societies in Opposition: The Republic of China and the People's Republic of China After Forty Years*, edited by R.H. Myers.

Hu Fo, and Chu Yun-han. "Electoral Competition and Political Democratization." In *Political Change in Taiwan*, edited by Cheng and Haggard.

Huang, Mab. *Intellectual Ferment for Political Reforms in Taiwan, 1971–1973*. Ann Arbor: Center for Chinese Studies, University of Michigan, 1976.

Huntington, Samuel P. *The Third Wave: Democratization in the Late Twentieth Century*. Norman: University of Oklahoma Press, 1991.

———. "Will More Countries Become Democratic?" *Political Science Quarterly* 99, no. 2 (Summer 1984): 193–218.

Jacobs, J. Bruce. *Local Politics in a Rural Chinese Cultural Setting: A Field Study of Mazu Township, Taiwan.* Canberra: Contemporary China Centre, Research School of Pacific Studies, Australian National University, 1980.

Joseph, William A., ed. *China Briefing, 1991*. Boulder, CO: Westview Press in cooperation with the Asia Society, 1992.

Kaplan, John. *The Court-Martial of the Kaohsiung Defendants*. Berkeley: Institute of East Asian Studies, University of California, 1981.

Karl, Terry Lynn. "Dilemmas of Democratization in Latin America." *Comparative Politics* 23 (October 1990): 1–21.

Kerr, George H. *Formosa Betrayed*. Boston: Houghton Mifflin Company, 1965.

———. *Formosa: Licensed Revolution and the Home Rule Movement, 1895–1945*. Honolulu: University Press of Hawaii, 1974.

Lai Tse-han, Ramon H. Myers, and Wei Wou. *A Tragic Beginning: The Taiwan Uprising of February 28, 1947*. Stanford: Stanford University Press, 1991.

Lasater, Martin L. *A Step Toward Democracy: The December 1989 Elections in Taiwan, Republic of China*. Washington, DC: American Enterprise Institute Press, 1990.

Lerman, Arthur J. *Taiwan's Politics: The Provincial Assemblyman's World*. Washington, DC: University Press of America, 1978.

Li Ch'ia. *T'ai-wan-jen ti ch'ou-lou mien* (The Ugly Side of the Taiwanese). Taipei: Vanguard Press, 1988.

Lijphart, Arend. *Democracy in Plural Societies: A Comparative Exploration*. New Haven: Yale University Press, 1977.

Lin Yu-t'i. *T'ai-wan chiao-yu mien-mu 40 nien* (Faces of Taiwan's Education Over Forty Years). Taipei: Cultural Division of *Tzu-li Wan-pao* (Independence Evening Post), 1987.

Linz, Juan J. "Totalitarian and Authoritarian Regimes." In *Handbook of Political Science,* vol. 3: *Macropolitical Theory*, edited by Fred I. Greenstein and Nelson W. Polsby. Reading, MA: Addison-Wesley, 1975.

Lipset, Seymour Martin. *Political Man*. Baltimore: Johns Hopkins University Press, 1981.

———. "Some Social Requisites of Democracy: Economic Development and Political Legitimacy." *American Political Science Review* 53 (March 1959): 69–103.

Liu, Leo Y. "Self-Determination, Independence, and the Process of Democratization in Taiwan." *Asian Profile* 19, no.3 (June 1991): 198–205.

Loewe, Michael. *The Pride That Was China*. New York: St. Martin's Press, 1990.

Long, Simon. *Taiwan: China's Last Frontier.* New York: St. Martin's Press, 1991.

Lui, Fei-lung. "The Electoral System and Voting Behavior in Taiwan." In *Political Change in Taiwan,* edited by Cheng and Haggard.

Lu, Ya-li. "Political Modernization in the ROC." In *Two Societies in Opposition: The Republic of China and the People's Republic of China After Forty Years,* edited by Myers.

———."Political Opposition in Taiwan." In *Political Change in Taiwan,* edited by Cheng and Haggard.

Meaney, Constance Squires. "Liberalization, Democratization, and the Role of the KMT." In *Political Change in Taiwan,* edited by Cheng and Haggard.

Mendel, Douglas. *The Politics of Formosan Nationalism.* Berkeley: University of California Press, 1970.

Mill, John Stuart. *Considerations on Representative Government.* Buffalo, NY: Prometheus Books, 1991. Originally published in 1861.

Moody, Peter W. *Political Change on Taiwan: A Study of Ruling Party Adaptability.* New York: Praeger, 1992.

Moser, Leo J. *The Chinese Mosaic: The Peoples and Provinces of China.* Boulder, CO: Westview, 1985.

Myers, Ramon H. "Political Theory and Recent Political Development in the Republic of China." *Asian Survey* 27, no.9 (September 1987): 1003–22.

———, ed. *Two Societies in Opposition: The Republic of China and the People's Republic of China After Forty Years.* Stanford: Hoover Institution Press, 1991.

Nathan, Andrew. *China's Crisis: Dilemmas of Reform and Prospects for Democracy.* New York: Columbia University Press, 1990.

———. "The Legislative Elections in Taiwan: Consequences of the Electoral System." *Asian Survey* 33, no.4 (April 1993): 424–38.

Nordlinger, Eric. "Political Development: Time Sequences and Rates of Change." In *Political Development and Social Change,* 2d ed., edited by Jason L. Finkle and Richard W. Gable. New York: John Wiley and Sons, 1966.

O'Donnell, Guillermo, Philippe C. Schmitter, and Laurence Whitehead, eds. *Transitions from Authoritarian Rule: Tentative Conclusions about Uncertain Democracies.* Baltimore: Johns Hopkins University Press, 1986.

P'eng Ming-min. *A Taste of Freedom: Memoirs of a Formosan Independence Leader.* New York: Holt, Rinehart and Winston, 1972.

Przeworski, Adam. *Democracy and the Market: Political and Economic Reforms in Eastern Europe and Latin America.* Cambridge: Cambridge University Press, 1991.

———. "Some Problems in the Study of the Transition to Democracy." In *Transitions from Authoritarian Rule: Comparative Perspectives,* edited by Guillermo O'Donnell, Philippe C. Schmitter, and Laurence Whitehead. Baltimore: Johns Hopkins University Press, 1986.

Pye, Lucian. *Politics, Personality and Nation Building: Burma's Search for Identity.* New Haven: Yale University Press, 1962.

Republic of China Government Information Office. *A Study of a Possible Communist Attack on Taiwan.* Sanchung: Government Information Office, 1991.

Republic of China Handbook, 1990 (and various years). Taipei: Kwang Hwa, 1990.

Rustow, Dankwart. "Transitions to Democracy: Toward a Dynamic Model." *Comparative Politics* 2 (April 1970): 337–63.

———. *A World of Nations: Problems of Political Modernization*. Washington, DC: The Brookings Institution, 1967.

Sartori, Giovanni. "Democracy." In *International Encyclopedia of the Social Sciences*, vol. 4, edited by David Sills. New York: Macmillan and The Free Press, 1968.

Schmitter, Philippe C., and Terry Lynn Karl. "What Democracy Is . . . and Is Not." *Journal of Democracy* 2, no.3 (Summer 1991): 75–88.

Schumpeter, Joseph A. *Capitalism, Socialism and Democracy*. New York: Harper and Brothers, 1950.

Share, Donald, and Scott Mainwaring. "Transitions Through Transaction: Democratization in Brazil and Spain." In *Political Liberalization in Brazil: Dynamics, Dilemmas, and Future Prospects*, edited by Wayne A. Selcher. Boulder, CO: Westview Press, 1986.

Shaw Yu-ming. *Beyond the Economic Miracle: Reflections on the Republic of China on Taiwan, Mainland China, and Sino-American Relations*. Taipei: Kwang Hwa, 1989.

Stepan, Alfred. *Rethinking Military Politics: Brazil and the Southern Cone*. Princeton: Princeton University Press, 1988.

Sun Yat-sen Institute of Social Sciences and Philosophy, Academia Sinica. *Taiwan ti-chu she-hui i-hsiang tiao-cha: Pa-shih-nien pa-yueh ting-chi tiao-cha pao-kao* (General Survey of Social Attitudes in Taiwan). Taipei: Sun Yat-sen Institute of Social Sciences and Philosophy, Academia Sinica, 1992.

Sung Tz'o-lai. *T'ai-wan-jen ti tzu-wo chui-hsun* (The Taiwanese Pursuit of the Self). Taipei: Vanguard Press, 1988.

"Taiwan Feelings, Chinese Heart." *Yuan Chien* (Global Views Monthly) 62 (July 15, 1991): 123.

Tang Mei-chuan. *Urban Chinese Families*. Taipei: National Taiwan University Press, 1978.

Tien Hung-mao. *The Great Transition: Political and Social Change in the Republic of China*. Stanford: Hoover Institution Press, 1988.

———. "Social Change and Political Development in Taiwan." In *Taiwan in a Time of Transition*, edited by Feldman, Kau, and Kim.

———. "Transformation of an Authoritarian Party State: Taiwan's Development Experience." In *Political Change in Taiwan*, edited by Cheng and Haggard.

Ts'ai Ling, and Ramon H. Myers. "Achieving Consensus Amidst Adversity: The Conference to Decide the Republic of China's Destiny." *American-Asian Review* 9, no.2 (Summer 1991); and 9, no.3 (Fall 1991): 1–40.

Tu Wei-ming. "A Confucian Perspective on Global Consciousness and Local Awareness." *IHJ Bulletin* 11 (Winter 1991): 1–5.

———. "Cultural China: The Periphery as the Center." *Daedalus* 120 (Spring 1991): 1–32.

U.S. Congress. *Country Reports on Human Rights Practices for 1993*. Washington, DC: U.S. Government Printing Office, February 1994.

Verba, Sidney. "Comparative Political Culture." In *Political Culture and Political Development*, edited by Lucian Pye and Sidney Verba. Princeton: Princeton University Press, 1965.

Wang Fu-chang. "The Unexpected Resurgence: Ethnic Assimilation and Competition in Taiwan, 1945–1988." Ph.D. dissertation, University of Arizona, 1989.

Weiner, Myron. "Empirical Democratic Theory and the Transitions from Authoritarianism to Democracy." *PS* 20 (Fall 1987): 861–66.

Wilson, Richard W. *Learning to Be Chinese: The Political Socialization of Children in Taiwan.* Cambridge: MIT Press, 1970.

Winckler, Edwin. "National, Regional, and Local Politics." In *The Anthropology of Taiwanese Society*, edited by Ahern and Gates.

———. "Taiwan: Changing Dynamics." In *China Briefing, 1991*, edited by William A. Joseph. Boulder, CO: Westview Press in cooperation with the Asia Society, 1992.

Index

Alan M. Wachman is the American Co-Director of the Johns Hopkins University-Nanjing University Center for Chinese and American Studies on the campus of Nanjing University in China. He received both an A.B. in East Asian art history and a Ph.D. in political science from Harvard University and a master's degree in international relations from The Fletcher School of Law and Diplomacy. His research about Taiwan was informed by three years of work and study in Taichung and Taipei .